BRITISH HISTORICAL FACTS

1760–1830

BRITISH
HISTORICAL FACTS
1760–1830

CHRIS COOK

AND

JOHN STEVENSON

ARCHON BOOKS
Hamden, Connecticut

First published 1980 by
THE MACMILLAN PRESS LTD
London and Basingstoke
and in the U.S.A. as an ARCHON BOOK
an imprint of
THE SHOE STRING PRESS, INC.
995 Sherman Avenue
Hamden, Connecticut

Phototypeset in V.I.P. Baskerville by
Western Printing Services Ltd, Bristol
Printed in Great Britain

ARCHON ISBN 0–208–01868–9

LC 79–57639

Contents

ACKNOWLEDGEMENTS ix

1. **THE MONARCHY**
Biographical Details of Monarchs and
   their Issue 1
Allowances to Members of the Royal Family 3
Grants in One Sum to Members of the
   Royal Family, 1760–1820 5
Regnal Years, 1760–1830 7
Office-holders of the Household 9

2. **MINISTRIES AND ADMINISTRATIONS**
Chronological List 11
Composition of Each Ministry 11
Biographical Details of Major Ministers 20

3. **SELECTED HOLDERS OF PUBLIC OFFICE**
Offices 26
Holders 27

4. **THE PEERAGE AND ORDERS OF KNIGHTHOOD**
Creations and Promotions within the
   Higher Peerage 37
The Orders of Knighthood 40
      Order of the Garter: Creations, 1760–1830 40
      Order of the Thistle 42
      Order of the Bath 43
      Order of St Patrick 45
      Order of St Michael and St George 46

5. **PARLIAMENT AND ELECTIONS**
House of Commons 47
      Speakers 47
      Contested Elections for the Speakership 47
      Chairmen of Ways and Means 47
      Clerks of the House 47
      Parliamentary Sessions 48
      Composition of the House 48
      Public Petitions 49
      Social Status of Members 49
House of Lords 49

      Lord Chairmen of Committees   49
      Officers   50
      Composition of the House   50
      Party Leaders, 1783–1830   50
      Scottish Representative Peers   51
      Irish Representative Peers   52
   The Franchise   53
   Patronage   59

6. **FOREIGN AFFAIRS**
   British Treaties, 1756–1830   60
   Principal British Diplomatic Representatives,
      1760–1830   70
   International Conferences and Congresses,
      1800–30   79

7. **THE ARMED FORCES**
   Outlines of British Campaigns, 1755–1830   80
   Principal Battles, 1755–1830   92
   Strength and Cost of the Army, 1755–1830   97
   Loans and Subsidies to Foreign States during
      the Wars of 1793–1814   99
   Annual Parliamentary Votes for the Navy, 1755–1830   101
   Military Office-holders   102
   Biographical Details of Major Commanders, 1755–1830   103
   Bibliography   111

8. **THE EMPIRE AND INDIA**
   Main Territories under British Rule by 1830   113
   The American Colonies   113
   Major Events in Irish History   115
   Holders of Important Office concerned
      with India   120
   Colonial Governors   121

9. **RADICALISM, TRADE UNIONS AND POLITICAL REFORM**
   Trade Unions   128
      Chronology of Trade Union
         Developments   128
      The Combination Acts   129
   Political Reform   132
      The Parliamentary Reform Movement,
         1760–1829   132
      The Reform Crisis, 1830–2   136
      Major Reform Societies and Clubs   137
      Biographical Details of Major
         Reformers   140

10. **LAW AND ORDER**
Principal Judges   144
Major Developments in Public Order   145
Popular Disturbances in Britain (excluding Ireland)   147
Criminal Statistics   154
The Abolition of Capital Offences, 1808–30   155

11. **THE PRESS**
Newspaper Legislation, Taxes and Prices   157
National Newspaper Press – Chronology of
  Main Events   157
Provincial Newspaper Press   158
Bibliography   161

12. **RELIGION**
Religious Statistics   162
    The Church of England   162
    The Catholic Church   163
    The New Dissent   163
The Church of England   164
    Archbishops and Bishops   164
    Plurality and Non-residence   166
    Revenues from Bishoprics, 1760   167
    Missionary and Benevolent Societies   167
    The Clapham Sect   168
Chronology of the New Dissent   168
    Protestant Dissenters   168
    Methodists   169
    Baptists   169
Roman Catholicism   170
    Popes, with Family Name   170
    Chronology of Principal Events   170
    Main Centres of Roman Catholic Refugees, 1794   171
Wales   172
Scotland   172
    Chronology   172
    Dioceses of the Episcopal Church   173
    Primus of Episcopal Church   173
    Roman Catholics   173
Ireland   174
    Chronology   174
    Division of Population among Creeds   175
    Dioceses of Church of Ireland, 1714–1830 175

13. **SELECTED HOLDERS OF LOCAL GOVERNMENT OFFICE**
Lord Lieutenants, England   176
Lord Lieutenants, Wales   179

14. **THE ECONOMY**
    Population, 1761–1831   181
    Principal Urban Populations, 1801 and 1831   181
    Prices   182
    Average Price of Wheat in England and Wales, 1771–1830   182
    Industrial Production, 1801–30   183
    Raw Cotton Imports and Consumption   183
    Enclosure Acts, 1760–1830   184
    The Corn Laws   184
    Trade   185
    Shipping and Shipbuilding   185
    Public Income and Expenditure   186
    The National Debt   187
    Yield on Consols   187
    Income Tax: Rates and Yields, 1799–1816   187
    Country Banks in England and Wales, 1784–1830   188
    Canal Acts, 1759–1827   188
    Distribution of the Labour Force, 1801–31   191

15. **SOCIAL DEVELOPMENTS**
    Major Social Legislation and Developments   192
    Hospital Foundations, 1714–1830   192
    Charities and Philanthropic Societies   193
    Education   194
    Poor Relief, 1783–1831   194
    Friendly Societies   194

    BIBLIOGRAPHICAL NOTE   196

Acknowledgements

Like the companion volume in this series, *British Historical Facts, 1830–1900*, the compilation of this book owes a very large debt to the pioneering efforts of David Butler, whose *British Political Facts 1900–1975* provided both the original idea and model for this latest volume. Much work for this book was undertaken at Nuffield College, Oxford. Both authors would like to record their thanks to the Warden and Fellows of the College for making its facilities so readily available.

Inevitably, for a reference work on a period as far back as 1760 to 1830, there is a difference in emphasis in this volume compared to its companions in the series. Diplomatic and military affairs occupy more space. There are details on the peerage and orders of knighthood that would be inappropriate in later volumes. Inevitably, party politics and electoral statistics cannot be as fully treated, but riots, public order and political reform come to the fore.

No volume of this type can ever hope to be definitive. The editors hope, however, that they have gathered together as many of the most useful facts and figures as can be included within the confines of a medium-sized reference work. Suggestions for additional material to be included in subsequent editions of this book will be welcomed.

Several people have contributed to the compilation of this book. The chapter on the armed forces was compiled by Stephen Brooks. Alan Gilbert and Anthony Bax provided much of the material for the chapter on religion. Jackie Johns gave valued advice on early trade unionism. Amongst others whom we would like to thank are Sheila Fairfield, Philip Riden and Philip Woods.

Finally, a very special debt is due to two people. John Brooke has encouraged the compilation of this book from the outset. His advice and guidance have been greatly appreciated. John Sainty, whose own definitive work on office-holders constitutes a towering achievement of scholarship, has generously given of his time to guide the authors from some, at least, of the pitfalls of compiling a work of reference for this period.

Sheffield and London   CHRIS COOK
June 1979   JOHN STEVENSON

1   The Monarchy

Biographical Details of Monarchs and their Issue

George III

Born 24 May 1738, the son of Frederick, Prince of Wales, and Augusta, daughter of Frederick II, Duke of Saxe-Gotha. He acceded to the throne on 25 October 1760 and died on 29 January 1820. On 8 September 1761 he married Charlotte, daughter of Charles Louis, Duke of Mecklenburg-Strelitz. Because of his incapacity, the Prince of Wales became regent on 5 February 1811.

His marriage produced the following children:

(1) **George:**	later George IV (q.v.) Born 12 Aug 1762.	
(2) **Frederick:**	Born 16 Aug 1763. Created Duke of York 29 Nov 1784. Died 5 Jan 1827.	
(3) **William:**	later William IV (q.v.). Born 21 Aug 1765.	
(4) **Charlotte:**	Born 29 Sep 1766. Died 5 Oct 1828. Married, 18 May 1797, Frederick Charles, later King of Württemberg.	
(5) **Edward:**	Born 2 Nov 1767. Created Duke of Kent 24 Apr 1799. Died 23 Jan 1820.	
(6) **Augusta:**	Born 8 Nov 1768. Died 22 Sep 1840.	
(7) **Elizabeth:**	Born 22 May 1770. Died 10 Jan 1840. Married, 7 Apr 1818, Frederick Joseph, Prince of Hesse-Homburg.	
(8) **Ernest Augustus:**	Born 5 June 1771. Died 18 Nov 1851. Created Duke of Cumberland, 24 Apr 1799. Succeeded as King of Hanover 20 June 1837.	
(9) **Augustus:**	Born 27 Jan 1773. Died 21 Apr 1843. Created Duke of Sussex 27 Nov 1801.	
(10) **Adolphus:**	Born 24 Feb 1774. Died 8 July 1850. Created Duke of Cambridge 27 Nov 1801.	
(11) **Mary:**	Born 25 Apr 1776. Died 30 Apr 1857. Married, 22 July 1816, William, Duke of Gloucester.	
(12) **Sophia:**	Born 3 Nov 1777. Died 27 May 1848.	
(13) **Octavia:**	Born 23 Feb 1779. Died 3 May 1783.	
(14) **Alfred:**	Born 22 Sep 1780. Died 26 Aug 1782.	

(15) **Amelia:**   Born 7 Aug 1783. Died 2 Nov 1810.

George IV

Born 12 Aug 1762, the son of George III and Charlotte. He acceded to the throne on 29 Jan 1820 and died on 26 June 1830. On April 1795 he married Caroline, daughter of Charles, Duke of Brunswick-Wolfenbüttel. The marriage produced one child:

Charlotte: Born 7 Jan 1796. Died 6 Nov 1817. She married, 2 May 1816, Prince Leopold, the third son of Francis, Duke of Saxe-Coburg-Saalfeld.

William IV

Born 21 Aug 1765, the son of George III and Charlotte. He acceded 26 June 1830 and died 20 June 1837. On 11 July 1818 he married Adelaide, daughter of George, Duke of Saxe-Meiningen. The marriage produced two children:

(1) **Charlotte:**   Born 27 Mar 1819. She died the same day.
(2) **Elizabeth:**   Born 10 Dec 1820. Died 4 Mar 1821.

William IV's illegitimate children included George Augustus Frederick Fitzclarence, born in 1794 and created Earl of Munster in 1831, together with nine other children by Mrs Jordan.

A note on the Royal Style

By proclamation of 1 Jan 1801, after the Union with Ireland, George III was styled 'By the Grace of God, of the United Kingdom of Great Britain and Ireland, King, Defender of the Faith'. The title 'King of France' was dropped. In 1814 Hanover became a Kingdom.

Allowances to Members of the Royal Family

Total of Annuities to Royal Family, at intervals, during the period 1760–1819

Grantees, with their Relationship to the Sovereign

Grantee	Relationship	1760 £	1770 £	1780 £	1790 £	1800 £	1810 £	1819 £
Dowager Princess of Wales	Mother	60,000	60,000	–	–	–	–	–
Duke of York*	Brother	12,000	–	–	–	–	–	–
Duke of Gloucester (Wm. Henry)*	Brother	8,000	9,000	9,000	17,000	17,000	–	–
Duke of Cumberland (Hy. Fredk.)*	Brother	8,000	8,000	8,000	–	–	–	–
Princess Amelia	Aunt	12,000	12,000	12,000	–	–	–	–
Duke of Cumberland (son of Geo. II)	Uncle	15,000 / 25,000	–	–	–	–	–	–
Queen Charlotte	Wife	–	58,000	58,000	58,000	58,000	58,000	70,000
Prince of Wales	Son	–	–	–	60,000	60,000	60,000	65,000
Princess of Wales	Daughter-in-law	–	–	–	–	6,000	6,000	35,000
Princess Charlotte of Wales	Granddaughter	–	–	–	–	–	7,000	–
Leopold of Saxe-Coburg	Granddaughter's husband	–	–	–	–	–	–	50,000
Six younger sons	Sons	–	–	11,000	12,000	12,000	12,000	12,000
Duke of York	Son	–	–	–	–	14,000	14,000	14,000
Duchess of York	Daughter-in-law	–	–	–	–	4,000	4,000	4,000
Duke of Clarence	Son	–	–	–	–	2,500	2,500	2,500
Duke of Kent	Son	–	–	–	–	12,000	18,000	24,000
Duke of Cumberland	Son	–	–	–	–	12,000	18,000	18,000
Duke of Sussex	Son	–	–	–	–	12,000	18,000	18,000
Duke of Cambridge	Son	–	–	–	–	–	18,000	18,000

Allowances to Members of the Royal Family – (cont.)

Princess Royal (Duchess of Württemberg)		—	—	—	—	5,000†	5,000†	5,000†
Princess Augusta Sophia	Daughter	—	—	—	—	—	*4,000*	*4,000* / 9,000
Princess Elizabeth	Daughter	—	—	—	—	—	*4,000*	*5,000* / 9,000
Princess Mary (Duchess of Gloucester)	Daughter	—	—	—	—	—	*4,000*	*5,000* / 9,000
Princess Sophia	Daughter	—	—	—	—	—	*4,000*	*4,000* / 9,000
Princess Amelia	Daughter	—	—	—	—	—	*4,000*	–
Duke of Gloucester	Nephew	—	—	—	—	—	*14,000*	*14,000*
Prince of Mecklenburg-Strelitz	Nephew of Queen	—	—	—	—	1,788	1,788	1,788
Princess Sophia of Gloucester	Niece of King	—	—	—	—	—	*7,000*	*7,000*
Civil List £		*115,000*	*148,000*	*99,000*	*130,000*	*138,500*	*158,500*	*102,500*
Consolidated Fund £		25,000	16,000	16,000	34,000	142,788	207,788	327,788

NOTE: Figures in *italics*, on this and following pages, mean a charge on Civil List Fund; ordinary figures a charge on the Consolidated Fund.

* These three princes, grandsons of George II, each received an annuity of £4,000 per annum from 1759. These annuities were increased in 1760.

† This annuity (of £5,416 Irish currency) was charged by Act of the Irish Parliament on the Irish Consolidated Fund.

Total of Annuities in the Reigns of George IV and William IV 1820–1830

	1820 £	1825 £	1829 £	1830 £
Queen Caroline	50,000	–	–	–
Queen Adelaide	–	–	–	50,000
Prince Leopold of Saxe-Coburg, afterwards King of the Belgians	50,000	50,000	50,000	50,000
Duke of York	26,000	26,000	–	–
Duchess of York	4,000	–	–	–
Duke of Clarence	26,500	26,500	32,500	–
Duchess of Kent	6,000	6,000	6,000	6,000
Education of Princess Victoria		6,000	6,000	6,000
Duke of Cumberland	18,000	18,000	21,000	21,000
Education of Prince George of Cumberland	–	6,000	6,000	6,000
Duke of Sussex	18,000	18,000	21,000	21,000
Duke of Cambridge	24,000	24,000	27,000	27,000
Duchess of Württemberg	5,000	–	–	–
Princess Augusta Sophia	13,000	13,000	13,000	13,000
Princess Elizabeth	1,000 ⎱ 13,000 ⎰	1,000 ⎱ 13,000 ⎰	1,000 ⎱ 13,000 ⎰	14,000
Princess Mary Duchess of Gloucester	1,000 ⎱ 13,000 ⎰	1,000 ⎱ 13,000 ⎰	1,000 ⎱ 13,000 ⎰	14,000
Princess Sophia	13,000	13,000	13,000	13,000
Duke of Gloucester	14,000	14,000	14,000	14,000
Princess Sophia of Gloucester	7,000	7,000	7,000	7,000
Prince of Mecklenburg-Strelitz	1,788	1,788	1,788	1,788
	302,288	255,288	244,288	213,788
	2,000	2,000	2,000	50,000

Grants in One Sum to Members of the Royal Family, 1760–1820

Grantees, with their Relationship to the Sovereign		Date of Grant	Grant in One Sum
Sisters of George III:			
Princess Augusta		5 Dec 1763	80,000[1]
Princess Caroline		24 Mar 1767	40,000[2]
The Prince of Wales	Son	1787	161,000[3]
		1788	55,200[4]
		1793	40,000[5]
		1812	100,000[6]

Grantees, with their Relationship to the Sovereign		Date of Grant	Grant in One Sum
Princess Charlotte of Wales	Grand-daughter	1808	1,493 ⎫
		1809	1,835 ⎪
		1810	1,656 ⎬ 7
		1811	1,652 ⎪
		1812	1,652 ⎪
		1813	1,489 ⎭
		1816	60,000[8]
The four younger sons of George III		1787	8,500 ⎫
		1788	6,000 ⎬ 9
		1789	6,000 ⎭
The three ditto		1790	8,500 ⎫
		1791	8,500 ⎪
		1792	8,500 ⎪
		1793	8,500 ⎪
		1794	8,500 ⎪
		1795	8,500 ⎬ 10
		1796	9,000 ⎪
		1797	9,000 ⎪
		1798	9,000 ⎪
		1799	2,250 ⎭
The Duke of York	Son	1793	5,265 ⎫
		1794	26,307 ⎪
		1795	4,501 ⎬ 11
		1796	6,021 ⎪
		1800	12,642 ⎭
The Duke of Clarence	Son	5 July 1786	3,500 ⎫
		5 July 1787	3,500 ⎪
		5 July 1788	3,500 ⎪
		5 July 1789	9,875 ⎪
		5 July 1790	12,000 ⎪
		5 July 1791	3,000 ⎬ 12
		5 Apr 1795	2,500 ⎪
		5 Apr 1796	3,816 ⎪
		16 June 1801	8,000 ⎪
		16 June 1802	7,000 ⎭
		8 Apr 1803	20,000 ⎫ 13
		15 Oct 1813	20,000 ⎭
The Duke of Kent	Son	10 Oct 1805	10,000 ⎫
		8 Apr 1806	10,000 ⎬ 14
		5 July 1806	6,000 ⎭
The Duke of Cumberland	Son	14 Oct 1805	15,000 ⎫ 15
		8 Apr 1806	5,000 ⎭

Grantees, with their Relationship to the Sovereign		Date of Grant	Grant in One Sum
The Duke of Sussex	Son	8 Apr 1806	20,000[16]
The Duke of Cambridge	Son	5 July 1801 5 July 1802	6,000 } 4,000 } [17]
Princess Royal (Duchess of Württemberg)		1797	80,000[18]
TOTALS £ 377,954[19] 576,200			

NOTES

[1] On marriage to Duke of Brunswick-Wolfenbüttel. Supply Grant.
[2] On marriage to King of Denmark. Supply Grant.
[3] Supply Grant, for Prince's debts.
[4] Supply Grant for works at Carlton House.
[5] Civil Service List, advanced as a loan, of which £13,000 was repaid.
[6] Out of Supplies on becoming Regent.
[7] Paid out of Civil List.
[8] Voted for expenses of her marriage.
[9] Out of Civil List.
[10] Ditto.
[11] Ditto.
[12] Ditto.
[13] Out of Admiralty Droits.
[14] Out of Admiralty Droits. £1000 out of £6000 subsequently repaid.
[15] Out of Admiralty Droits.
[16] Ditto.
[17] Out of Civil List.
[18] Voted for marriage portion.
[19] Including amounts above stated to have been repaid.

Regnal Years, 1760–1830

George III

1	25 Oct 1760 24 Oct 1761		5	25 Oct 1764 24 Oct 1765
2	25 Oct 1761 24 Oct 1762		6	25 Oct 1765 24 Oct 1766
3	25 Oct 1762 24 Oct 1763		7	25 Oct 1766 24 Oct 1767
4	25 Oct 1763 24 Oct 1764		8	25 Oct 1767 24 Oct 1768

9	25 Oct 1768 24 Oct 1769	30	25 Oct 1789 24 Oct 1790
10	25 Oct 1769 24 Oct 1770	31	25 Oct 1790 24 Oct 1791
11	25 Oct 1770 24 Oct 1771	32	25 Oct 1791 24 Oct 1792
12	25 Oct 1771 24 Oct 1772	33	25 Oct 1792 24 Oct 1793
13	25 Oct 1772 24 Oct 1773	34	25 Oct 1793 24 Oct 1794
14	25 Oct 1773 24 Oct 1774	35	25 Oct 1794 24 Oct 1795
15	25 Oct 1774 24 Oct 1775	36	25 Oct 1795 24 Oct 1796
16	25 Oct 1775 24 Oct 1776	37	25 Oct 1796 24 Oct 1797
17	25 Oct 1776 24 Oct 1777	38	25 Oct 1797 24 Oct 1798
18	25 Oct 1777 24 Oct 1778	39	25 Oct 1798 24 Oct 1799
19	25 Oct 1778 24 Oct 1779	40	25 Oct 1799 24 Oct 1800
20	25 Oct 1779 24 Oct 1780	41	25 Oct 1800 24 Oct 1801
21	25 Oct 1780 24 Oct 1781	42	25 Oct 1801 24 Oct 1802
22	25 Oct 1781 24 Oct 1782	43	25 Oct 1802 24 Oct 1803
23	25 Oct 1782 24 Oct 1783	44	25 Oct 1803 24 Oct 1804
24	25 Oct 1783 24 Oct 1784	45	25 Oct 1804 24 Oct 1805
25	25 Oct 1784 24 Oct 1785	46	25 Oct 1805 24 Oct 1806
26	25 Oct 1785 24 Oct 1786	47	25 Oct 1806 24 Oct 1807
27	25 Oct 1786 24 Oct 1787	48	25 Oct 1807 24 Oct 1808
28	25 Oct 1787 24 Oct 1788	49	25 Oct 1808 24 Oct 1809
29	25 Oct 1788 24 Oct 1789	50	25 Oct 1809 24 Oct 1810

			George IV
	25 Oct 1810	1	29 Jan 1820
51	5 Feb 1811		28 Jan 1821
	24 Oct 1811		
52	25 Oct 1811	2	29 Jan 1821
	24 Oct 1812		28 Jan 1822
53	25 Oct 1812	3	29 Jan 1822
	24 Oct 1813		28 Jan 1823
54	25 Oct 1813	4	29 Jan 1823
	24 Oct 1814		28 Jan 1824
55	25 Oct 1814	5	29 Jan 1824
	24 Oct 1815		28 Jan 1825
56	25 Oct 1815	6	29 Jan 1825
	24 Oct 1816		28 Jan 1826
57	25 Oct 1816	7	29 Jan 1826
	24 Oct 1817		28 Jan 1827
58	25 Oct 1817	8	29 Jan 1827
	24 Oct 1818		28 Jan 1828
59	25 Oct 1818	9	29 Jan 1828
	24 Oct 1819		28 Jan 1829
60	25 Oct 1819	10	29 Jan 1829
	29 Jan 1820		28 Jan 1830
		11	29 Jan 1830
			26 Jun 1830

The bracketed entries 51–60 are labelled } Regency

Office-holders of the Household

Lord Steward of the Household

1760	D of Rutland	Oct 1789	D of Dorset
1761	E of Talbot	Feb 1799	E of Leicester
May 1782	E of Carlisle	Aug 1802	E of Dartmouth
Feb 1783	D of Rutland	May 1804	E of Aylesford
Apr 1783	E of Dartmouth	Feb 1812	E of Cholmondeley
Dec 1783	D of Chandos	Dec 1821	M of Conyngham

Treasurer of the Household

1760	E of Thomond	1783	C. Greville
1761	E of Powis	1784	E of Courtown
1765	Ld Edgcumbe	1793	Vt Stopford
1766	J. Shelly	1806	Ld Ossulston
1777	E of Carlisle	1807	Vt Stopford
1779	Ld Onslow and Cranley	1812	Vt Jocelyn
1780	Vt Cranbourn		Ld Cavendish Bentinck
1782	E of Effingham	1826	Sir W. H. Freemantle

Master of the Horse

1760	E of Huntingdon
1761	D of Rutland
1766	E of Hertford
	D of Ancaster and Kesteven
1788	D of Northumberland
1780	D of Montagu
1790	D of Montrose
1795	E of Westmorland
1798	E of Chesterfield
1804	M of Hertford
1806	E of Carnarvon
1807	D of Montrose
1821	D of Dorset
1827	D of Leeds

2 Ministries and Administrations*

Chronological List

Date of Formation	Name	Year(s) Covered
June 1757	Pitt–Newcastle	1757–61
Oct 1761	Bute–Newcastle	1761–62
May 1762	Bute	1762–63
Apr 1763	Grenville	1763–65
July 1765	1st Rockingham	1765–66
July 1766	Chatham	1766–68
Oct 1768	Grafton	1768–70
Jan 1770	North	1770–82
Mar 1782	2nd Rockingham	1782
July 1782	Shelburne	1782–83
Apr 1783	Fox–North	1783
Dec 1783	Pitt	1783–1801
Feb 1801	Addington	1801–04
May 1804	Pitt	1804–06
Feb 1806	Ministry of All the Talents	1806–07
Mar 1807	Portland	1807–09
Oct 1809	Perceval	1809–12
June 1812	Liverpool	1812–27
Apr 1827	Canning	1827
Aug 1827	Goderich	1827–28
Jan 1828	Wellington	1828–30

Composition of Each Ministry

Pitt–Newcastle 1757–61
(formed June 1757)

1st Ld Treas.	**D of Newcastle**	2 July 57	*Sec. of State*	**W. Pitt**	27 June 57
Chanc. Exch.	**H. Bilson Legge**	2 July 57	*(South)*		
	Vt Barrington	19 Mar 61	*Sec. of State*	**E of Holdernesse**	
Ld Pres.	**Earl Granville**	17 June 51	*(North)*		29 June 57
Ld Chanc.	**Sir R. Henley**	16 Jan 61		**E of Bute**	25 Mar 61
	(Ld Kpr 30 June 57–		*B.o.T.*	**E of Halifax**	1 Nov 48
	16 Jan 61)		*Admir.*	**Ld Anson**	2 July 57

* An asterisk indicates that the person concerned was not in the Cabinet. For the sources used, see Bibliographical Note, pp. 196–7.

11

Pitt–Newcastle 1757–61 *(contd.)*

P.S.	Earl Temple	5 July 57	*Treas. of Navy*	G. Grenville	25 Nov 56
D. Lanc.	Ld Edgcumbe	22 Dec 43		(new patent	18 Mar 61)
	E of Kinnoull	24 Dec 58	*Sec. at War*	Vt Barrington	14 Nov 55
Master-Gen.	Earl Ligonier	1 July 59		C. Townshend	18 Mar 61
of Ordnance			*Pay.-Gen.*	H. Fox	July 57

Bute–Newcastle 1761–2
(formed Oct 1761)

1st Ld Treas.	D of Newcastle	29 June 57	*P.S.*	Earl Temple	5 July 57
Chanc. Exch.	Vt. Barrington	19 Mar 61		(Seal in commission	16 Oct–
Ld Pres.	Earl Granville	17 June 51			25 Nov 61)
Ld Chanc.	Ld Henley	16 Jan 61		D of Bedford	25 Nov 61
Sec. of State	E of Egremont	9 Oct 61	*D. Lanc.*	E of Kinnoull	24 Jan 58
(South)			*Master-Gen.*	Earl Ligonier	1 July 59
Sec. of State	E of Bute	25 Mar 61	*of Ordnance*		
(North)			*Treas. of Navy*	C. Grenville	25 Nov 56
B.o.T.	Ld Sandys	21 Mar 61	*Sec. at War*	C. Townshend	18 Mar 61
Admir.	Ld Anson	2 July 57	*Pay.-Gen.*	H. Fox	July 57

Bute 1762–3
(formed May 1762)

1st Ld Treas.	E of Bute	26 May 62		E of Halifax	19 June 62
Chanc. Exch.	Sir F. Dashwood	29 May 62		G. Grenville	2 Jan 63
Ld Pres.	Earl Granville	17 June 51	*P.S.*	D of Bedford	25 Nov 61
Ld Chanc.	Ld Henley	16 Jan 61	*D. Lanc.*	E of Kinnoull	24 Jan 58
Sec. of State	E of Egremont	9 Oct 61		Ld Strange	13 Dec 62
(South)			*Master-Gen.*	Earl Ligonier	1 July 59
Sec. of State	G. Grenville	27 May 62	*of Ordnance*		
(North)	E of Halifax	14 Oct 62	*Treas. of Navy*	Vt Barrington	8 May 62
B.o.T.	Ld Sandys	21 Mar 61	*Sec. at War*	C. Townshend	18 Mar 61
	C. Townshend	1 Mar 63		Ld Mendip	17 Dec 62
Admir.	Ld Anson	2 July 57	*Pay.-Gen.*	H. Fox	July 57

Grenville 1763–5
(formed Apr 1763)

1st Ld Treas.	G. Grenville	16 Apr 63	*Sec. of State*	E of Halifax	14 Oct 62
Chanc. Exch.	G. Grenville	16 Apr 63	*(North)*	E of Sandwich	9 Sep 63
Ld Pres.	D of Bedford	9 Sep 63	*B.o.T.*	Ld Wycombe	20 Apr 63
Ld Chanc.	Sir R. Henley	16 Jan 61		E of Hillsborough	9 Sep 63
Sec. of State	E of Egremont	9 Oct 61	*Admir.*	E of Sandwich	23 Apr 63
(South)	E of Halifax	9 Sep 63		E of Egmont	10 Sep 63

Grenville 1763–5 *(contd.)*

P.S.	**D of Marlborough**		*Treas. of Navy*	**Vt Barrington**	2 June 62
		22 Apr 63	*Sec. at War*	**Ld Mendip**	17 Dec 62
D. Lanc.	**Ld Strange**	13 Dec 62	*Pay.-Gen.*	**H. Fox**	July 57
Master-Gen. of Ordnance	**M of Granby**	1 July 63			

1st Rockingham 1765–6 (formed July 1765)

1st Ld Treas.	**M of Rockingham**		*Admir.*	**E of Egmont**	10 Sep 63
		13 July 65	*P.S.*	**D of Newcastle-upon-Tyne**	
Chanc. Exch.	**W. Dowdeswell**	16 July 65			15 July 65
Ld Pres.	**E of Winchilsea and Nottingham**	12 July 65	*D. Lanc*	**Ld Strange**	13 Dec 62
Ld Chanc.	**Sir R. Henley**	16 Jan 61	*Master-Gen. of Ordnance*	**M of Granby**	1 July 63
Sec. of State (South)	**H. Conway**	12 July 65	*Treas. of Navy*	**Vt Howe**	Aug 65
	D of Richmond	23 May 66	*Sec. at War*	**Vt Barrington**	19 July 65
Sec. of State (North)	**D of Grafton**	12 July 65	*Pay.-Gen.*	**C. Townshend**	May 65
	H. Conway	23 May 66			
B.o.T.	**E of Dartmouth**	20 July 65			

Chatham 1766–8 (formed July 1766)

1st Ld Treas.	**D of Grafton**	2 Aug 66	*Am. Cols*	**Ld Harwich**	20 Jan 68
Chanc. Exch.	**C. Townshend**	2 Aug 66	*Admir.*	**Sir E. Hawke**	10 Dec 66
	Ld Mansfield	11 Sep 67	*P.S.*	**E of Chatham**	30 July 66
	Ld North	6 Oct 67		(Seal in commission Feb–Mar 68. Chatham resumed office 21 Mar 68.)	
Ld Pres.	**E of Northington**	30 July 66			
	Earl Gower	23 Dec 67			
Ld Chanc.	**Ld Camden**	30 July 66	*D. Lanc.*	**Ld Strange**	13 Dec 62
Sec. of State (South)	**E of Shelburne**	30 July 66	*Master-Gen. of Ordnance*	**M of Granby**	1 July 63
Sec. of State (North)	**H. Conway**	23 May 66	*Treas. of Navy*	**Vt Howe**	9 Aug 65
	Vt Weymouth	20 Jan 68	*Sec. at War*	**Vt Barrington**	19 July 65
B.o.T.	**E of Hillsborough**	16 Aug 66	*Pay.-Gen.*	**C. Townshend**	May 65
	Vt Clare	18 Dec 66		**Ld North and G. Cooke**	10 Dec 66
	E of Hillsborough	20 Jan 68		**G. Cooke and T. Townshend**	23 Dec 67

Grafton 1768–70 (formed Oct 1768)

1st Ld Treas.	**D of Grafton**	2 Aug 66	*Chanc. Exch.*	**Ld North**	6 Oct 67

Grafton 1768–70 (contd.)

Ld Pres.	**Earl Gower**	23 Dec 67	*Admir.*	**Sir E. Hawke**	10 Dec 66
Ld Chanc.	**Ld Camden**	30 July 66	*Am. Cols*	**Ld Harwich**	20 Jan 68
	C. Yorke	17 Jan 70	*P.S.*	**E of Bristol**	2 Nov 68
Sec. of State (South)	**Vt Weymouth**	21 Oct 68	*D. Lanc.*	**Ld Strange**	13 Dec 62
Sec. of State (North)	**E of Rochford**	21 Oct 68	*Master-Gen. of Ordnance*	**M of Granby**	1 July 63
B.o.T.	**E of Hillsborough**		*Treas. of Navy*	**Vt Howe**	9 Aug 65
		20 Jan 68	*Sec. at War*	**Vt Barrington**	19 July 65

North 1770–82
(formed Jan 1770)

1st Ld Treas.	**Ld North**	28 Jan 70		**Ld Sackville-Germain**	
Chanc. Exch.	**Ld North**	6 Oct 67			10 Nov 75
Ld Pres.	**Earl Gower**	23 Dec 67		**E of Carlisle**	6 Nov 79
	Earl Bathurst	24 Nov 79		**Ld Grantham**	9 Dec 80
Ld Chanc.	(Seal in commission		*Am. Cols*	**Ld Harwich**	20 Jan 68
	20 Jan 70–23 Jan 71)			**E of Dartmouth**	14 Aug 72
	Ld Apsley (Earl Bathurst 1775)	23 Jan 71		**Ld Sackville-Germain**	10 Nov 75
	Ld Thurlow	3 June 78		**W. Ellis**	17 Feb 82
Sec. of State (South)	**Vt Weymouth**	21 Oct 68		(office abolished same year)	
	E of Rochford	19 Dec 70	*Admir.*	**Sir E. Hawke**	10 Dec 66
	Vt Weymouth	9 Nov 75		**E of Sandwich**	12 Jan 71
	E of Hillsborough		*P.S.*	**E of Halifax**	26 Feb 70
		24 Nov 79		**E of Suffolk and Berkshire**	
Sec. of State (North)	**E of Rochford**	21 Oct 68			22 Jan 71
	E of Sandwich	19 Dec 70		**D of Grafton**	12 June 71
	E of Halifax	22 Jan 71		**E of Dartmouth**	10 Nov 75
	E of Suffolk and Berkshire		*D. Lanc.*	**Ld Strange**	13 Dec .?
		12 June 71		**Ld Hyde (E of Clarendon 1776)**	14 June 71
	Vt Weymouth (sole secretary)	7 Mar 79	*Master-Gen. of Ordnance*	**M of Granby**	1 July 63
	Vt Stormont	27 Oct 79		**Vt Townshend**	1 Oct 72
	(Secretariat reorganised		*Treas. of Navy*	**Sir G. Elliot**	19 Mar 70
	Mar 1782)			**Ld Mendip**	12 June 77
B.o.T.	**E of Hillsborough**		*Sec. at War*	**Vt Barrington**	19 July 65
		20 Jan 68		**C. Jenkinson (later Ld Liverpool)**	16 Dec 78
	E of Dartmouth	31 Aug 72			

2nd Rockingham 1782
(formed Mar 1782)

1st Ld Treas.	**M of Rockingham**	27 Mar 82	*Home O.*	**E of Shelburne**	27 Mar 82
Chanc. Exch.	**Ld J. Cavendish**	1 Apr 82	*For. O.*	**C. J. Fox**	27 Mar 82
Ld Pres.	**Ld Camden**	27 Mar 82	*B.o.T.*	**Ld Grantham**	9 Dec 80
Ld Chanc.	**Ld Thurlow**	3 June 78	*Admir.*	**Vt Keppel**	30 Mar 82

Pitt 1804–6 (contd.)

Ld Pres.	D of Portland	30 July 01	*Admir.*	Vt Melville	15 May 04
	H. Addington			Ld Barham	30 Apr 05
	(Vt Sidmouth 1805)		*P.S.*	E of Westmorland	
		14 Jan 05			14 Feb 98
	Earl Camden	10 July 05	*D. Lanc.*	Ld Mulgrave	6 June 04
Ld Chanc.	Ld Eldon	14 Apr 01		E of Buckinghamshire	
Home O.	Ld Hawkesbury	12 May 04			14 Jan 05
For. O.	Ld Harrowby	14 May 04		Ld Harrowby	10 July 05
	Ld Mulgrave	11 Jan 05	*Master-Gen.*	E of Chatham	16 June 01
B.o.T.	Ld Hawkesbury		*of Ordnance*		
		23 Aug 86	*Treas. of Navy*	G. Canning*	29 May 04
	D of Montrose	6 June 04	*Sec. at War*	W. Dundas*	15 May 04
War and Cols	Earl Camden	12 May 04	*Master of*	Earl Bathurst*	7 July 04
	Vt Castlereagh	10 June 05	*Mint*		
Bd Control	Vt Castlereagh	12 July 02			

All The Talents 1806–7
(formed Feb 1806)

1st Ld Treas.	Ld Grenville	11 Feb 06		T. Grenville	29 Sep 06
Chanc. Exch.	Ld H. Petty	5 Feb 06	*P.S.*	Vt Sidmouth	5 Feb 06
Ld Pres.	Earl Fitzwilliam	19 Feb 06		Ld Holland	15 Oct 06
	Vt Sidmouth	8 Oct 06	*D. Lanc.*	E of Derby*	12 Feb 06
Ld Chanc.	Ld Erskine	7 Feb 06	*Master-Gen.*	E of Moira	14 Feb 06
Home O.	Earl Spencer	5 Feb 06	*or Ordnance*		
For. O.	C. J. Fox	7 Feb 06	*Treas. of Navy*	R. B. Sheridan*	22 Feb 06
	Vt Howick	24 Sep 06	*Sec. of War*	R. Fitzpatrick*	7 Feb 06
B.o.T.	Ld Auckland	5 Feb 06	*Master of*	Ld Spencer*	20 Feb 06
War and Cols	W. Windham	14 Feb 06	*Mint*	C. Bathurst*	27 Oct 06
Bd Control	Ld Minto*	12 Feb 06	*Ld. Chief*	Ld Ellenborough	Feb 06
	T. Grenville	16 July 06	*Justice of the*		
	G. Tierney	1 Oct 06	*King's Bench*		
Admir.	C. Grey (Vt Howick,		*Min. without*	Earl Fitzwilliam	8 Oct 06
	Apr 06)		*Portfolio*		
		11 Feb 06			

Portland 1807–9
(formed Mar 1807)

1st Ld Treas.	D of Portland	31 Mar 07	*War and Cols*	Vt Castlereagh	25 Mar 07
Chanc. Exch.	S. Perceval	26 Mar 07	*Bd Control*	R. Dundas*	6 Apr 07
Ld Pres.	Earl Camden	26 Mar 07		E of Harrowby	17 July 09
Ld Chanc.	Ld Eldon	1 Apr 07		R. Dundas*	13 Nov 09
Home O.	Ld Hawkesbury (E of		*Admir.*	Ld Mulgrave	4 Apr 07
	Liverpool 1808)	25 Mar 07	*P.S.*	E of Westmorland	
For. O.	G. Canning	25 Mar 07			25 Mar 07
B.o.T.	Earl Bathurst	26 Mar 07	*D. Lanc.*	S. Perceval	30 Mar 07

Portland 1807–9 (contd.)

Master-Gen. of Ordnance	**E of Chatham**	4 Apr 07	*Sec. at War*	**J. M. Pulteney*** **Ld Gower**	30 Mar 07 27 June 09
Treas. of Navy	**G. Rose***	15 Apr 07	*Master of Mint*	**Earl Bathurst***	25 Apr 07

Perceval 1809–12
(formed Oct 1809)

1st Ld Treas.	**S. Perceval**	4 Oct 09		**C. P. Yorke**	1 May 10
Chanc. Exch.	**S. Perceval**	26 Mar 07		**Vt Melville**	24 Mar 12
Ld Pres.	**Earl Camden**	26 Mar 07	*P.S.*	**E of Westmorland**	
	Vt Sidmouth	8 Apr 12			25 Mar 07
Ld Chanc.	**Ld Eldon**	1 Apr 07	*D. Lanc.*	**S. Perceval**	30 Mar 07
Home O.	**R. Ryder**	1 Nov 09	*Master-Gen.*	**E of Chatham**	4 Apr 07
For. O.	**Earl Bathurst**	11 Oct 09	*of Ordnance*	**E of Mulgrave**	5 May 10
	Ld Wellesley	6 Dec 09	*Treas. of Navy*	**G. Rose***	15 Apr 07
	Vt Castlereagh	4 Mar 12	*Sec. at War*	**Vt Palmerston**	27 Oct 09
B.o.T.	**Earl Bathurst**	26 Mar 07	*Master of*	**Earl Bathurst**	25 Apr 07
War and Cols	**E of Liverpool**	31 Oct 09	*Mint*		
Bd Control	**R. Dundas (Vt Melville 1811)**	13 Nov 09	*Mins without portfolio*	**D of Portland** **E of Harrowby**	Oct 09 Nov09–June 12
	E of Buckinghamshire	7 Apr 12		**Earl Camden**	Apr–June 12
Admir.	**Ld Mulgrave**	4 Apr 07			

Liverpool 1812–27
(formed June 1812)

1st Ld Treas.	**E of Liverpool**	18 June 12	*Admir.*	**Vt Melville**	24 Mar 12
Chanc. Exch.	**N. Vansittart**	9 June 12	*P.S.*	**E of Westmorland**	
	F. J. Robinson	21 Jan 23			25 Mar 07
Ld Pres.	**E of Harrowby**	11 June 12	*D. Lanc.*	**C. Bathurst**	23 June 12
Ld Chanc.	**Ld Eldon**	1 Apr 07		**E of Buckinghamshire**	
Home O.	**Vt Sidmouth**	11 June 12			23 Aug 12
	R. Peel	17 Jan 22		**N. Vansittart**	13 Feb 23
For. O.	**Vt Castlereagh**	4 Mar 12	*Master-Gen.*	**E of Mulgrave**	5 May 10
	G. Canning	16 Sep 22	*of Ordnance*	**D of Wellington**	1 Jan 19
B.o.T.	**Earl Bathurst**	26 Mar 07	*Treas. of Navy*	**G. Rose***	15 Apr 07
	E of Clancarty	29 Sep 12		**F. J. Robinson**	12 Feb 18
	F. J. Robinson	24 Jan 18		**W. Huskisson**	8 Feb 23
	W. Huskisson	31 Jan 23	*Sec. at War*	**Vt Palmerston***	27 Oct 09
War and Cols	**Earl Bathurst**	11 June 12	*Master of*	**E of Clancarty***	30 Oct 12
Bd Control	**E of Buckinghamshire**		*Mint*	**W. Wellesley Pole**	
		7 Apr 12			28 Sep 14
	G. Canning	20 June 16		**T. Wallace***	9 Oct 23
	C. Bathurst	16 Jan 21	*Min. without*	**Earl Camden**	June–Dec 12
	C. W. Williams Wynn		*portfolio*	**E of Mulgrave**	Jan 19–May 20
		8 Feb 22			

Canning 1827
(formed Apr 1827)

1st Ld Treas.	G. Canning	10 Apr 27	Admir.	D of Clarence	17 Apr 27
Chanc. Exch.	G. Canning	20 Apr 27	P.S.	D of Devonshire	30 Apr 27
Ld Pres.	E of Harrowby	11 June 12		E of Carlisle	16 July 27
Ld Chanc.	Ld Lyndhurst	2 May 27	D. Lanc.	N. Vansittart	13 Feb 23
Home O.	W. Sturges Bourne	30 Apr 27	Master-Gen. of Ordnance	M of Anglesey	30 Apr 27
	M of Lansdowne	16 July 27	Treas. of Navy	W. Huskisson	8 Feb 23
For. O.	Vt Dudley and Ward	30 Apr 27	Sec. at War	Vt Palmerston	27 Oct 09
B.o.T.	W. Huskisson	31 Jan 23	Master of Mint	G. Tierney	29 May 27
War and Cols	Vt Goderich	30 Apr 27	Min. without portfolio	M of Lansdowne	May–July 27
Bd Control	C. W. Williams Wynn	8 Feb 22		D of Portland	May–Aug 27

Goderich 1827–8
(formed Aug 1827)

1st Ld Treas.	Vt Goderich	31 Aug 27	P.S.	E of Carlisle	16 July 27
Chanc. Exch.	J. C. Herries	3 Sep 27	D. Lanc.	Ld Bexley	13 Feb 23
Ld Pres.	D of Portland	17 Aug 27	Master-Gen. of Ordnance	M of Anglesey	30 Apr 27
Ld Chanc.	Ld Lyndhurst	2 May 27			
Home O.	M of Lansdowne	16 July 27	Treas. of Navy	C. Grant	10 Sep 27
For. O.	Vt Dudley and Ward	30 Apr 27	Sec. at War	Vt Palmerston	27 Oct 09
B.o.T.	C. Grant	3 Sep 27	Master of Mint	G. Tierney	29 May 27
War and Cols	W. Huskisson	3 Sep 27	1st Comm. of Woods and Forests	W. Sturges Bourne	July 27
Bd Control	C. W. Williams Wynn	8 Feb 22			
Admir.	D of Clarence	17 Apr 27			

Wellington 1828–30
(formed Jan 1828)

1st Ld Treas.	D of Wellington	22 Jan 28	War and Cols	W. Huskisson	3 Sep 27
Chanc. Exch.	H. Goulburn	22 Jan 28		Sir G. Murray	30 May 28
Ld Pres.	E of Bathurst	26 Jan 28	Bd Control	C. W. Williams Wynn	8 Feb 22
Ld Chanc.	Ld Lyndhurst	2 May 27		Vt Melville	31 July 28
Home O.	R. Peel	26 Jan 28		Ld Ellenborough	24 Sep 28
For. O.	E of Dudley	30 Apr 27	Admir.	D of Clarence	17 Apr 27
	E of Aberdeen	2 June 28		Vt Melville	17 Sep 28
B.o.T.	C. Grant	3 Sep 27	P.S.	Ld Ellenborough	26 Jan 28
	W. V. Fitzgerald	11 June 28		E of Rosslyn	10 June 29
	J. C. Herries	2 Feb 30			

Wellington 1828–30 (contd.)

D. Lanc.	**Vt Gordon**	26 Jan 28	*Sec. at War*	**Vt Palmerston**	27 Oct 09
	C. Arbuthnot*	2 June 28		**H. Hardinge***	31 May 28
Master-Gen.	**M of Anglesey**	30 Apr 27	*Master of*	**J. C. Herries**	12 Feb 28
of Ordnance	**Vt Beresford**	28 Apr 28	*Mint*		
Treas. of Navy	**W. Fitzgerald**	25 Feb 28			

Biographical Details of Major Ministers

The following 45 names include all who held the positions of Prime Minister and First Lord of the Treasury, or Chancellor of the Exchequer, Home Secretary, Foreign Secretary and, before 1782, selected secretaries. Peers are listed under the last title they held (e.g. for Shelburne see Lansdowne). Major offices only are given.

Barrington, 2nd Vt   William Wildman Barrington (1717–93)
MP, Berwick 1740–54; Plymouth 1754–78. Chancellor of the Exchequer 1761–2; Treasurer of the Navy 1762–5; Secretary at War 1765–78; Joint Postmaster-General 1782.

Bathurst, 3rd Earl   Henry Bathurst (1762–1834)
MP, Cirencester 1783–94. Lord of the Admiralty 1783–9; Lord of the Treasury 1789–91; Teller of the Exchequer 1790–1834; Commissioner of the India Board 1793–1802; Clerk of the Crown 1801–34; Master of the Mint 1804–6, 1807–12; President of the Board of Trade 1807–12; Foreign Secretary 1809; Secretary for War and the Colonies 1812–27; Lord President of the Council 1828–30. Succeeded as 3rd Earl Bathurst 1794.

Bexley, 1st B   Nicholas Vansittart (1766–1851)
MP, Hastings 1796–1802; Old Sarum 1802–12; East Grinstead 1812; Harwich 1812–23. Secretary of the Treasury 1801–4, 1806–7; Chief Secretary for Ireland 1805; Chancellor of the Exchequer 1812–23; Chancellor of the Duchy of Lancaster 1823–8. Created Baron Bexley 1823.

Bute, 3rd E of   John Stuart (1713–1792)
Secretary of State, 1761–62. Succeeded Newcastle as First Lord of the Treasury, 1762. Resigned 1763. Succeeded as Earl, 1723.

Canning, George (1770–1827)
MP, Newport 1794–6; 1806–7; Wendover 1796–1802; Tralee 1802–6; Hastings 1807–12; Liverpool 1812–22; Harwich 1823–6; Newport 1826–7; Seaford 1827. Under-Secretary for Foreign Affairs 1796–9; India Board 1799–1800; Paymaster-General 1800–1; Treasurer of Navy 1804–6; Foreign Secretary 1807–9, 1822–7; President India Board 1816–21; Prime Minister and Chancellor of Exchequer 1827.

Cavendish, Lord John (1732–96)
MP, Weymouth and Melcombe Regis 1754–61; Knaresborough

1761–8; York 1768–90; Derbyshire 1794–6. Chancellor of the Exchequer 1782, 1783.

Chatham, 1st E of William Pitt (1708–78)

MP, Old Sarum 1735–47; Seaford 1747–54; Aldborough 1754–6; Okehampton 1756–7; Bath 1757–66. Vice-Treasurer of Ireland 1746; Paymaster-General 1746–55. Secretary of State 1756–7, 1757–61. Privy Seal (Prime Minister) 1766–8. Leader of the House of Commons 1756–61.

Chichester, 2nd E of Thomas Pelham (1756–1826)

MP, Sussex 1780–1801. Chief Secretary to Lord Lieutenant of Ireland 1783–4, 1795–8; Home Secretary 1801–3; Chancellor of the Duchy of Lancaster 1803–4; Joint Postmaster-General 1807–23; Postmaster-General 1823–6. Created Baron Pelham of Stanmer 1801. Succeeded as 2nd Earl of Chichester 1805.

Le Despenser, 15th B Francis Dashwood (1708–81)

MP, New Romney 1741–61; Weymouth and Melcombe Regis 1761–3. Chancellor of the Exchequer 1762–3.

Dowdeswell, William (1721–75)

MP, Tewkesbury 1747–54; Worcestershire 1761–75. Chancellor of the Exchequer 1765–6.

Fox, Charles James (1749–1806)

MP, Midhurst 1768–74; Malmesbury 1774–80; Westminster 1780–1806. Foreign Secretary 1782, 1783, 1806. Leader of the House of Commons 1782, 1783.

Goulburn, Henry (1784–1856)

MP, Horsham 1808–12; St Germans 1812–18; West Looe 1818–26; Armagh 1826–31; Cambridge University 1831–56. Under-Secretary for War and the Colonies 1812–21; Commissioner for Peace with the United States 1814; Chief Secretary for Ireland 1821–7; Chancellor of the Exchequer 1828–30, 1841–6; Home Secretary 1834–5.

Grafton, 3rd D of Augustus Henry Fitzroy (1735–1811)

MP, Bury St Edmunds 1756. Secretary of State for the Northern Department 1765–6. Nominal head of the Chatham Administration 1766. Prime Minister 1768–70. Lord Privy Seal 1771–5. Returned as Lord Privy Seal 1782. Succeeded as Duke of Grafton 1757.

Grantham, 2nd B Thomas Robinson (1738–86)

MP, Christchurch 1761–70; Junior Lord of Trade 1766–70. Vice-Chamberlain of the Household 1770–1; Ambassador to Madrid 1771–9; First Lord of Trade and Plantations 1780–2; Foreign Secretary 1782–3. First Baron Grantham 1770.

Grenville, George (1712–70)

MP, Buckingham 1741–70. Treasurer of the Navy 1756–62. Secretary of State 1762. Lord of the Admiralty 1762–3. Chancellor of the Exchequer 1763–5. Leader of the House of Commons 1761–2, 1763–5. First Lord of the Treasury 1763–5.

Grenville, B William Wyndham Grenville (1759–1834)

MP, Buckingham 1782–4; Buckinghamshire 1784–90. Chief Secretary for Ireland 1782–3; Paymaster and Joint Paymaster 1783–9; Vice-President of the Board of Trade 1786–9; Speaker 1789; Home Secretary 1789–90; President of the Board of Control 1790–3; Foreign Secretary 1791–1801; Prime Minister 1806–7. Created Baron Grenville 1790.

Grey, 2nd Earl Charles Grey (1764–1845)

MP, Northumberland 1786–1807; Appleby 1807; Tavistock 1807. First Lord of the Admiralty 1806; Foreign Secretary 1806–07; Prime Minister 1830–34. Styled Viscount Howick 1806. Succeeded as Earl Grey 1807.

Guildford, 2nd E of Frederick North (1732–92)

MP, Banbury 1754–90. A Lord of the Treasury 1759–65; Joint Paymaster-General 1766–7; Chancellor of the Exchequer 1767–82; 1st Lord of the Treasury (Prime Minister) 1770–82. Secretary of State for Colonial Affairs Apr–Dec 1783 (Fox–North coalition). Styled Lord North 1752–90. Earl of Guildford 1790.

Harrowby, 1st E of Dudley Ryder (1762–1847)

MP, Tiverton 1784–1809. Vice-President of the Board of Trade 1790–1801; Foreign Secretary 1804–5; Chancellor of the Duchy of Lancaster 1805–6; Ambassador to Berlin 1805–6; President of the India Board July–Nov 1809; Minister without Portfolio 1809–12; Lord President of the Council June 1812–Aug 1827. Created Viscount Sandon and Earl of Harrowby 1809.

Herries, John Charles (1778–1855)

MP, Harwich 1823–41; Stamford 1847–53. Commissary-in-Chief 1811–16; Financial Secretary to the Treasury 1823–7; Chancellor of the Exchequer 1827–8; Master of the Mint 1828–30; President of the Board of Trade 1830; Secretary at War 1834–5; President of the Board of Control 1852.

Holland, 1st B Henry Fox (1705–74)

MP, Hindon 1735–41; Windsor 1741–61; Dunwich 1761–3. A Lord of the Treasury 1743; Secretary at War 1746–54, Secretary of State 1755–6; Paymaster-General 1757–65; Bute's Leader in the House of Commons, 1762–3. Baron Holland 1763.

Huskisson, William (1770–1830)

MP, Morpeth 1796–1802; Liskeard 1804–7; Harwich 1807–12; Chichester 1812–23; Liverpool 1823–30. Secretary to the Treasury 1804–5, 1807–9; Treasurer of the Navy and President of the Board of Trade 1823–7; Colonial Secretary and Leader of the House of Commons 1827–8.

Lansdowne, 1st M of William Petty (1737–1805)

MP, Chipping Wycombe 1760–1; President of the Board of Trade Apr–Sep 1763; Secretary of State for the Southern Department

1766–8; Home Secretary Mar–July 1782; 1st Lord of the Treasury (Prime Minister July 1782–Apr 1783. Succeeded his father as Earl of Shelburne 1761. Created Marquess of Lansdowne 1784.

Lansdowne, 3rd M of   Henry Petty-Fitzmaurice (1780–1863)
MP, Calne 1802–6; University of Cambridge 1806–7; Camelford 1807–9. Chancellor of the Exchequer 1806–7; Cabinet Minister without office May 1827–8, 1852–63; Home Secretary July 1827–Jan 1828; Lord President of the Council 1830–4, 1835–41, 1846–52; Lord Lieutenant of Wiltshire 1827–63. Succeeded as Marquess of Lansdowne 1809.

Leeds, 5th D of   Francis Godolphin Osborne (1751–99)
MP, Eye Mar–Sep 1774; Helston 1774–5. A Lord of the Bedchamber 1776–7; Lord Chamberlain to the Queen Consort 1777–80; Foreign Secretary 1783–91. Styled Marquess of Carmarthen 1761–89. Succeeded as Duke of Leeds 1789.

Liverpool, 2nd E of   Robert Banks Jenkinson (1770–1828)
MP, Appleby 1790–6; Rye 1796–1803. Master of the Mint 1799–1801; Foreign Secretary 1801–4; Home Secretary 1804–6, 1807–9; Secretary for War and Colonies 1809–12; First Lord of Treasury (Prime Minister) 1812–27. Baron Hawkesbury 1803. Earl of Liverpool 1808.

Londonderry, 2nd M of   Robert Stewart (1769–1822)
MP, Down 1790–4, 1801–5, 1812–21; Tregony 1794–6; Orford 1796–7, 1821–2; Boroughbridge 1806; Plympton 1806–12. A Lord of the Treasury 1797–1804; Chief Secretary for Ireland 1799–1801; President of India Board 1802–6; Secretary for War and Colonies 1805–6, 1807–9; Foreign Secretary 1812–22. Styled Viscount Castlereagh. Succeeded as Marquess of Londonderry 1821.

Melville, 1st Vt   Henry Dundas (1742–1811)
MP, Midlothian 1774–82; Newport (I. of W.) 1782; Midlothian 1782–90; Edinburgh 1790–1802. Lord Advocate 1775–83; Treasurer of the Navy 1782–3, 1784–1800; Home Secretary 1791–4; President of the Board of Control 1793–1801; Secretary of War 1794–1801; First Lord of the Admiralty, 1804–5. Created Viscount Melville and Baron Dunira 1802.

Mulgrave, 1st E of   Sir Henry Phipps (1755–1831)
MP, Totnes 1784–90; Scarborough 1790–4. Chancellor of the Duchy of Lancaster 1804–5; Foreign Secretary Jan 1805–Feb 1806; 1st Lord of the Admiralty Apr 1807–Apr 1810; Master of the Ordnance 1810–18. Created Earl of Mulgrave 1812.

Newcastle, 1st D of   Thomas Pelham-Holles (1693–1768)
Secretary of State for the Southern Department, 1724–54; First Lord of the Treasury 1754–6, 1757–62; Lord Privy Seal July 1765 to Aug 1766. Created Earl of Clare 1714 and Duke of Newcastle 1715.

Palmerston, 3rd Vt   Henry John Temple (1784–1865)
MP, Newport (I. of W.) 1807–11; Cambridge University 1811–31;

Bletchingley 1831–2; South Hampshire 1832–4; Tiverton 1835–65. A Lord of the Admiralty 1807–9; Secretary at War 1809–28; Foreign Secretary 1830–4, 1835–41, 1846–51; Home Secretary 1852–5; Prime Minister 1855–8, 1859–65. Succeeded as Viscount Palmerston 1802.

Peel, Sir Robert (1788–1850)
MP, Cashel 1809–12; Chippenham 1812–17; Oxford University 1817–29; Westbury 1829; Tamworth 1830–50. Chief Secretary for Ireland 1812–18; Home Secretary 1822–7, 1828–30; Chancellor of the Exchequer 1834–5; Prime Minister 1834–5, 1841–5 and 1845–6.

Perceval, Spencer (1762–1812)
MP, Northampton 1796–1812; Attorney-General 1802–6; Chancellor of the Exchequer and of the Duchy of Lancaster 1807–9; Prime Minister and Chancellor of the Exchequer 1809–12.

Pitt, William (1759–1806)
MP, Appleby 1781–4; Cambridge University 1784–1806. Chancellor of the Exchequer 1782–3; Prime Minister and Chancellor of the Exchequer 1783–1801, 1804–6.

Portland, 3rd D of   William Henry Cavendish-Bentinck (1738–1809)
MP, Weobley 1761–2. Viceroy of Ireland 1782; Prime Minister 1783, 1807–9; Home Secretary 1794–1801; Lord President of the Council 1801–5. Styled Marquess of Titchfield. Succeeded as 3rd Duke of Portland 1762.

Ripon, 1st E of   Frederick John Robinson (1782–1859)
MP, Carlow Borough 1806–7; Ripon 1807–27. President of the Board of Trade and Treasurer of the Navy 1818–23; Chancellor of the Exchequer 1823–7; Secretary for War and Colonies Apr–Aug 1827, 1830–3; Prime Minister Aug 1827–Jan 1828; Lord Privy Seal Apr 1833–May 1834; President of the Board of Trade 1841–3; President of the Board of Control 1843–6. Created 1st Viscount Goderich 1827 and Earl of Ripon 1833.

Rockingham, 2nd M of   Charles Watson-Wentworth (1730–1782)
Lord-Lieutenant of the North and West Ridings of Yorkshire July 1751–Dec 1762; a Lord of the Bedchamber 1751–62; First Lord of the Treasury July 1765–July 1766, Mar 1782 till death. Styled Viscount Higham from 1734. Succeeded as Marquess of Rockingham 1750.

Ryder, Richard (1766–1832)
MP, Tiverton 1795–1830. Lord Commissioner of the Treasury, Privy Councillor and Judge Advocate-General 1807; Home Secretary 1809–12.

Sidmouth, 1st Vt   Henry Addington (1757–1844)
MP, Devizes, 1784–1805. Speaker of the House of Commons 1789–1801; First Lord of the Treasury and Chancellor of the Exchequer 1801–4; Lord President of the Council 1805; Lord Privy Seal 1806; Lord President of the Council 1806–7, 1812; Home Secretary

1812–22; Cabinet Minister without office 1822–4. Created Viscount Sidmouth 1805.

Spencer, 2nd Earl   George John Spencer (1758–1834)
MP, Northampton 1780–2; Surrey 1782–3. A Lord of the Treasury Mar–July 1782; Lord Privy Seal July–Dec 1794; First Lord of the Admiralty 1794–1801; Home Secretary 1806–7. Styled Viscount Althorp 1765–83. Succeeded as Earl Spencer 1783.

Spencer, 3rd Earl   John Charles Spencer (1782–1845)
MP, Okehampton 1804–6; Northamptonshire 1806–32; South Northamptonshire 1832–4. A Lord of the Treasury 1806–7, 1830–4; Chancellor of the Exchequer and a Commissioner for Indian Affairs 1830–4. Styled Viscount Althorp 1783–1834. Earl Spencer 1834.

Sydney, 1st Vt   Thomas Townshend (1733–1800)
MP, Whitchurch 1754–83. A Lord of the Treasury 1765–6; Joint Paymaster of the Forces 1767–8; Secretary at War Mar–July 1782; Home Secretary July 1782–Apr 1783, Dec 1783–Jan 1789. Created Baron Sydney 1783, Viscount Sydney 1789.

Townshend, Charles (1725–67)
MP, Great Yarmouth 1747–56; Saltash 1756–61; Harwich 1761–7. Lord of the Admiralty 1754–5; Secretary at War 1761–2; President of the Board of Trade 1763. Paymaster-General 1765–6; Chancellor of the Exchequer, 1766–7.

Wellesley, 1st M   Richard Colley Wellesley (1760–1842)
MP, Trim 1780–1; Beeralston 1784–6; Saltash 1786–7; Windsor 1787–96; Old Sarum 1796–7. Junior Lord of the Treasury 1786–97; Governor-General of Bengal 1797–1805; Ambassador to Spain 1809; Foreign Secretary 1809–12; Viceroy of Ireland 1821–8, 1833–4. Succeeded as Earl of Mornington 1781. Created Baron Wellesley 1797, Marquis Wellesley 1799.

Wellington, 1st D of   Arthur Wellesley (1769–1852)
MP, Trim 1790–5; Rye 1806; Mitchell 1807; Newport 1807–9. Chief Secretary for Ireland 1807–9. Master-General of the Ordnance 1819–27; Prime Minister 1828–30. Secretary of State all departments and Prime Minister Nov–Dec 1834. Foreign Secretary 1834–5; Minister without Portfolio 1841–6. Created Earl Wellington 1812, Marquis 1812, Duke of Wellington 1814.

Yorke, Charles Philip (1764–1834)
MP, Cambridgeshire 1790–1810; St Germans 1810; Liskeard 1812–18. Secretary at War 1801–3; Home Secretary 1803–4; First Lord of the Admiralty 1810–11.

Sources: For a detailed note on sources most frequently consulted, see Bibliographical Note, pp. 196–7.

3 Selected Holders of Public Office

Offices

1 Prime Minister
2 Lord Chancellor
3 Lord President of the Council
4 Lord Privy Seal
5 Secretary of State for the Northern Department
6 Secretary of State for the Southern Department
7 Secretary of State for the Home Department
8 Secretary of State for Foreign Affairs
9 Secretary of State for the American Colonies
10 Secretary of State for War and the Colonies
11 Chancellor of the Exchequer
12 First Lord of the Admiralty
13 President of the Board of Control
14 President of the Board of Trade
15 Vice-President of the Board of Trade
16 Chancellor of the Duchy of Lancaster
17 Lord-Lieutenant of Ireland
18 Chief Secretary for Ireland
19 Secretary at War
20 Paymaster-General
21 Master-General of the Ordnance
22 Treasurer of the Navy
23 Master of the Mint
24 Attorney-General
25 Solicitor-General
26 Under-Secretaries of State for the Northern Department
27 Under-Secretaries of State for the Southern Department
28 Permanent Under-Secretary to the Home Department
29 Non-Permanent (later Parliamentary) Under-Secretary for the Home Department
30 Parliamentary Under-Secretaries of State for Foreign Affairs
31 Permanent Under-Secretary of State for Foreign Affairs
32 Parliamentary Under-Secretary of State for Foreign Affairs

33 Under-Secretaries of State for the Colonies
34 Permanent Under-Secretary of State for the Colonies
35 Under-Secretary of State for War and Colonies
36 Deputy Secretaries at War
37 Senior (Parliamentary) Secretaries to the Treasury
38 Junior (Financial) Secretaries to the Treasury

Holders

1 Prime Minister*

June 57	D of Newcastle	Dec 83	W. Pitt
May 62	E of Bute	Mar 01	H. Addington
Apr 63	G. Grenville	May 04	W. Pitt
July 65	M of Rockingham	Feb 06	Ld Grenville
July 66	E of Chatham	Mar 07	D of Portland
Oct 68	D of Grafton	Oct 09	S. Perceval
Jan 70	Ld North	June 12	E of Liverpool
Mar 82	M of Rockingham	Apr 27	G. Canning
July 82	E of Shelburne	Aug 27	Vt Goderich
Apr 83	D of Portland	Jan 28	D of Wellington

2 Lord Chancellor

June 57	E of Northington	Dec 83	Ld Thurlow
July 66	Ld Camden	June 92	Seal in commission
Jan 70	C. Yorke	Jan 93	E of Rosslyn
Jan 70	Seal in commission	Apr 01	Ld Eldon
Jan 71	Earl Bathurst	Feb 06	Ld Erskine
June 78	Ld Thurlow	Apr 07	E of Eldon
Apr 83	Seal in commission	May 27	Ld Lyndhurst

3 Lord President of the Council

June 51	Earl Granville	Sep 96	E of Chatham
Sep 63	D of Bedford	July 01	D of Portland
July 65	E of Winchilsea and Nottingham	Jan 05	Vt Sidmouth
July 66	E of Northington	July 05	Earl Camden
Dec 67	Earl Gower	Feb 06	Earl Fitzwilliam
Nov 79	Earl Bathurst	Oct 06	Vt Sidmouth
Mar 82	Ld Camden	Mar 07	Earl Camden
Apr 83	Vt Stormont	Apr 12	Vt Sidmouth
Dec 83	Earl Gower	June 12	E of Harrowby
Dec 84	Earl Camden	Aug 27	D of Portland
July 94	Earl Fitzwilliam	Jan 28	Earl Bathurst
Dec 94	E of Mansfield		

* There was no office of Prime Minister as it is known today. Generally, administrations were led by a minister who held an important office, such as First Lord of the Treasury, although occasionally leadership of an administration could be shared. When the head of the administration was a peer, leadership of the House of Commons was not attached to any particular office and was exercised by a senior Government spokesman who sat in the Cabinet by virtue of this position. See Sir L. Namier and J. Brooke, *The History of Parliament: The House of Commons, 1754–1790* (London: HMSO, 1964) pp. 538–9.

4   Lord Privy Seal

July	57	Earl Temple	Dec	83	D of Rutland

July 57   Earl Temple   Dec 83   D of Rutland
Oct 61   Seal in commission   Mar 84   Seal in commission
Nov 61   D of Bedford   Nov 84   M of Stafford
Apr 63   D of Marlborough   July 94   D of Marlborough
July 65   D of Newcastle-upon-Tyne   Dec 94   E of Chatham
July 66   E of Chatham   Feb 98   E of Westmorland
Nov 68   E of Bristol   Feb 06   Vt Sidmouth
Feb 70   E of Halifax   Oct 06   Ld Holland
Jan 71   E of Suffolk and Berkshire   Mar 07   E of Westmorland
June 71   D of Grafton   Apr 27   D of Devonshire
Nov 75   E of Dartmouth   July 27   E of Carlisle
Mar 82   D of Grafton   Jan 28   Ld Ellenborough
Apr 83   E of Carlisle   June 29   E of Rosslyn

5   Secretary of State for the Northern Department

Mar 54   E of Holdernesse   Jan 68   Vt Weymouth
Mar 61   E of Bute   Oct 68   E of Rochford
May 62   G. Grenville   Dec 70   E of Sandwich
Oct 62   E of Halifax   Jan 71   E of Halifax
Sep 63   E of Sandwich   June 71   E of Suffolk and Berkshire
July 65   D of Grafton   Mar 79   Vt Weymouth
May 66   H. S. Conway   Oct 79   Vt Stormont

6   Secretary of State for the Southern Department

June 57   W. Pitt   July 66   E of Shelburne
Oct 61   E of Egremont   Oct 68   Vt Weymouth
Sep 63   E of Halifax   Dec 70   E of Rochford
July 65   H. S. Conway   Nov 75   Vt Weymouth
May 66   D of Richmond   Nov 79   E of Hillsborough

7   Secretary of State for the Home Department

Mar 82   E of Shelburne   May 04   Ld Hawkesbury
July 82   Ld Sydney   Feb 06   Earl Spencer
Apr 83   Ld North   Mar 07   E of Liverpool
Dec 83   Earl Temple   Nov 09   R. Ryder
Dec 83   Ld Sydney   June 12   Vt Sidmouth
June 89   Ld Grenville   Jan 22   R. Peel
June 91   H. Dundas   Apr 27   W. Sturges-Bourne
July 94   D of Portland   July 27   M of Lansdowne
July 01   Ld Pelham   Jan 28   R. Peel
Aug 03   C. P. Yorke

8   Secretary of State for Foreign Affairs

Mar 82   C. J. Fox   Dec 83   D of Leeds
July 82   Ld Grantham   June 91   Ld Grenville
Apr 83   C. J. Fox   Feb 01   Ld Hawkesbury
Dec 83   Earl Temple   May 04   Ld Harrowby

Jan 05	Ld Mulgrave	Dec 09	Marquis Wellesley
Feb 06	C. J. Fox	Mar 12	M of Londonderry
Sep 06	Earl Grey	Sep 22	G. Canning
Mar 07	G. Canning	Apr 27	E of Dudley
Oct 09	Earl Bathurst	June 28	E of Aberdeen

9   Secretary of State for the American Colonies

Jan 68	E of Hillsborough	Nov 75	Vt Sackville
Aug 72	E of Dartmouth	Feb 82	W. Ellis

10   Secretary of State for War and the Colonies

July 94	H. Dundas	Oct 09	E of Liverpool
Mar 01	E of Buckinghamshire	June 12	Earl Bathurst
May 04	Earl Camden	Apr 27	Vt Goderich
June 05	Vt Castlereagh	Sep 27	W. Huskisson
Feb 06	W. Windham	May 28	Sir G. Murray
Mar 07	Vt Castlereagh		

11   Chancellor of the Exchequer

July 57	H. B. Legge	Dec 83	W. Pitt
Mar 61	Vt Barrington	Mar 01	H. Addington
May 62	Ld Le Despenser	May 04	W. Pitt
Apr 63	G. Grenville	Feb 06	Ld H. Petty
July 65	W. Dowdeswell	Mar 07	S. Perceval
Aug 66	C. Townshend	June 12	Ld Bexley
Sep 67	Ld Mansfield	Jan 23	Vt Goderich
Apr 82	Ld J. Cavendish	Apr 27	G. Canning
July 82	W. Pitt	Sep 27	J. C. Herries
Apr 83	Ld J. Cavendish	Jan 28	Henry Goulburn

12   First Lord of the Admiralty

July 57	Ld Anson	July 88	E of Chatham
June 62	E of Halifax	Dec 94	Earl Spencer
Jan 63	G. Grenville	Feb 01	E of St Vincent
Apr 63	E of Sandwich	May 04	Vt Melville
Sep 63	E of Egmont	Apr 05	Ld Barham
Sep 66	Sir C. Saunders	Feb 06	Earl Grey
Dec 66	Sir E. Hawke	Sep 06	T. Grenville
Jan 71	E of Sandwich	Apr 07	Ld Mulgrave
Mar 82	Vt Keppel	May 10	C. P. Yorke
Jan 83	Vt Howe	Mar 12	Vt Melville
Apr 83	Vt Keppel	Apr 27	D of Clarence
Dec 83	Earl Howe	Sep 28	Vt Melville

13   President of the Board of Control

Sep 84	Vt Sydney	May 01	E of Dartmouth
Mar 90	Ld Grenville	July 02	Vt Castlereagh
June 93	H. Dundas	Feb 06	Ld Minto

July 06   T. Grenville   June 16   G. Canning
Oct   06   G. Tierney   Jan 21   C. Bathurst
Apr   07   R. Saunders-Dundas   Feb 22   C. W. W. Wynn
July 09   E of Harrowby   July 28   Vt Melville
Nov   09   R. Saunders-Dundas   Sep 28   Ld Ellenborough
Apr   12   E of Buckinghamshire

14   President of the Board of Trade

Nov 48   E of Halifax   Dec 80   Ld Grantham
Mar 61   Ld Sandys   Mar 84   Ld Sydney
Mar 63   C. Townshend   Aug 86   E of Liverpool
Apr 63   E of Shelburne   June 04   D of Montrose
Sep 63   E of Hillsborough   Feb 06   Ld Auckland
July 65   E of Dartmouth   Mar 07   Earl Bathurst
Aug 66   E of Hillsborough   Sep 12   E of Clancarty
Dec 66   Earl Nugent   Jan 18   F. J. Robinson
Jan 68   E of Hillsborough   Jan 23   W. Huskisson
Aug 72   E of Dartmouth   Sep 27   C. Grant
Nov 75   Ld G. Sackville-Germain   June 28   W. V. Fitzgerald
Nov 79   E of Carlisle   Feb 30   J. C. Herries

15   Vice-President of the Board of Trade

Aug 86   W. Grenville   Mar 07   G. Rose
Aug 89   M of Graham   Sep 12   F. J. Robinson
Oct 90   D. Ryder   Jan 18   T. Wallace
Nov 01   Ld Glenbervie   Apr 23   C. Grant
Feb 04   N. Bond   Feb 28   T. F. Lewis
June 04   G. Rose   May 28   T. P. Courtenay
Feb 06   Earl Temple

16   Chancellor of the Duchy of Lancaster

Jan 58   E of Kinnoull   Jan 05   E of Buckinghamshire
Dec 62   Ld Strange   July 05   E of Harrowby
June 71   E of Clarendon   Feb 06   E of Derby
Apr 82   Ld Ashburton   Mar 07   S. Perceval
Aug 83   E of Derby   June 12   C. Bathurst
Dec 83   E of Clarendon   Aug 12   E of Buckinghamshire
Sep 86   Ld Liverpool   Feb 23   Ld Bexley
Nov 03   Ld Pelham   Jan 28   E of Aberdeen
June 04   Ld Mulgrave   June 28   C. Arbuthnot

17   Lord-Lieutenant of Ireland

Jan 57   D of Bedford   Oct 72   E of Harcourt
Apr 61   E of Halifax   Dec 76   E of Buckinghamshire
Apr 63   E of Northumberland   Nov 80   E of Carlisle
June 65   Vt Weymouth   Apr 82   D of Portland
Aug 65   E of Hertford   Aug 82   M of Buckingham
Oct 66   E of Bristol   May 83   E of Northington
Aug 67   Vt Townshend   Feb 84   D of Rutland

Nov 87	M of Buckingham		June 13	E Whitworth
Oct 89	E of Westmorland		Oct 17	Earl Talbot
Dec 94	Earl Fitzwilliam		Aug 21	King George IV
Mar 95	Earl Camden		Sep 21	Earl Talbot
June 98	M Cornwallis		Dec 21	Marquis Wellesley
Apr 01	E of Hardwicke		Feb 28	M of Anglesey
Mar 06	D of Bedford		Jan 29	D of Northumberland
Apr 07	D of Richmond			

18   Chief Secretary for Ireland

Jan 57	R. Rigby		Dec 93	S. Douglas
Apr 61	W. G. Hamilton		Dec 94	Vt Milton
July 64	E of Drogheda		Mar 95	T. Pelham
June 65	Sir C. Bunbury Bt		Nov 98	Vt Castlereagh
Aug 65	Vt Beauchamp		May 01	C. Abbot
Oct 66	A. H. Hervey		Feb 02	W. Wickham
July 67	T. Jones		Feb 04	Sir E. Nepean Bt
Aug 67	Ld F. Campbell		Mar 05	N. Vansittart
Jan 69	Sir G. Macartney		Sep 05	C. Long
Nov 72	Sir J. Blaquiere		Mar 06	W. Elliot
Dec 76	Sir R. Heron Bt		Apr 07	Sir A. Wellesley
Nov 80	W. Eden		Apr 09	R. Saunders-Dundas
Apr 82	R. Fitzpatrick		Oct 09	W. W. Pole
Aug 82	W. W. Grenville		Aug 12	R. Peel
May 83	W. Windham		Aug 18	C. Grant
Aug 83	T. Pelham		Dec 21	H. Goulburn
Feb 84	T. Orde		Apr 27	Vt Melbourne
Nov 87	A. FitzHerbert		June 28	Ld F. Leveson Gower
Apr 89	R. Hobart		July 30	Sir H. Hardinge

19   Secretary at War

Nov 55	Vt Barrington		July 94	W. Windham
Mar 61	C. Townshend		Feb 01	C. Yorke
Dec 62	Ld Mendip		Aug 03	C. Bragge
July 65	Vt Barrington		May 04	W. Dundas
Dec 78	Ld Hawkesbury		Feb 06	R. Fitzpatrick
Mar 82	T. Townshend		Mar 07	J. M. Pulteney
July 82	Sir G. Yonge		June 09	Ld Gower
Apr 83	R. Fitzpatrick		Oct 09	Vt Palmerston
Dec 83	Sir G. Yonge		May 28	H. Hardinge

20   Paymaster-General

July 57	H. Fox		Jan 84	W. Grenville
July 65	C. Townshend		Apr 84	W. Grenville and Ld Mulgrave
Dec 66	Ld North and G. Cooke		Sep 89	Ld Mulgrave and M of Graham
Dec 67	G. Cooke and T. Townshend		Mar 91	D. Ryder and T. Steele
Dec 68	R. Rigby		July 00	T. Steele and G. Canning
Mar 82	E. Burke		Mar 01	T. Steele and Ld Glenbervie
July 82	I. Barre		Jan 03	T. Steele and J. H. Addington
Apr 83	E. Burke		July 04	G. Rose and Ld Somerset

Feb 06 Earl Temple and Ld Townshend   Aug 17 Sir C. Long
Apr 07 C. Long and Ld Somerset   July 26 W. Vesey Fitzgerald
Nov 13 C. Long and F. J. Robinson   July 28 J. Calcraft

21 Master-General of the Ordnance

July 59 Earl Ligonier   June 01 E of Chatham
July 63 D of Rutland   Feb 06 E of Moira
Oct 72 Vt Townshend   Apr 07 E of Chatham
Mar 82 D of Richmond   May 10 E of Mulgrave
Dec 83 Vt Townshend and D of   Jan 19 D of Wellington
        Richmond   Apr 27 M of Anglesey
Feb 95 C. M. Cornwallis   Apr 28 Vt Beresford

22 Treasurer of the Navy

Nov 56 G. Grenville   Nov 01 C. Bragge
June 62 Vt Barrington   June 03 G. Tierney
Aug 65 Vt Howe   May 04 G. Canning
Mar 70 Sir G. Elliot   Feb 06 R. B. Sheridan
June 77 Ld Mendip   Apr 07 G. Rose
Apr 82 I. Barre   Feb 18 F. J. Robinson
Aug 82 H. Dundas   Feb 23 W. Huskisson
Apr 83 C. Townshend   Sep 27 C. Grant
Jan 84 H. Dundas   Feb 28 W. Fitzgerald
June 00 D. Ryder

23 Master of the Mint

Feb 60 Vt Chetwynd   July 04 Earl Bathurst
Feb 69 Earl Cadogan   Feb 06 Ld Spencer
Jan 84 E of Effingham   Oct 06 C. Bathurst
Feb 89 E of Chesterfield   Apr 07 Earl Bathurst
Jan 90 E of Leicester   Oct 12 E of Clancarty
July 94 Sir G. Yonge   Sep 14 W. Wellesley Pole
Feb 99 Ld Hawkesbury   Oct 23 T. Wallace
Apr 01 Ld Arden   May 27 G. Tierney
July 02 J. Smyth   Feb 28 J. C. Herries

24 Attorney-General

Oct 60 C. Pratt   Feb 93 J. Scott
Jan 62 C. Yorke   July 99 J. Mitford
Dec 63 F. Norton   Feb 01 E. Law
Sep 65 C. Yorke   Apr 02 S. Perceval
Aug 66 W. De Grey   Feb 06 A. Piggot
Jan 71 E. Thurlow   Apr 07 V. Gibbs
June 78 A. Wedderburn   June 12 T. Plumer
July 80 J. Wallace   May 13 W. Garrow
Apr 82 Ld Kenyon   May 17 S. Shepherd
May 83 J. Wallace   July 19 R. Gifford
Mar 84 R. Pepper Arden   Jan 24 J. Singleton Copley
June 88 A. Macdonald   Sep 26 C. Wetherell

Apr 27 J. Scarlett   June 29 J. Scarlett
Feb 28 C. Wetherell

25 Solicitor-General

Oct   60 C. Yorke   Feb 93 J. Mitford
Jan   62 F. Norton   July 99 W. Grant
Dec   63 W. De Grey   Feb 01 S. Perceval
Aug   66 E. Willes   May 02 T. Manners Sutton
Jan   68 J. Dunning   Feb 05 V. Gibbs
Mar   70 E. Thurlow   Feb 06 S. Romilly
Jan   71 A. Wedderburn   Apr 07 T. Plumer
June 78 J. Wallace   June 12 W. Garrow
Sep   80 J. Mansfield   May 13 R. Dallas
Apr   82 J. Lee   Dec 13 S. Shepherd
Nov   82 R. Pepper Arden   May 17 R. Gifford
Apr   83 J. Lee   July 19 J. Singleton Copley
Nov   83 J. Mansfield   Jan 24 C. Wetherell
Dec   83 R. Pepper Arden   Sep 26 N. Conyngham Tindal
Mar   84 A. Macdonald   June 29 E. Burtenshaw Sugden
June 88 J. Scott

26 Under-Secretaries of State for the Northern Department

1760 M. P. Movin   1769 R. Sutton
      W. Fraser   S. Porten
1761 E. Weston   1770 R. Phelps
      C. Jenkinson   W. Fraser
1762 E. Weston   1771 E. Sedgwick
      E. Sedgwick   L. Stanhope
      L. Stanhope   W. Eden
1763 R. Phelps   W. Fraser
      J. Rivers   1772 W. Fraser
1765 R. Stonehewer   T. Whately
      W. Fraser   1773 W. Eden
1766 W. Fraser   1779 W. Fraser
      W. Burke   B. L'Anglois
1768 W. Fraser
      D. Hume
      R. Wood

27 Under-Secretaries of State for the Southern Department

1756 R. Wood   1768 R. Wood
      J. Rivers   W. Fraser
1762 E. Sedgwick   1773 F. Willis
      L. Stanhope   Sir S. Porten
1765 W. Burke   1775 Sir S. Porten
      M. P. Morin   Sir A. Chamier
      J. C. Roberts   1779 R. Bell

28   Permanent Under-Secretary to the Home Department

Mar 82	J. Bell		Feb 06	J. Beckett
Apr 82	E. Nepean		June 17	H. Hobhouse
Dec 91	J. King		July 27	S. M. Phillipps

29   Non-Permanent (later Parliamentary) Under-Secretary to the Home Department

Apr 82	E. Nepean		Aug 03	R. Pole Carew
Apr 82	T. Orde		July 04	J. H. Smyth
July 82	H. Strachey		Feb 06	C. W. Williams Wynn
Apr 83	G. A. North		Nov 07	C. C. C. Jenkinson
Feb 84	J. T. Townshend		Feb 10	H. Goulburn
June 89	S. Bernard		Aug 12	J. H. Addington
July 94	T. Brodrick		Apr 18	H. Clive
Mar 96	C. Greville		Jan 22	G. R. Dawson
Mar 98	W. Wickham		Apr 27	S. Perceval
Feb 01	E. Finch Hatton		July 27	T. Spring Rice
Aug 01	Sir G. Shee		Jan 28	W. Y. Peek

30   Parliamentary Under-Secretaries of State for Foreign Affairs*

1782	R. B. Sheridan		1783	St A. St John
	W. Fraser			W. Fraser
	G. Maddison, *vice* Sheridan		1789	J. Bland Burgess
				D. Ryder

31   Permanent Under-Secretary of State for Foreign Affairs

Feb 90	G. Aust		Oct 09	W. R. Hamilton
Oct 95	G. Hammond (res. 1806)		July 17	J. Planta
Mar 07	G. Hammond		Apr 27	J. Backhouse

32   Parliamentary Under-Secretary of State for Foreign Affairs

Aug 89	J. Bland Burgess		Mar 07	Vt FitzHarris
Jan 96	G. Canning		Aug 07	C. Bagot
Apr 99	J. H. Frere		Dec 09	C. C. Smith
Sep 00	E. Fisher		Feb 12	E. Cooke
Feb 01	Ld Harvey		Jan 22	E of Clanwilliam
Nov 03	C. Arbuthnot		Jan 23	Ld Conyngham
June 04	W. Eliot		July 24	Ld Howard de Walden
Feb 05	R. Ward		Jan 26	M of Clanricarde
Feb 06	G. Walpole and Sir F. Vincent Bt		June 28	Ld Dunglas

* There were originally two Under-Secretaries of State for Foreign Affairs, both parliamentary. In 1790 one of the Under-Secretaryships was made a permanent appointment. In 1824 a third Under-Secretary (parliamentary) was appointed, but this was discontinued in 1827.

33 Under-Secretaries of State for the Colonies

1768	R. Philips
	J. Pownall
1772	W. Knox

1776	C. D'Oyly
1778	T. De Grey
1780	B. Thompson

34 Permanent Under-Secretary of State for the Colonies

1825   R. W. Hay

35 Under-Secretary of State for War and Colonies

1794	E. Nepean Bt (War only)
1795	W. Huskisson (War only)
1801	J. Sullivan
1804	E. Cooke
1806	Sir G. Shee Bt
	Sir J. Cockburn
1807	E. Cooke, *vice* Shee
	C. W. Steward, *vice* Cockburn

1809	F. J. Robinson, *vice* Stewart
	C. Jenkinson, *vice* Cooke
	H. E. Bunbury, *vice* Robinson
1810	R. Peel, *vice* Jenkinson
1812	H. Goulburn, *vice* Peel
1821	R. W. Horton, *vice* Goulburn
1828	Ld Stanley, *vice* Horton
	Ld Leveson Gower, *vice* Stanley
	H. Twiss, *vice* Gower

36 Deputy Secretaries at War

1797	M. Lewis
1803	F. Nison

1810	W. Merry
1826	L. Sulivan

37 Senior (Parliamentary) Secretaries to the Treasury

Apr	1758	J. West
May	1762	S. Martin
Apr	1763	J. Dyson
Aug	1763	C. Jenkinson
July	1765	W. Mellish
Sep	1765	C. Lowndes
Aug	1767	G. Cooper
Apr	1782	H. Strachey
July	1782	T. Orde
Apr	1783	R. Burke

Dec	1783	G. Rose
Mar	1801	J. H. Addington
July	1802	N. Vansittart
May	1804	W. Sturges Bourne
Feb	1806	N. Vansittart
Apr	1807	Hon. H. Wellesley
Apr	1809	C. Arbuthnot
Feb	1823	S. R. Lushington
Apr	1827	J. Planta
Nov	1830	E. Ellice

38 Junior (Financial) Secretaries to the Treasury

May	1758	S. Martin
May	1762	J. Dyson
Apr	1763	C. Jenkinson
Aug	1763	T. Whately
July	1765	C. Lowndes

Sep	1765	G. Cooper
Aug	1767	T. Bradshaw
Oct	1770	J. Robinson
Apr	1782	R. Burke
July	1782	G. Rose

Apr	1783	R. B. Sheridan
Dec	1783	T. Steele
Feb	1791	C. Long
Apr	1801	N. Vansittart
July	1802	J. Sargent
May	1804	W. Huskisson
Feb	1806	J. King
Sep	1806	W. H. Fremantle

Apr	1807	W. Huskisson
Dec	1809	R. Wharton
Jan	1814	S. R. Lushington
Feb	1823	J. C. Herries
Sep	1827	T. F. Lewis
Jan	1828	G. R. Dawson
Nov	1830	T. Spring Rice

SOURCES: For a detailed note on sources consulted, see Bibliographical Note, pp. 196–7.

4 The Peerage and Orders of Knighthood

Creations and Promotions within the Higher Peerage*

(S) = in the Peerage of Scotland
(I) = in the Peerage of Ireland

Date of Patent	Original Name	New Title
Mar 1761	John West, Ld Delawarr	Earl Delawarr
Mar 1761	William Talbot, Ld Talbot	Earl Talbot
Apr 1761	John Spencer	Vt Spencer
May 1762	Edward Noel, Ld Wentworth	Vt Wentworth
Apr 1763	John Ward, Ld Ward	Vt Dudley and Ward
May 1764	Robert Henley, Ld Henley	E of Northington
Oct 1765	William Bouverie, Vt Folkestone	E of Radnor
Nov 1765	John Spencer, Vt Spencer	Earl Spencer
Aug 1766	Rt Hon. William Pitt	E of Chatham
Sep 1766	John Ligonier, Ld Ligonier	Earl Ligonier
Oct 1766	Charles Maynard, Ld Maynard	Vt Maynard
Nov 1766	Henry Percy, E of Northumberland	D of Northumberland
Nov 1766	George Brudenell Montagu, E of Cardigan	D of Montagu
Aug 1772	Wills Hill, Ld Harwich	E of Hillsborough
June 1776	Thomas Bruce, Ld Bruce	E of Ailesbury
June 1776	Thomas Villiers, Ld Hyde	E of Clarendon
June 1776	William Murray, Ld Mansfield	E of Mansfield
June 1776	Robert Hampden Trevor, Ld Trevor	Vt Hampden
Mar 1781	George Edgcumbe, Ld Edgcumbe	Vt Edgcumbe and Valletort
Feb 1782	George Germaine (Ld George Sackville)	Vt Sackville
Apr 1782	Hon. Augustus Keppel	Vt Keppel
Apr 1782	Richard Howe	Vt Howe
May 1784	George, Ld Abergavenny	E of Abergavenny and Vt Neville
May 1784	George, Ld de Ferrers	E of Leicester
May 1784	Henry, Ld Paget	E of Uxbridge
May 1784	Sir James Lowther	E of Lonsdale
July 1784	Alexander, D of Gordon(S)	E of Norwich
July 1784	John, B Talbot	Earl Talbot
July 1784	Richard, B Grosvenor	Earl Grosvenor
Nov 1784	Prince Frederick (2nd son of George III)	D of York and Albany
Dec 1784	George, Earl Temple	M of Buckingham
Dec 1784	William, B Wycombe	M of Lansdowne
July 1785	Edward, B Beaulieu	E of Beaulieu
Mar 1786	Granville, Earl Gower	M of Stafford

* In addition to sources cited in the bibliography, the most useful aid in compiling these lists is A. F. Turberville, *The House of Lords in the Age of Reform* (London, 1958).

Date of Patent	Original Name	New Title
Mar 1786	Charles, B Camden	Earl Camden
Aug 1786	John, D of Atholl(S)	Earl Strange and Baron Murray
Aug 1786	James, E of Abercorn	Vt Hamilton
Oct 1786	George, Vt Townshend	Marquis Townshend
Aug 1788	Richard, Vt Howe	Earl Howe
May 1789	Prince William Henry (3rd son of George III)	D of Clarence
June 1789	Thomas, B Sydney	Vt Sydney
Aug 1789	George, Vt Mount Edgcumbe	E of Mount Edgcumbe and Valletort
Aug 1789	James, E of Salisbury	M of Salisbury
Aug 1789	Thomas, Vt Weymouth	M of Bath
Sep 1789	Hugh, B Fortescue	Earl Fortescue and Vt Ebrington
Oct 1790	John James, E of Abercorn(S)	M of Abercorn
Nov 1790	Henry, B Digby	E of Digby and Vt Coleshill
May 1792	Joseph, B Milton	E of Dorchester and Vt Milton
	David, Vt Stormont(S)	E of Mansfield
Oct 1792	Charles, Earl Cornwallis	Marquis Cornwallis
July 1793	Francis, E of Hertford	M of Hertford
July 1793	Henry, B Porchester	E of Carnarvon
Apr 1796	George, E of Stamford	E of Warrington
May 1796	John, E of Bute(S)	M of Bute and E of Windsor
June 1796	Charles, Baron Hawkesbury	E of Liverpool
June 1796	Samuel, Baron Hood	Vt Hood of Whitley
July 1796	Charles Meadowes Pierrepont	Vt Newark
June 1797	Sir John Jervis	E of St Vincent and B Jervis
Oct 1797	Adam Duncan	Vt Duncan of Camperdown
Oct 1797	James, E of Lonsdale	Vt Lowther
Apr 1799	Prince Edward (4th son of George III)	D of Kent and Strathearn, E of Dublin
Apr 1799	Prince Ernest Augustus	D of Cumberland and Teviotdale, E of Armagh
June 1800	Alexander, B Bridport	Vt Bridport
Dec 1800	James, B Malmesbury	E of Malmesbury and Vt FitzHarris
Dec 1800	Charles, B Cadogan	E of Cadogan and Vt Chelsea
Feb 1801	Henry, E of Exeter	M of Exeter
Apr 1801	Alexander, Ld Loughborough	E of Rosslyn
June 1801	Thomas Egerton, B Grey de Wilton	E of Wilton and Vt Grey de Wilton
June 1801	Charles Marsham, B Romney	E of Romney and Vt Marsham of the Mote
June 1801	Thomas, B Pelham of Stanmer	E of Chichester

Date of Patent	Original Name	New Title
June 1801	George, B Onslow	E of Onslow and Vt Cranleigh
June 1801	William, B Craven	E of Craven and Vt Uffington
Nov 1801	Prince Adolphus Frederick (7th son of George III)	D of Cambridge
Nov 1801	Prince Augustus Frederick (6th son of George III	E of Sussex
	Sir William Lowther	Vt Lowther of Whitehaven
Feb 1802	Assheton, B Curzon	Vt Curzon of Penn
Dec 1802	Henry Dundas	Vt Melville and B Dunira
May 1804	Edward, B Clive	E of Powys
Jan 1805	Henry Addington	Vt Sidmouth
	Sir James St Clair Erskine	E of Rosslyn
Nov 1805	William, B Nelson	Earl Nelson of Trafalgar and Merton
Apr 1806	Horatio, B Walpole	E of Orford
Apr 1806	Charles, B Grey	Earl Grey and Vt Howick
Apr 1806	Charles, Vt Newark	Earl Manvers
Apr 1807	William, Vt Lowther	E of Lonsdale
Nov 1807	Gerard, B Lake	Vt Lake
Nov 1807	William, B Cathcart	Vt Cathcart
July 1809	Dudley, B Harrowby	E of Harrowby
Sep 1809	Sir Arthur Wellesley	Vt Wellington of Talavera, later E, M and finally D of Wellington and Marquis Douro (May 1814)
Sep 1812	Henry, B Mulgrave	E of Mulgrave and Vt Normanby
Sep 1812	Charles, E of Northampton	M or Northampton
Sep 1812	John, Earl Camden	Marquess Camden
Sep 1812	Edward, B Harewood	E of Harewood and Vt Lascelles
June 1813	Charles, B Whitworth (I)	Vt Whitworth
June 1814	George, E of Aberdeen(S)	Vt Gordon
June 1814	George, B Keith	Vt Keith
June 1814	William, Vt Cathcart	Earl Cathcart
July 1815	Henry William, E of Uxbridge	M of Anglesey
Aug 1815	Granville Leveson Gower	Vt Granville of Stone Park
Nov 1815	James, B Verulam	E of Verulam and Vt Grimston
Nov 1815	John, B Brownlow	E of Brownlow and Vt Alford
Nov 1815	John, B Eliot	E of St Germans
Nov 1815	George James, E of Cholmondeley	M of Cholmondeley
Nov 1815	John, B Bovingdon	E of Morley and Vt Bovingdon
Nov 1815	Charles, Vt Whitworth	Earl Whitworth

Date of Patent	Original Name	New Title
Dec 1815	William, B Beauchamp of Powys	Earl Beauchamp and M of Hastings and E of Rawdon
Feb 1817	Francis, E of Moira and B Hastings	Vt Elmley
	Thomas Grosvenor	E of Wilton
July 1821	John, B Eldon	E of Eldon and Vt Encombe
July 1821	John Somers Cocks, B Somers	Earl Somers and Eastnor
July 1821	John, B Rous	E of Stradbroke
July 1821	Charles, E of Ailesbury	M of Ailesbury
July 1821	Richard, Vt Curzon	Earl Howe
July 1821	Edward, Vt Falmouth	E of Falmouth
July 1821	Richard, E of Donoughmore (I)	Vt Hutchinson of Knocklofty
Feb 1822	Richard, M of Buckingham	D of Buckingham and Chandos
Apr 1823	William, B Beresford	Vt Beresford
	Edward Jervis	Vt St Vincent
July 1823	Charles, M of Londonderry (I)	Earl Vane and Vt Seaham
	William Eliot	E of St Germans
Dec 1823	Richard, E of Clancarty (I) and B Trench of Gorbally	Vt Clancarty
Dec 1826	William Pitt, B Amherst	E of Amherst and Vt Holmesdale
Feb 1827	Stapleton, B Combermere	Vt Combermere
Apr 1827	Rt Hon. Frederick John Robinson	Vt Goderich
	John Hely-Hutchinson	Vt Hutchinson of Knocklofty
Oct 1827	John Frederick, B Cawdor	Earl Cawdor
Oct 1827	William, E of Darlington	M of Cleveland
Oct 1827	John, Vt Dudley and Ward	E of Dudley

The Orders of Knighthood

Order of the Garter: Creations, 1760–1830

Date	Person	Died
27 May 1762	William Henry, Pr. of Brunswick-Lüneburg (later D of Gloucester and Edinburgh)	Aug 1805
27 May 1762	3rd E of Bute	Mar 1792
23 Apr 1764	Adolphus Frederick, D of Mecklenburg-Strelitz	June 1794
23 Apr 1764	5th E of Halifax	June 1771
26 Dec 1765	George Augustus Frederick, Pr. of Wales (later George IV)	June 1830
26 Dec 1765	Charles William Ferdinand, Pr. (later D) of Brunswick-Wolfenbüttel	Nov 1806
26 Dec 1765	15th E of Albemarle	Oct 1772
21 Dec 1767	Henry Frederick, Pr. of Brunswick-Lüneburg (later D of Cumberland and Strathearn)	Sep 1790
12 Dec 1768	4th D of Marlborough	Jan 1817
20 Sep 1769	3rd D of Grafton	Mar 1811

Date	Person	Died
11 Feb 1771	2nd Earl Gower (later 1st M of Stafford)	Oct 1803
19 June 1771	Frederick, Pr. of Brunswick-Lüneburg (later D of York and Albany)	Jan 1827
18 June 1772	Ld North (later 4th E of Guildford)	Aug 1792
3 June 1778	20th E of Suffolk	Mar 1779
3 June 1778	4th E of Rochford	Sep 1781
3 June 1778	3rd Vt Weymouth (later 1st M of Bath)	Nov 1796
19 Apr 1782	William Henry, Pr. of Brunswick-Lüneburg (later William IV)	
19 Apr 1782	8th D of Richmond	Dec 1806
19 Apr 1782	5th D of Devonshire	July 1811
19 Apr 1782	3rd E of Shelburne (later M of Lansdowne)	May 1805
3 Oct 1782	4th D of Rutland	Oct 1787
2 June 1786	Edward, Pr. of Brunswick-Lüneburg (later D of Kent and Strathearn)	Jan 1820
2 June 1786	Ernest Augustus, Pr. of Brunswick-Lüneburg (later D of Cumberland and King of Hanover)	Nov 1851
2 June 1786	Augustus Frederick, Pr. of Brunswick-Lüneburg (later D of Sussex)	Apr 1843
2 June 1786	William, Landgrave of Hesse-Cassel (later Elector of the Holy Roman Empire)	Feb 1821
2 June 1786	5th D of Beaufort	Oct 1803
2 June 1786	1st M of Buckingham	Feb 1813
2 June 1786	2nd E (later 1st M) Cornwallis	Oct 1805
9 Apr 1788	3rd D of Dorset	July 1799
9 Apr 1788	4th D of Northumberland	July 1817
15 Dec 1790	Ernest Lewis, D of Saxe-Gotha	Apr 1804
15 Dec 1790	5th D of Leeds	Jan 1799
15 Dec 1790	2nd E of Chatham	Sep 1835
12 June 1793	1st M of Salisbury	June 1823
12 June 1793	16th E of Westmorland	Dec 1841
12 June 1793	8th E of Carlisle	Sep 1825
28 May 1794	3rd D of Buccleuch	Jan 1812
16 July 1794	William Frederick, Pr. of Brunswick-Lüneburg (later D of Gloucester and Edinburgh)	Apr 1857
16 July 1794	3rd D of Portland	Oct 1809
2 June 1797	1st E Howe	Aug 1799
1 Mar 1799	2nd E Spencer	Nov 1834
14 Aug 1799	2nd E (later 1st M Camden)	Oct 1840
3 June 1801	3rd D of Roxburghe	Mar 1804
25 Nov 1803	5th D of Rutland	Jan 1857
25 Nov 1803	3rd E of Hardwicke	Nov 1834
17 Jan 1805	6th D of Beaufort	Nov 1835
17 Jan 1805	1st M of Abercorn	Jan 1818
17 Jan 1805	30th E of Pembroke	Oct 1827
17 Jan 1805	9th E of Winchilsea	Aug 1826
17 Jan 1805	6th E of Chesterfield	Aug 1815
27 May 1805	3rd E of Dartmouth	Nov 1810
22 Mar 1806	2nd M of Stafford (later D of Sutherland)	July 1833
18 July 1807	5th M of Hertford	June 1822
18 July 1807	2nd E of Lonsdale	Mar 1844
3 Mar 1810	Marquess Wellesley	Sep 1842
26 Mar 1812	9th D of Richmond	Aug 1819

Date	Person	Died
26 Mar 1812	4th D of Montrose	Dec 1836
12 June 1812	2nd E of Moira (later 1st M of Hastings)	Nov 1826
19 June 1812	4th D of Newcastle	Jan 1851
4 Mar 1813	M of Wellington (later D)	Sep 1852
27 July 1813	Alexander I, Emperor of All the Russias	Sep 1825
21 Apr 1814	Louis XVIII, King of France	Sep 1824
9 June 1814	Francis I, Emperor of Austria	Mar 1835
9 June 1814	Frederick William III, King of Prussia	June 1840
9 June 1814	2nd E of Liverpool	Dec 1828
9 June 1814	Vt Castlereagh (later 2nd M of Londonderry)	Aug 1822
10 Aug 1814	Ferdinand VII, King of Spain	Sep 1833
10 Aug 1814	William Frederick, Pr. of Orange (King of the Netherlands)	Dec 1843
23 May 1816	Leopold, D of Saxe-Coburg-Saalfeld (later King of the Belgians)	Dec 1865
24 July 1817	3rd E Bathurst	July 1834
19 Feb 1818	1st M of Anglesey	Apr 1854
25 Nov 1819	5th D of Northumberland	Feb 1847
7 June 1820	2nd M (1st D) of Buckingham	Jan 1839
13 Feb 1822	Frederick IV, King of Denmark	Dec 1839
13 Feb 1822	John VI, King of Portugal	Mar 1826
22 July 1822	1st M Cholmondeley	Apr 1827
22 Nov 1822	6th M of Hertford	Mar 1842
16 July 1823	2nd M of Bath	Mar 1837
9 Mar 1825	Charles X, King of France	Nov 1836
30 Jan 1826	5th D of Dorset	July 1843
16 Mar 1827	Nicholas I, Emperor of All the Russias	Mar 1855
10 May 1827	6th D of Leeds	July 1838
10 May 1827	6th D of Devonshire	Jan 1858
10 May 1827	2nd M of Exeter	Jan 1867
13 May 1829	10th D of Richmond	Oct 1860
10 June 1829	3rd E of Ashburnham	Oct 1830

Order of the Thistle

History of the Order

On 29 May 1687, James II ordered Letters Patent to be made out for 'reviving and restoring the Order of the Thistle to its full glory, lustre and magnificency'. The earlier history of the Order remains obscure. During the reign of William and Mary the Order remained in abeyance. It was revived again by Anne on 31 December 1703. These 1703 statutes were later modified on 17 February 1715 by George II and on 8 May 1827 by George IV. By this last modification the number of Knights of the Order was extended from 12 to 16.

Creations, 1760–1830

Date	Person	Died
13 Apr 1763	9th Ld Cathcart	Aug 1776
13 Apr 1763	3rd E of March (D of Queensberry)	Dec 1810
7 Aug 1765	4th D of Argyll	Nov 1770

Date	Person	Died
23 Dec 1767	3rd D of Buccleuch	(res.) May 1794
23 Dec 1767	3rd D of Atholl	Nov 1774
23 Dec 1767	8th E of Carlisle	(res.) June 1793
26 Oct 1768	4th M of Lothian	Apr 1775
2 Nov 1768	7th Vt Stormont (E of Mansfield)	Sep 1796
28 Nov 1768	3rd D of Roxburghe	Mar 1804
5 Apr 1770	William Henry, Pr. of Brunswick-Lüneburg (William IV)	June 1837
4 Mar 1771	3rd E of Rosebery	Mar 1814
18 Aug 1773	2nd E of Northington	July 1786
11 Jan 1775	4th D of Gordon	June 1827
1 Nov 1775	7th E of Galloway	Nov 1806
11 Oct 1776	5th M of Lothian	Jan 1815
3 Mar 1786	8th D of Hamilton	Aug 1799
29 Nov 1786	4th E of Ailesbury	Apr 1814
14 June 1793	4th D of Montrose	(res.) Mar 1812
30 May 1794	4th Earl Poulett	Jan 1819
26 July 1797	17th E of Morton	July 1827
23 Apr 1800	4th D of Atholl	Sep 1830
23 Nov 1805	10th Baron (1st E) Cathcart	June 1843
16 Mar 1808	4th E of Aberdeen	Dec 1860
22 May 1812	4th D of Buccleuch	Apr 1819
22 May 1812	12th E of Eglintoun	Dec 1819
23 May 1814	8th E of Galloway	Mar 1834
23 May 1814	2nd E of Abergavenny	Mar 1843
23 Feb 1815	1st Baron Erskine	Nov 1823
20 May 1819	5th E (1st M) of Ailesbury	Jan 1856
26 Apr 1820	6th M of Lothian	Apr 1824
22 May 1820	8th M of Tweeddale	Oct 1876
17 July 1821	1st Baron (1st M) Ailsa	Sep 1846
17 July 1821	8th E of Lauderdale	Sep 1839
17 July 1821	2nd Vt Melville	June 1851
17 July 1821	6th M of Queensberry	Dec 1837
10 May 1827	5th E of Aboyne (9th M of Huntley)	June 1853
10 May 1827	3rd Earl Brooke	Aug 1853
3 Sep 1827	4th E of Fife	Mar 1857
3 Sep 1827	23rd E of Moray	Jan 1848

Order of the Bath

History of the Order

The Order is of very ancient origin. After some time in abeyance, it was revived and remodelled by George I by statute dated 18 May 1725. After this date, the Order consisted of the Sovereign, a Great Master and 36 Companions. In 1815, the Order was again remodelled and very much enlarged – partly to reward services in the campaigns against Napoleon. For reasons of space, the very many creations after 1815 are omitted.

Creations 1760–1815

Mar 1761	1st Ld Carysfort	Mar 1761	Sir James Gray
Mar 1761	Lt-Gen. Hon. Joseph Yorke (Ld Dover)	Mar 1761	Sir William Beauchamp
		Mar 1761	Sir John Gibbons

Mar 1761	Admiral George Pocock
Mar 1761	Sir Jeffrey Amherst (Ld Amherst)
Mar 1761	John Griffin (4th Ld Howard de Walden)
Mar 1761	Francis Blake Delaval
Mar 1761	Charles Frederick
Mar 1761	George Warren
May 1761	Charles Saunders
Jan 1764	Charles Cook (E of Belmont)
Apr 1764	1st Ld Clive
Dec 1765	Andrew Mitchell
Dec 1765	William Draper
Dec 1767	Pr. Frederick, Bp of Osnaburgh (D of York)
Oct 1768	Sir Horace Mann
May 1770	Sir John Moore
May 1770	Sir John Lindsay
June 1770	Eyre Coote
Feb 1771	Sir Charles Montagu
Feb 1771	Ralph Payne (Ld Lavington)
Feb 1771	William Lynch
Jan 1772	Sir Charles Hotham
Jan 1772	William Hamilton
Feb 1772	Robert Murray Keith
May 1772	George Macartney (Ld, Vt, and E Macartney)
Feb 1773	James Adolphus Oughton
June 1773	Robert Gunning
Aug 1774	John Blaquiere (Ld Blaquiere)
Feb 1775	William Gordon
Dec 1775	John Irwin
July 1776	Guy Carleton (Ld Dorchester)
Oct 1776	Hon. William Howe (Vt Howe)
Nov 1776	John Clavering
Apr 1777	Sir Henry Clinton
Dec 1778	Edward Hughes
Feb 1779	James Harris (Ld, E of Malmesbury)
Mar 1779	Hector Monro
May 1779	Randal Williams (6th E, 1st M of Antrim)
Nov 1780	Richard Peirson
Nov 1780	Thomas Wroughton
Nov 1780	Sir George Bridges Rodney (Ld Rodney)
Dec 1781	2nd Vt Ligonier
May 1782	John Jervis (E of St Vincent)
Jan 1783	George Augustus Elliot (Ld Heathfield)
Jan 1783	Charles Grey (Ld, Earl Grey)
Jan 1785	Robert Boyd
Sep 1785	Frederick Haldimand
Sep 1785	Archibald Campbell
Dec 1786	William Fawcett
Dec 1786	Robert Monckton (4th Vt Galway)
May 1788	Sir George Yonge
May 1788	Alexander Hood (Ld, Vt Bridport)
June 1788	Robert Sloper
Dec 1791	Morton Eden (Ld Henley)
Aug 1792	William Augustus Pitt
Aug 1792	Hon. John Vaughan
Aug 1792	William Medows
Aug 1792	Robert Abercromby
Sep 1793	Charles Whitworth (Ld Whitworth)
May 1794	Hon. George Keith Elphinstone (Ld, Vt Keith)
May 1794	Sir John Borlase Warren
Nov 1794	Adam Williamson
July 1795	Sir Joseph Banks
July 1795	Ralph Abercromby
Feb 1796	Hugh Cloberry Christian
Jan 1797	Alured Clarke
Jan 1797	James Henry Craig
May 1797	Horatio Nelson (Ld, Vt Nelson)
Feb 1798	John Colpoys
Feb 1799	Hon. Charles Stuart
Jan 1800	Henry Harvey
Jan 1800	Sir Andrew Mitchell
May 1801	Thomas Graves
May 1801	John Hely-Hutchinson (Ld Hutchinson and 2nd E of Donoughmore)
June 1801	Thomas Trigge
June 1801	John Thomas Duckworth
Sep 1801	Sir James Saumarez
May 1802	Eyre Coote
Feb 1803	John Francis Craddock
Apr 1803	Sir David Dundas
May 1804	Hon. Arthur Paget
Aug 1804	Hon. Arthur Wellesley (D of Wellington)
Sep 1804	Hon. George James Ludlow
Sep 1804	John Moore
Sep 1804	Samuel Hood
Jan 1806	7th E of Northesk
Jan 1806	Sir Richard John Strachan
Mar 1806	Hon. Alexander Cochrane
Sep 1806	Sir John Stuart
Oct 1806	Philip Francis
Oct 1806	Sir George Hilario Barlow

Mar	1808	Percy Clinton Sydney (6th Vt Strangford)
Oct	1808	Richard Goodwin Keats
Apr	1809	Sir David Baird
Apr	1809	George Beckwith
Apr	1809	Hon. John Hope (Ld Niddry)
Apr	1809	Brent Spencer
Apr	1809	Thomas Cochrane (10th E of Dundonald, expelled July 1814, readmitted Sep 1847)
Sep	1809	John Cope Sherbrooke
Oct	1810	William Carr Beresford (Ld Beresford)
Feb	1812	Thomas Graham (Ld Lynedoch)
Feb	1812	Rowland Hill (Ld, Vt Hill)
Feb	1812	Sir Samuel Auchmuty
Mar	1812	Henry Wellesley (Ld Cowley)
June	1812	Hon. Edward Paget
Aug	1812	Sir Stapleton Cotton (Ld, Vt Combermere)
Sep	1812	Charles Stuart (Ld Stuart de Rothesay)
Oct	1812	Isaac Brock
Feb	1813	Hon. George Cranfield Berkeley
Feb	1813	Sir George Nugent
Feb	1813	William Keppel
Feb	1813	Sir John Doyle
Feb	1813	William Cavendish-Bentinck
Feb	1813	James Leith
Feb	1813	Thomas Picton
Feb	1813	Hon. Galbraith Lowry Cole
Feb	1813	Hon. Charles William Stewart (Ld Stewart, 3rd M of Londonderry)
June	1813	Hon. Alexander Hope
June	1813	Henry Clinton
Sep	1813	9th E of Dalhousie
Sep	1813	Hon. William Stuart
Sep	1813	George Murray
Sep	1813	Hon. Edward Michael Pakenham
July	1814	William Young
Aug	1814	William, Pr. of Orange (William I, King of the Netherlands)

Order of St Patrick

History of the Order

The Order was instituted by George III by warrant dated 5 February 1783. The fifteen original knights (the 'Knights Founders') were nominated on 5 February 1783, invested on 11 March and installed on 17 March. Through ill-health, the Earl of Ely was absent from both the investiture and installation. Hence he is not considered to be one of the Knights Founders.

The Knights of St Patrick

The Original Knights (5 February 1783)

Name	Date of Death
Prince Edward (later D of Kent and Strathearn)	Jan 1820
2nd D of Leinster	Oct 1804
12th E (later M) of Clanricarde	Dec 1797
6th E of Antrim	July 1791
6th E of Westmeath	Sep 1792
5th E of Inchiquin (later M of Thomond)	Feb 1808
6th E (later M) of Drogheda	Dec 1822
2nd E of Tyrone (later M of Waterford)	Dec 1800
2nd E of Shannon	May 1807
2nd E of Clanbrassil	Feb 1798
2nd E of Mornington (later Marquis Wellesley)	Sep 1842
2nd E of Arran	Oct 1809

Name	*Date of Death*
2nd E of Courtown	Mar 1810
1st E of Charlemont	Aug 1799
1st E of Bective	Feb 1795
E of Ely	died May 1783 without being invested

Subsequent Creations, 1784–1830

Feb 1784	Earl Carysfoot	Apr 1828
Dec 1794	Vt Loftus (later M of Ely)	Mar 1806
Mar 1795	E of Clermont	Sep 1806
Mar 1798	E of Ormond and Ossory	Aug 1820
Mar 1798	Vt Dillon	Nov 1813
Aug 1800	E of Altamont (later M of Sligo)	Jan 1809
Jan 1801	Marquess Conyngham	Dec 1832
Mar 1806	M of Waterford	July 1826
May 1806	M of Headfort	Oct 1829
Nov 1806	E of Roden	June 1820
Nov 1807	M of Ely	Sep 1845
Apr 1808	E of Shannon	Apr 1842
Feb 1809	Earl O'Neill	Mar 1841
Nov 1809	M of Thomond	Aug 1846
Mar 1810	M of Sligo	Jan 1845
Apr 1810	E of Enniskillen	Mar 1840
Dec 1813	E of Longford	May 1835
Aug 1821	D of Cumberland (later King of Hanover)	Nov 1851
Aug 1821	M of Donegal	Oct 1844
Aug 1821	E of Caledon	Apr 1839
Aug 1821	Earl Talbot	quit for Garter 1844
Aug 1821	E of Ormond and Ossory	May 1838
Aug 1821	E of Meath	Mar 1851
Aug 1821	E of Fingal	July 1836
Aug 1821	E of Courtown	June 1835
Aug 1821	E of Roden	Mar 1870

Order of St Michael and St George

History of the Order

The Order was not founded until 27 April 1818. Its membership was originally confined to 'natives of the United States, of the Ionian islands, and of the island of Malta and its dependencies, and to such other subjects of his Majesty as may hold high and confidential situation in the Mediterranean'.

During the period up to 16 August 1832 (when the Order was enlarged) membership consisted of the King of the United Kingdom as Sovereign, the Grand Master, 8 Knights Grand Cross (including the Grand Master), 12 Knights Commanders, and 24 Knights.

5 Parliament and Elections

House of Commons

Speakers

Date of Election	Name	Birth and Death	Constituency
23 Jan 1728	Arthur Onslow	1691–1768	Surrey
3 Nov 1761	Sir John Cust	1718–1770	Grantham
22 Jan 1770	Sir Fletcher Norton	1716–1789	Guildford
31 Oct 1780	Charles Wolfran Cornwall	1735–1789	Winchelsea
5 Jan 1789	William Wyndham Grenville	1759–1834	Buckinghamshire
8 June 1789	Henry Addington	1757–1844	Truro
11 Feb 1801	Sir John Mitford	1748–1830	Northumberland
10 Feb 1802	Charles Abbot	1757–1829	Woodstock
2 June 1817	Charles Manners-Sutton	1780–1858	Scarborough
19 Feb 1835	James Abercromby	1776–1858	Edinburgh

Contested Elections for the Speakership

Date	Successful Candidate	Voting
22 Jan 1770	Sir Fletcher Norton	237–121
1 Oct 1780	Charles Wolfran Cornwall	203–134
5 Jan 1789	William Wyndham Grenville	215–144
8 June 1789	Henry Addington	215–142
2 June 1817	Charles Manners-Sutton	312–152

Chairmen of Ways and Means

19 Nov 1754	Job Staunton Charlton
17 Nov 1761	Marshe Dickinson
15 Feb 1765	John Paterson
14 Nov 1768	Sir Charles Whitworth
30 Nov 1778	John Ord
31 May 1784	Thomas Gilbert

Clerks of the House

1768	J. Hatsell
1820	J. H. Ley

Parliamentary Sessions

Date for which Summoned	Date of Dissolution
31 May 1754	20 Mar 1761
19 May 1761	11 Mar 1768
10 May 1768	30 Sep 1774
29 Nov 1774	1 Sep 1780
31 Oct 1780	25 Mar 1784
18 May 1784	11 June 1790
12 July 1796	5 Nov 1800*
22 Jan 1801	29 June 1802
31 Aug 1802	24 Oct 1806
13 Dec 1806	29 Apr 1807
22 June 1807	29 Sep 1812
24 Nov 1812	10 June 1818
4 Aug 1818	29 Feb 1820
21 Apr 1820	2 June 1826
25 July 1826	24 July 1830
14 Sep 1830	23 Apr 1831

* By proclamation dated 5 Nov 1800 the members of the Great Britain Parliament were summoned to meet on 22 Jan 1801 as Members of the First Parliament of the United Kingdom and Ireland.

Composition of the House

Period	England	Wales	Scotland	Ireland	County	Borough	Univ.	Total
1707–1800	489	24	45	–	122	432	4	558
1801–26	489	24	45	100	186	467	5	658
1826–32	489	24	45	100	188	465	5	658

During the period 1760–1800, the House of Commons returned 558 members, representing 314 constituencies. The detailed breakdown of these figures was as follows:

England, 489 Members, 245 constituencies:
  40 counties, returning 2 Members each;
  196 boroughs, returning 2 Members each;
  2 boroughs (London and the combined constituency of Weymouth and Melcombe Regis), returning 4 Members each;
  5 boroughs (Abingdon, Banbury, Bewdley, Higham Ferrers and Monmouth), returning 1 Member each;
  2 universities (Oxford and Cambridge) returning 2 Members each.

Wales, 24 Members, 24 constituencies:
  12 counties, returning 1 Member each;
  12 boroughs, returning 1 Member each.

Scotland, 45 Members, 45 constituencies;
  27 counties, returning 1 Member each;
  3 pairs of counties, 1 county in each pair alternating with the other in returning 1 Member;
  1 burgh (Edinburgh), returning 1 Member;
  14 groups of burghs, each returning 1 Member.

As a result of the Act of Union, total membership of the House of Commons increased to 658, with Ireland returning exactly 100 Members. The Irish representation was as follows:

	County	Borough	Univ	Total
32 two-Member counties	64			
2 two-Member boroughs (Cork, Dublin)		4		
31 single-Member boroughs		31		
Trinity College, Dublin			1	
Total, Ireland	64	35	1	100
Total, England, Scotland and Wales	122	432	4	558
Total, United Kingdom	186	467	5	658

The only other change in representation occurred in 1821, with the disfranchisement of Grampound, a two-member borough constituency. To recompense, the seats thus released were given to Yorkshire, which as a result had four seats. This reform was effective from 1826.

Public Petitions

A feature of the work of the House of Commons during the early part of the nineteenth century was the public petitions which occupied a great part of the time of the House of Commons. It was not until 1839 that these debates were discontinued and their place was gradually taken by Questions to Ministers.

Session	No. of Petitions Presented
1785	298
1801	192
1812–13	1,699
1827	3,635
1833	10,394
1843	33,898

Social Status of Members

	1761	1768	1774	1780	1784	1790	1796*	1802	1806	1807	1812	1818	1820	1826	1830
Baronets	68	64	78	75	83	73	85	84	73	70	78	72	69	67	84
Irish peers	18	24	18	20	19	19	16	7	9	10	6	4	6	7	3
Ed. sons Eng. peers	27	25	20	25	27	42	38	40	45	47	38	50	46	57	66
Yr. sons Eng. peers	51	46	44	44	37	40	51	57	60	61	58	71	62	66	57
Sons of Scottish peers	11	10	13	10	10	7	11	8	10	7	4	2	5	6	5
Sons of Irish peers	7	7	15	14	11	12	28	28	34	30	31	26	25	25	23
Sons of peeresses	3	3	1	–	–	1	–	3	4	4	6	4	3	4	1
Other	373	379	369	370	371	364	429	431	423	429	437	429	442	426	419
Total	558	558	558	558	558	558	658	658	658	658	658	658	658	658	658

*Includes 100 Irish members returned in 1801.
SOURCE: G. P. Judd IV, *Members of Parliament 1734–1832* (New Haven, 1955).

House of Lords

Lord Chairman of Committees

(The Lords' equivalent of Deputy Speaker: the Lord Chancellor acts as Speaker.)

10 Nov 1814	E of Shaftesbury
4 Feb 1851	Ld Redesdale

Officers

Clerk of the Parliaments

1740	Cowper, A.
1788	Rose, G.
1818	Rose, G. H.
1855	Shaw Lefevre, J. G.

Gentleman Usher of the Black Rod	Yeoman Usher of the Black Rod	Serjeant-at-Arms
1747 Bellenden, Hon. H.	1754 Quarme, R.	1745 Jephson, R.
1761 Robinson, Sir S.	1787 Quarme, R.	1789 Watson, W.
1765 Molyneux, Sir F.	1830 Pulman, J.	1818 Seymour, G. F.
1812 Tyrwhitt, Sir T.	1860 Clifford, R. C. S.	1841 Perceval, A.
1832 Clifford, Sir A. W. J.		

Deputy Serjeant-at-Arms

By 1730	Hollinshead, T.
By 1776	Macklay, F.
By 1813	Butt, W.
1841	Goodbody, G. W.

Composition of the House

Date	Sovereign and Regnal Year	Remarks	Dukes	Mar-quises	Earls	Vis-counts	Barons	Repres-enting Scotland	Repres-enting Ireland	Arch-bishops and Bishops	Total
1714	1 George I	After the Union with Scotland in 1707	23	2	74	11	67	16		26	219
1727	1 George II		31	1	71	15	62	16		26	222
1760	1 George III		25	1	81	12	63	16		26	224
1820	1 George IV	After the Union with Ireland in 1801	25	17	100	22	134	16	28	30	372
1830	1 William IV		23	18	103	22	160	16	28	30	400
1837	1 Victoria		24	19	111	19	192	16	28	30	439

Party Leaders, 1783–1830

The Prime Minister has always been Leader of the House in which he sits. If a peer, the Prime Minister was always Leader in the House of Lords – the only exception during this period was during the short ministry of the Duke of Portland (1807–9).

If the Prime Minister was in the Commons, it was part of the duties of one of the Secretaries of State to be responsible for the conduct of government business in the Lords. Normally this task was undertaken by the Home Secretary but it was not always so. Thus, Lord Grenville led the Lords from 1790 to 1801 as Foreign Secretary.

3rd E Temple	Dec 1783
1st Ld Sydney	Dec 1783 – June 1789
5th D of Leeds	June 1789 – Nov 1790

1st Ld Grenville	Nov 1790 – Feb 1801
Ld Pelham	July 1801 – Aug 1803
Ld Hawkesbury	Nov 1803 – Feb 1806
1st Ld Grenville	Feb 1806 – Mar 1807
2nd E of Liverpool	Mar 1807 – Apr 1827
1st Vt Goderich	Apr 1827 – Jan 1828
1st D of Wellington	Jan 1828 – Nov 1830

SOURCE: J. Sainty, *House of Lords Record Office Memo No. 31.*

Scottish Representative Peers

The provisions for electing the Scottish representative peers were contained in the Scottish Union with England Act 1707 (1706, c.7) and the Union with Scotland Act 1707 (6 Ann c.78). Later legislation, in 1847 and 1851, introduced certain changes.

There were 16 Scottish representative peers, elected for the period of each Parliament, with by-elections held when necessary to fill such vacancies as occurred. Elections were held in Edinburgh, with peers entitled to vote either in person, or by proxy, or by sending a signed list. The Lord Clerk Register (or the Clerks of Session) acted as Returning Officers.

The Lord Clerk Register

1756–60	Alexander Hume Campbell
1760–68	Earl of Morton
1768–1816	Lord Frederick Campbell
1816–21	Archibald Colquhoun
1821–45	Rt Hon. William Dundas

Elections of Scottish Representative Peers

Date		General or By-election	Number of Peers Present
1761	5 May	G	39
	12 Aug	B	22
1763	8 Mar	B	20
1766	21 Aug	B	23
1767	1 Oct	B	28
1768	26 Apr	G	37
	21 Dec	B	17
1770	17 Jan	B	23
1771	2 Jan	B	28
1774	15 Nov	G	34
1776	24 Jan	B	13
	13 June	B	13
	14 Nov	B	15
1778	24 Sep	B	15
1780	17 Oct	G	26
1782	24 July	B	14
1784	8 May	G	40
1787	28 Mar	B	19
1788	10 Jan	B	18

Date		General or By-election	Number of Peers Present
1790	24 July	G	33
1793	7 Aug	B	13
1794	23 Oct	B	11
1796	30 June	G	25
1798	15 Aug	B	11
1802	10 Aug	G	29
1803	16 June	B	13
1804	14 Nov	B	15
1806	4 Dec	G	18
1807	9 June	G	20
1812	13 Nov	G	29
1817	17 Apr	B	13
1818	24 July	G	27
1819	18 Mar	B	10
1820	11 Apr	G	21
1821	2 Aug	B	10
1823	2 Oct	B	11
1824	8 July	B	6
1825	2 June	B	8
1826	13 July	G	25
1828	10 Apr	B	10
1830	2 Sep	G	21

SOURCE: J. Fergusson, *The Sixteen Peers of Scotland 1707–1959* (Oxford, 1960). All elections from 1760 to 1830 took place in the Palace of Holyrood House.

Irish Representative Peers

The provisions for the election of the Irish representative peers (before later modification in 1857 and 1882) were contained in an act of the Irish Parliament (40 Geo III c.29) and the Union with Ireland Act 1800 (39 and 40 Geo III c.67).

The Original 28 Peers (elected 2 Aug 1800)

John Thomas	13th E of Clanricarde	Robert	2nd Vt Wicklow
George Frederick	7th E of Westmeath	Thomas	1st Vt Northland
Thomas	2nd E of Bective	Laurence	Vt Oxmantown
Robert	2nd E of Roden	Charles Henry	2nd Vt O'Neill
John Denis	3rd E of Altamont	Francis	1st Vt Bandon
John	2nd E of Glendore	Richard Hely	1st Vt Donoughmore
Thomas	2nd E of Longford	Hugh	1st Vt Carleton
John	1st E of Erne	Richard	11th B Calier
Otway	1st E of Desart	Edmund Henry	2nd B Glentworth
Robert	1st E of Leitrim	George	1st B Callen
Richard	2nd E of Lucan	Charles	Ld Somerton
Robert	1st E of Londonderry	Richard	1st Vt Longueville
Henry	1st Earl Conyngham	Robert	1st B Rossmore
Francis	2nd E of Llandaff	James	B Tyrawly

Elections on Vacancy of Irish Representative Peers 1800–1830

Date	New Peer	Replacing
15 Jan 1805	2nd E of Enniskillen	E of Desart
15 Jan 1805	2nd E of Caleden	E of Leitrim
17 Dec 1806	2nd E of Charlemont	E of Llandaff
15 July 1807	3rd E of Kingston	E of Rosse
23 Jan 1809	2nd E of Clancarty	E of Clanricarde
19 Apr 1809	Vt Mountjoy	M of Sligo
23 Jan 1810	2nd E of Rosse	E of Normanton
7 Jan 1812	2nd E of Gosford	Vt Longueville
5 Apr 1815	2nd E of Mountcashel	E of Westmeath
7 Mar 1816	4th E of Mayo	E of Wicklow
7 Mar 1816	5th Ld Farnham	E of Glandore
7 Mar 1816	2nd M of Thomond	B Callen
21 Mar 1819	3rd E of Carrick	Vt Northland
10 May 1819	E of Belmore	E of Glengall
16 Oct 1820	1st Ld Dufferin	E of Roden
	5th Vt Powerscourt	M of Londonderry
8 Feb 1822	3rd E of Wicklow	B Tyrawly
14 Feb 1823	1st Vt Lorton	E of Mountcashell
5 Feb 1824	2nd Vt Gort	Vt Powerscourt
2 Feb 1826	5th Ld Farnham	E of Donoughmore
24 Nov 1826	3rd E of Mountcashel	Vt Carleton
4 Feb 1830	2nd E of Glengall	E of Blessington
22 Mar 1830	3rd Vt Doneraile	M of Headfort

The Franchise*

Types

Scot and Lot (SL): right of voting vested in inhabitant householders paying poor rate.

Householder (H): also known as 'potwalloper' franchise. Right of voting vested in all inhabitant householders not receiving alms or poor relief.

Burgage (B): franchise attached to property in the borough.

Corporation (C): right of voting confined to the corporation.

Freeman (FM): right of voting belonged to the freemen of the borough (in the City of London in the livery, rather than in the freemen as a whole).

Freeholder (FH): right of voting lay with the freeholders.

* Both editors would like to acknowledge the help and assistance of John Brooke. The following tables are based both on his figures and on his general format.

English Boroughs, 1830

Electors	SL	H	B	C	FM	FH	Total
Over 5,000	1	1	–	–	5	–	7
1,001 to 5,000	6	2	–	–	24	4	36
601 to 1,000	7	5	–	–	9	1	22
301 to 600	10	1	–	–	13	–	24
101 to 300	8	5	10	1	11	1	36
51 to 100	4	–	10	2	5	–	21
50 or fewer	2	–	15	26	13	–	56
Total	38	14	35	29	80	6	202

English Counties

Constituency	MPs	Electors (est.)	Pop. 1831
Bedfordshire	2	2,000	95,483
Berkshire	2	3,000	145,389
Buckinghamshire	2	4,000	146,529
Cambridgeshire	2	3,000	143,955
Cheshire	2	5,000	334,391
Cornwall	2	2,500	302,440
Cumberland	2	4,000	169,681
Derbyshire	2	4,000	237,170
Devon	2	3,000	494,478
Dorset	2	3,000	159,252
Durham	2	3,000	253,910
Essex	2	6,000	317,507
Gloucestershire	2	6,000	387,019
Hampshire	2	5,000	314,280
Herefordshire	2	4,000	111,211
Hertfordshire	2	4,000	143,341
Huntingdonshire	2	2,000	53,192
Kent	2	8,000	479,155
Lancashire	2	8,000	1,336,854
Leicestershire	2	6,000	197,003
Lincolnshire	2	5,000	317,465
Middlesex	2	3,000	1,358,330
Monmouthshire	2	1,500	98,130
Norfolk	2	6,000	390,054
Northamptonshire	2	3,000	179,336
Northumberland	2	2,000	237,000
Nottinghamshire	2	3,000	225,000
Oxfordshire	2	4,000	152,156
Rutland	2	800	19,385
Shropshire	2	4,000	222,938
Somerset	2	8,000	404,200
Staffordshire	2	5,000	410,512
Suffolk	2	5,000	296,317
Surrey	2	4,000	486,326
Sussex	2	4,000	272,340
Warwickshire	2	4,000	336,610
Westmorland	2	2,000	55,041

Constituency	MPs	Electors (est.)	Pop. 1831
Wiltshire	2	3,000	240,156
Worcestershire	2	4,000	211,563
Yorkshire	2*	20,000	1,371,675

* Increased to 4 in 1821.

English Boroughs

Constituency	Type of Seat	MPs	Electors (est.)	Constituency	Type of Seat	MPs	Electors (est.)
Abingdon	SL	1	250	Chipping Wycombe	FM	2	50
Aldborough	SL	2	50	Christchurch	C	2	70
Aldeburgh	FM	2	50	Cirencester	H	2	800
Amersham	SL	2	70	Clitheroe	B	2	102
Andover	C	2	24	Cockermouth	B	2	278
Appleby	B	2	250	Colchester	FM	2	1,500
Arundel	SL	2	200	Corfe Castle	SL	2	100
Ashburton	B	2	250	Coventry	FM	2	2,500
Aylesbury	H	2	500	Cricklade	FH	2	200–1,000
Banbury	C	1	18	Dartmouth	FM	2	50–
Barnstaple	FM	2	350	Derby	FM	2	700
Bath	C	2	30	Devizes	C	2	30
Bedford	FM	2	1,000	Dorchester	SL	2	400
Bere Alston	B	2	30–	Dover	FM	2	1,000
Berwick-on-Tweed	FM	2	600	Downton	B	2	100
Beverley	FM	2	1,000	Droitwich	C	2	14
Bewdley	FM	1	50–	Dunwich	FM	2	40–
Bishop's Castle	FM	2	150	Durham	FM	2	1,500
Bletchingley	B	2	90	East Grinstead	B	2	36
Bodmin	C	2	36	East Looe	FM	2	50
Boroughbridge	B	2	64	East Retford	FM	2	150
Bossiney	FM	2	30–	Evesham	FM	2	1,000
Boston	FM	2	250	Exeter	FM	2	1,500
Brackley	C	2	33	Eye	SL	2	200
Bramber	B	2	36	Fowey	SL	2	100
Bridgnorth	FM	2	1,000	Gatton	SL	2	2
Bridgwater	SL	2	250	Gloucester	FM	2	2,000
Bridport	SL	2	200	Grampound	FM	2*	50
Bristol	FM	2	5,000	Grantham	FM	2	400
Buckingham	C	2	13	Great Bedwyn	B	2	120
Bury St Edmunds	C	2	37	Great Grimsby	FM	2	200
Callington	SL	2	50	Great Marlow	SL	2	250
Calne	C	2	25	Great Yarmouth	FM	2	800
Cambridge	FM	2	150	Guildford	FM	2	200
Camelford	FM	2	20	Harwich	C	2	32
Canterbury	FM	2	1,500	Haslemere	FH	2	100
Carlisle	FM	2	1,000	Hastings	FM	2	50–
Castle Rising	FM	2	50	Hedon	FM	2	150
Chester	FM	2	1,500	Helston	C	2	30–
Chichester	SL	2	500	Hereford	FM	2	1,000
Chippenham	B	2	129	Hertford	FM	2	500

Constituency	Type of Seat	MPs	Electors (est.)	Constituency	Type of Seat	MPs	Electors (est.)
Heytesbury	B	2	26	Northallerton	B	2	200
Higham Ferrers	FM	1	80	Northampton	H	2	1,000
Hindon	H	2	200	Norwich	FM	2	3,000
Honiton	H	2	700	Nottingham	FM	2	2,000
Horsham	B	2	80	Okehampton	FM	2	300
Huntingdon	FM	2	200–	Old Sarum	B	2	7
Hythe	FM	2	100	Orford	FM	2	50–
Ilchester	H	2	200	Oxford	FM	2	1,000
Ipswich	FM	2	700	Penryn	SL	2	200
King's Lynn	FM	2	300	Peterborough	SL	2	400
Kingston-upon-Hull	FM	2	1,200	Petersfield	B	2	70
				Plymouth	FM	2	200
Knaresborough	B	2	100	Plympton Erle	FM	2	100
Lancaster	FM	2	2,500	Pontefract	B	2	320–400
Launceston	FM	2	30–	Poole	FM	2	100
Leicester	FM	2	2,500	Portsmouth	FM	2	100
Leominster	SL	2	500	Preston	H	2	800
Lewes	SL	2	200	Queenborough	FM	2	150
Lichfield	FM	2	700	Reading	SL	2	600
Lincoln	FM	2	1,000	Reigate	FH	2	200
Liskeard	FM	2	50	Richmond	B	2	270
Liverpool	FM	2	2,000	Ripon	B	2	150
London	FM	4	7,000	Rochester	FM	2	600
Lostwithiel	C	2	24	Rye	FM	2	40–
Ludgershall	FH	2	100	St Albans	FM	2	500
Ludlow	FM	2	500	St Germans	H	2	20
Lyme Regis	FM	2	50	St Ives	SL	2	200
Lymington	FM	2	50–	St Mawes	FM	2	25
Maidstone	FM	2	1,000	Salisbury	C	2	54
Maldon	FM	2	800–	Saltash	C	2	30–
Malmesbury	C	2	13	Sandwich	FM	2	700
Malton	B	2	300	Scarborough	C	2	50–
Marlborough	C	2	12–	Seaford	SL	2	100–
Midhurst	B	2	200	Shaftesbury	SL	2	300
Milborne Port	SL	2	120	Southampton	FM	2	500
Minehead	H	2	300	Southwark	SL	2	2,000
Mitchell	SL	2	50	Stafford	FM	2	400
Monmouth	FM	1	800	Stamford	SL	2	500
Morpeth	FM	2	250	Steyning	SL	2	100
Newark	SL	2	1,000	Stockbridge	SL	2	100
Newcastle-under-Lyme	FM	2	600	Sudbury	FM	2	800
				Tamworth	SL	2	300
Newcastle-upon-Tyne	FM	2	2,500	Taunton	H	2	500
				Tavistock	FH	2	100
Newport	B	2	200	Tewkesbury	FM	2	500
Newport (I. of W.)	C	2	24	Thetford	C	2	31
New Romney	C	2	40	Thirsk	B	2	50
New Shoreham	SL	2†	100–800†	Tiverton	C	2	25
Newton	C	2	36	Totnes	FM	2	100
Newtown (I. of W.)	B	2	40–	Tregony	H	2	150
New Windsor	SL	2	300	Truro	C	2	24
New Woodstock	FM	2	200	Wallingford	SL	2	200

Constituency	Type of Seat	MPs	Electors (est.)	Constituency	Type of Seat	MPs	Electors (est.)
Wareham	SL	2	500	Whitchurch	B	2	70
Warwick	SL	2	500	Wigan	FM	2	100
Wells	FM	2	250	Wilton	C	2	24
Weobley	B	2	100	Winchelsea	FM	2	40–
Wendover	H	2	150	Winchester	FM	2	70
Wenlock	FM	2	500	Wootton Bassett	SL	2	250
Westbury	B	2	69	Worcester	FM	2	2,000
West Looe	FM	2	50	Yarmouth	C	2	50
Westminster	SL	2	12,000	(I. of W.)			
Weymouth and Melcombe Regis	FH	4	300	York	FM	2	2,500

* None after 1821.
† Number of voters increased in 1771 with addition of 40s freeholders in the rape of Bramber.

Universities

	MPs	Electors
Cambridge	2	500
Oxford	2	500

Welsh Counties

Constituency	MPs	Electorate (approx)	Pop. 1831
Anglesey	1	700	48,325
Breconshire	1	1,200	47,763
Cardiganshire	1	800	64,780
Carmarthenshire	1	1,000	100,740
Carnarvonshire	1	500	66,448
Denbighshire	1	2,000	83,629
Flintshire	1	1,000	60,012
Glamorganshire	1	1,500	126,612
Merionethshire	1	600	35,815
Montgomery	1	1,300	66,482
Pembrokeshire	1	2,000	81,425
Radnorshire	1	1,000	24,651

Welsh Boroughs

Constituency	Type of Seat	MPs	Electorate (approx.)	Pop. 1831
Beaumaris	C	1	24	10,817
Brecon	FM	1	100	5,026
Cardiff Boroughs	FM	1	500	14,034
Cardigan Boroughs	FM	1	4,000	8,230
Carmarthen	FM	1	100	17,641
Carnarvon Boroughs	FM	1	1,000	7,642
Denbigh Boroughs	FM	1	500	14,245
Flint Boroughs	SL	1	600	31,327
Haverfordwest	FM	1	500	10,832
Montgomery	FM	1	70	18,680
New Radnor Boroughs	FM	1	1,000	8,410
Pembroke Boroughs	FM	1	500	12,366

Scottish Counties

Constituency	MPs	Electorate (approx.)	Pop. 1831
Aberdeenshire	1	180	177,657
Argyllshire	1	50	101,973
Ayrshire	1	200	145,055
Banffshire	1	120	48,604
Berwickshire	1	100	34,048
Dumfriesshire	1	50	73,770
Dunbartonshire	1	70	33,211
Edinburghshire	1	100	219,345
Elginshire	1	70	n.a.c.34,000
Fife	1	150	128,839
Forfarshire	1	100	139,606
Haddingtonshire	1	70	36,145
Inverness-shire	1	100	94,797
Kincardineshire	1	50	31,431
Kirkcudbrightshire	1	100	40,590
Lanarkshire	1	100	316,819
Linlithgowshire	1	40	23,291
Orkney and Shetland	1	30	58,239
Peebleshire	1	30	10,578
Perthshire	1	100	142,894
Renfrewshire	1	100	133,443
Ross-shire	1	50	74,820†
Roxburghshire	1	100	43,663
Selkirkshire	1	50	6,833
Stirlingshire	1	70	72,621
Sutherland	1	30	25,518
Wigtownshire	1	50	36,258
Buteshire ⎱ *	1	12	14,151
Caithness ⎰	1	20	34,529
Clackmannanshire ⎱ *	1	25	23,801
Kinross-shire ⎰	1	25	c.15,000
Nairnshire ⎱ *	1	20	c. 9,000
Cromartyshire ⎰	1	18	c. 9,000

* In alternate Parliaments one of each pair of counties was represented.
† This figure is the population for Ross and Cromarty.

Scottish Burghs*

Constituency	MPs	Electorate (approx.)	Pop. 1831
Aberdeen Burghs	1	87	58,019
Anstruther Easter Burghs	1	92	–
Ayr Burghs	1	83	22,626
Dumfries Burghs	1	95	c.20,000
Dysart Burghs	1	87	–
Edinburgh	1	33	162,156
Elgin Burghs	1	84	20,732

Constituency	MPs	Electorate (approx.)	Pop. 1831
Glasgow Burghs	1	87	202,426
Haddington Burghs	1	99	17,755
Inverness Burghs	1	72	19,674
Linlithgow Burghs	1	94	–
Perth Burghs	1	125	25,571
Stirling Burghs	1	103	37,769
Tain Burghs	1	82	–
Wigtown Burghs	1	75	8,675

* An indirect system of election operated in all the Scottish burghs except Edinburgh, where the 33 members of the Town Council elected 1 MP directly. In the other burghs, the Town Councils nominated 1 delegate each, a majority of electors in each district electing 1 MP.

Patronage

Between 1794 and 1816, four lists of Parliamentary patronage were compiled. The first was that drawn up by the Society of the Friends of the People and published in 1793 (*State of the Representation in England and Wales*). All the others were published by T. H. B. Oldfield – one in 1794 (*History of the Boroughs*, 2nd ed., II, pp. 477–84), compiled on the basis of the 1790 General Election, another in 1797 (*History of the Original Constitution of Parliaments*, pp. 531–43), incorporating the results of the 1796 elections, and a final edition in 1816 (*Representative History of Great Britain and Ireland*, VI, pp. 285–96). There are numerous wide discrepancies in these figures. The totals below are thus only a rough guide.

England and Wales

	1793	1794	1797	1816
Number of Members returned				
by peers: by nomination	92	92	93	115
by influence	72	103	124	103
by commoners: by nomination	80	102	74	85
by influence	57	54	70	52
by the Treasury etc.	7	8	9	16
Total (out of 513) for England and Wales	308	359	370	371

Scotland

	1793	1794	1797	1816
Returned by peers		30	20	31
commoners		9	13	14
the Treasury		–	12	–
Total (out of 558) for England, Wales and Scotland		398	415	416

SOURCE: *English Historical Documents, 1783–1832*, Vol. XI (London, 1959).

6 Foreign Affairs

British Treaties, 1756–1830

Date Signed	Subject	Place Signed
1756		
16 Jan	Treaty with Prussia	London
1758		
11 Apr	Treaty with Prussia	London
7 Dec	Convention with Prussia	London
1759		
17 Jan	Convention with Landgrave of Hesse-Cassel	London
9 Nov	Convention with Prussia	–
1760		
14 Jan	Treaty with Duke of Brunswick	Marburg
1 Apr	Convention with Hesse-Cassel	London
28 July	Treaty of peace and commerce with Morocco	Fez
12 Dec	Convention with Prussia	–
1761		
28 Jan	Renewal of peace with Tripoli	Tripoli
3 Mar	Protocol with Hesse	London
10 Aug	Convention with Brunswick for troops	Brunswick
14 May	Treaty of peace and commerce with Algiers	Algiers
22 June	Treaty of peace and commerce with Tunis	Bardo
22 July	Treaty of peace and commerce with Tripoli	Tripoli
3 Nov	Preliminary articles of peace with France and Spain (accession: Portugal, 22 Nov)	Fontainebleau
1763		
10 Feb	Definitive treaty of peace with France and Spain (accession: Portugal, 10 Feb)	Paris
21 Sep	Act of guarantee by Britain of treaty between France, Spain and Sardinia of 10 June 1763	London
1765		
27 Feb	Convention with France	London
3 Aug	Treaty of peace and commerce with Algiers	Algiers
1766		
5 Feb	Treaty of commerce and alliance with Sweden	Stockholm
1 July	Treaty of amity and commerce with Russia	St Petersburg
1771		
22 Jan	Spanish declaration and British counter-declaration concerning Falkland Islands	London

Date Signed	Subject	Place Signed
1776		
9 Jan	Treaty of subsidy with Duke of Brunswick	Brunswick
15 Jan	Treaty of subsidy with Landgrave of Hesse-Cassel	Cassel
5 Feb	Treaty of subsidy with Hesse-Hanau	Hanau
20 Apr	Subsidiary treaty with Prince of Waldeck	Arolsen
25 Apr	Ulterior convention with Hereditary Prince of Hesse-Cassel, as Regent of Hesse-Hanau	Hanau
11 Dec	Treaty with Landgrave of Hesse for corps of 1,067 men to serve in America	Cassel
11 Dec	Convention with Hesse-Cassel	Cassel
1777		
1 Feb	Treaty with Brandenburg-Anspach for corps of 1,200 infantry	Anspach
10 Feb	Treaty with Hereditary Prince of Hesse, as Regent of Hesse-Hanau	Hanau
1778		
23 Apr	Treaty of subsidy with Anhalt-Zerbst	Stade
1780		
12/28 Mar	Cartel with France for general exchange of all prisoners taken at sea and brought to Europe (with Additional Article, 16/22 June)	London/ Versailles
4 July	Explanatory article with Denmark concerning neutral trade	Copenhagen
1782		
30 Nov	Provisional articles of peace with USA	Paris
1783		
20 Jan	Preliminary articles of peace with France	Versailles
20 Jan	Preliminary articles of peace with Spain	Versailles
24 May	Additional articles with Morocco	Sallee
2 Sep	Preliminary articles of peace with the Netherlands	Paris
3 Sep	Definitive treaty of peace with France	Versailles
3 Sep	Definitive treaty of peace with Spain	Versailles
3 Sep	Definitive treaty of peace and friendship with USA	Paris
1784		
20 May	Definitive treaty of peace and amity with the Netherlands	Paris
1786		
14 July	Convention with Spain concerning America	London
26 Sep	Treaty of commerce and navigation with France	Versailles
1787		
15 Jan	Explanatory convention with France	Versailles
30 Aug	Reciprocal declaration with France to put in action 6 vessels of the line	Versailles
31 Aug	Explanatory convention with France concerning French commercial establishments in India	Versailles
28 Sep	Treaty of alliance with Landgrave of Hesse-Cassel	Cassel
2 Oct	Convention with Prussia	Berlin

Date Signed	Subject	Place Signed
27 Oct	Reciprocal declarations with France to stop the armament made on the occasion of the troubles in Holland	Versailles
1788		
15 Apr	Treaty of defensive alliance with the Netherlands	The Hague
13 June	Provisional treaty of defensive alliance with Prussia	Loo-en-Gueldre
13 Aug	Treaty of defensive alliance with Prussia	Berlin
1790		
9 Jan	Alliance with Prussia and Holland	Berlin
24 July	Exchange of declaration and counter-declaration with Spain	Madrid
28 Oct	Convention with Spain concerning America	Escurial
10 Dec	Convention with the Netherlands, Empire and Prussia concerning the Austrian Netherlands	The Hague
1791		
8 Apr	Treaty of peace with Morocco	Sallee
1793		
12 Feb	Convention with Spain	London
4 Mar	Articles with Elector of Brunswick-Lüneburg concerning body of troops entering British service	London
4 Mar	Preliminary articles with Hanover concerning deployment of Hanoverian troops on the continent in British pay	London
25 Mar	Commercial convention with Russia	London
25 Mar	Convention with Russia for concerted action against France	London
10 Apr	Treaty of subsidy with Landgrave of Hesse-Cassel	–
25 Apr	Treaty of alliance with Sardinia	London
25 May	Convention with Spain	Aranjuez
12 July	Convention with Sicily	Naples
14 July	Convention with Prussia	Mayence
23 Aug	Second convention with Landgrave of Hesse-Cassel	Maykammer
30 Aug	Convention with Emperor	London
21 Sep	Treaty of subsidy with Margrave of Baden	Carlsruhe
26 Sep	Treaty with Portugal	London
5 Oct	Treaty of subsidy with Landgrave of Hesse-Darmstadt	Langen-Candel
1794		
7 Jan	Article of agreement with Hanover for additional troops to be taken into British pay	London
11 Jan	Agreement with Spain	Madrid
19 Apr	Treaty of subsidy between Britain and the Netherlands, and Prussia	The Hague
19 Apr	Separate convention with the Netherlands	The Hague
8 Nov	Treaty of subsidy with Duke of Brunswick	Brunswick
19 Nov	Treaty of amity, commerce and navigation with USA	London
1795		
18 Feb	Treaty of defensive alliance with Russia	St Petersburg
4 May	Convention of loan with Emperor of Germany	Vienna
20 May	Treaty of defensive alliance with Emperor of Germany	Vienna

Date Signed	Subject	Place Signed
1796		
Jan	Treaty with Algiers concerning Corsica	–
4 May	Explanatory article with USA concerning trade and intercourse with American Indians	Philadelphia
10 June	Treaty of subsidy with Hesse-Darmstadt	Frankfurt
1797		
21 Feb	Treaty of commerce with Russia	St Petersburg
11 May	Declaration concerning Treaty of 21 Feb	Moscow
16 May	Convention of loan with Emperor of Germany	London
1798		
15 Mar	Explanatory article with USA concerning the River St Croix	London
16 July	Article of peace and commerce with Tripoli	Tripoli
13 Sep	Cartel for exchange of prisoners of war with France	London
25 Oct	Declaration with American Commissioners concerning the River St Croix	Providence
1 Dec	Treaty of alliance with King of the Two Sicilies	Naples
29 Dec	Provisional treaty with Russia	St Petersburg
1799		
5 Jan	Treaty of alliance with Turkey	Constantinople
22 June	Convention with Russia	St Petersburg
29 June	Declaration with Russia concerning treaty of Dec 1798	St Petersburg
1800		
18 Jan	Convention with Prince of Orange for receiving Dutch troops into British pay	–
11 Mar	Convention with Prince of Orange concerning Dutch ships surrendered 30 Aug 1799	–
16 Mar	Treaty of subsidy with Bavaria	Munich
2 Apr	First explanatory article of convention with Prince of Orange	–
20 Apr	Treaty of subsidy with Duke of Württemberg	Louisbourg
30 Apr	Treaty with Elector of Mayence	Pfora
10 June	Second explanatory article of convention with Prince of Orange	London
20 June	Convention with Emperor	Vienna
20 June	Secret convention granting Emperor an indemnity for his territorial losses	Vienna
15 July	Supplementary convention to Bavarian subsidy treaty of 16 Mar	Amberg
29 Aug	Preliminary convention with Denmark	Copenhagen
3 Sep	Treaty of peace and commerce with Algiers	Algiers
1801		
Jan	Treaty of commerce with Persia	–
Jan	Political treaty with Persia	–
19 Mar	Treaty with Algiers concerning Malta	Algiers
14 June	Treaty of peace with Morocco	Fez
17 June	Convention with Russia (accessions: Denmark, 23 Oct; Sweden, 30 Mar 1802)	St Petersburg
1 Oct	Preliminary articles of peace with France	London

Date Signed	Subject	Place Signed
20 Oct	Additional articles to convention of 17 June with Russia	Moscow
20 Oct	Explanatory declaration with Russia	Moscow
23 Oct	Convention with Denmark concerning neutral trade	Moscow
1802		
8 Jan	Convention of claims with USA	London
27 Mar	Definitive treaty of peace with France, Spain and Batavian Republic	Amiens
17 May	Postal convention with France	–
1803		
2 Jan	Articles of agreement with Batavian authorities on evacuation of Cape of Good Hope	The Cape
25 July	Explanatory convention with Sweden concerning treaty of 1661	London
1804		
3 Dec	Preliminary and secret convention with Sweden	Stockholm
1805		
11 Apr	Treaty of concert with Russia (accession: Austria, 9 Aug): additional articles 10 May and 24 July	St Petersburg
9 Aug	Declaration with Russia and Austria respecting future policy	St Petersburg
31 Aug	Treaty with Sweden concerning convention of 1804	Helsingborg
3 Oct	Treaty with Sweden	Beckascog
1807		
28 Jan	Articles of treaty of peace and amity with Prussia	Memel
17 June	Convention with Sweden	London
23 June	Convention of subsidy with Sweden	Stralsund
27 June	Convention of subsidy with Prussia	London
7 July	Treaty between commanders of British and Spanish troops	Buenos Aires
22 Oct	Convention of friendship and amity with Portugal	London
1808		
8 Feb	Convention of subsidy with Sweden	Stockholm
30 Mar	Treaty of alliance and subsidy with the Two Sicilies	Palermo
30 Aug	Convention for evacuation of Portugal by French army	Lisbon
1809		
5 Jan	Treaty of peace and commerce with Turkey	Dardanelles
14 Jan	Treaty of peace, friendship and alliance with Ferdinand VII of Spain (Additional Article 21 Mar)	London
1 Mar	Convention with Sweden	Stockholm
12 Mar	Preliminary treaty of friendship and alliance with Persia	Tehran
21 Apr	Convention of loan with Prince Regent of Portugal	London
24 Apr	Treaty of alliance with Austria	London
13 May	Treaty of alliance and subsidy with the Two Sicilies	Palermo
9 Sep	Treaty with Algiers renewing existing treaties	
1810		
19 Feb	Treaty of commerce and navigation with Portugal	Rio de Janeiro
19 Feb	Treaty of friendship and alliance with Portugal	Rio de Janeiro

Date Signed	Subject	Place Signed
1812		
14 Mar	Treaty of peace with Persia	Tehran
2 May	Treaty of commerce with Tunis	Bardo
10 May	Treaty of commerce with Tripoli	Tripoli
18 July	Treaty of peace, union and friendship with Russia	Orebro
18 July	Treaty of peace and friendship with Sweden	Orebro
12 Sep	Supplementary treaty of alliance and subsidy with the Two Sicilies	Palermo
1813		
3 Mar	Treaty of concert and subsidy with Sweden	Stockholm
12 May	Cartel for exchange of prisoners of war with USA	Washington
14 June	Convention with Prussia	Reichenbach
27 June	Convention with Russia	Reichenbach
6 July	Convention with Russia concerning holding German Legion in service of his Imperial Majesty	Peterswaldaw
30 Sep	Supplementary convention of concert and subsidy with Prussia	London
30 Sep	Supplementary convention of concert and subsidy with Russia	London
3 Oct	Preliminary treaty of alliance with Austria	Toplitz
16 Oct	Additional article with Tunis	Bardo
22 Oct	Separate and additional article to treaty of concert and subsidy with Sweden of 3 Mar.	Leipzig
5 Dec	Subsidiary agreement with Hanoverian government	London
1814		
14 Jan	Treaty of peace with Denmark (Additional Articles, 7 Apr)	Kiel
3 Feb	Armistice with Neapolitan forces	Naples
3 Feb	Subsidiary agreement with Sardinia	London
5 Feb	Convention with Spain for mutual restoration of vessels recaptured from the enemy	London
15 Feb	Convention with Austria, Prussia and Russia concerning territorial arrangements of peace with France	Troyes
1 Mar	Treaty of union, concert and subsidy with Austria	Chaumont
1 Mar	Treaty of union, concert and subsidy with Prussia	Chaumont
1 Mar	Treaty of union, concert and subsidy with Russia	Chaumont
18 Apr	Convention with French armies for surrender of Genoa	St François d'Albaro
23 Apr	Convention for suspension of hostilities with France	Paris
27 Apr	Accession of Britain to treaty between Austria, Prussia, Russia and Napoleon of 11 Apr	Paris
27 Apr	Convention of armistice between British and Austrian armies in Italy and French army	Turin
28 May	Military convention between Britain, Austria, Prussia and Russia, and France	Paris
30 May	Definitive treaty of peace and amity with France	Paris
2 June	Convention with Prussia and Russia concerning Russo-German Legion	Paris
14 June	Protocol of conference with Austria, Russia and Prussia concerning union of Holland and Belgium	Vienna

Date Signed	Subject	Place Signed
29 June	Supplementary convention with Austria	London
29 June	Supplementary convention with Prussia	London
29 June	Supplementary convention with Russia	London
4 July	Convention with Post Office of Hamburg	London
5 July	Treaty of friendship and alliance with Spain (Additional Articles, 28 Aug)	Madrid
13 Aug	Convention with the Netherlands concerning trade and colonies	London
13 Aug	Convention with Sweden concerning compensation for restoration of Guadeloupe to France	London
25 Nov	Definitive treaty of friendship and alliance with Persia	Tehran
24 Dec	Treaty of peace and amity with USA	Ghent
1815		
3 Jan	Treaty of defensive alliance with Austria and France (accessions: Bavaria, 26 Jan; the Netherlands, 31 Jan)	Vienna
22 Jan	Treaty with Portugal for restriction of slave trade	Vienna
8 Feb	Declaration by Britain, Austria, France, Portugal, Prussia, Russia, Spain and Sweden concerning universal abolition of slave trade	Vienna
20 Mar	Declaration of the Eight Powers (as above) on affairs of Swiss Confederation (accession: Swiss Confederation 27 May)	Vienna
25 May	Treaty of alliance with Austria, Prussia and Russia against Napoleon (accessions: France, 27 Mar; Hanover, 7 Apr; Portugal, 8 Apr; Sardinia, 9 Apr; Bavaria, 15 Apr; Princes and Free Towns of Germany, 27 Apr; the Netherlands, 28 Apr; Baden, 13 May; Switzerland, 20 May; Hesse-Darmstadt, 23 May; Saxony, 27 May; Württemberg, 30 May; Denmark, 1 Sep): supplemented by convention of 30 Apr	Vienna
29 Mar	Protocol of conferences between plenipotentiaries of the Eight Powers on the cessions of the King of Sardinia to the Canton of Geneva	Vienna
30 Apr	Additional convention of alliance and subsidy with Austria, Prussia and Russia	Vienna
2 May	Treaty of subsidy with Sardinia	Brussels
13 May	Naval convention with Naples	Naples
19 May	Treaty of subsidy with Baden	Brussels
19 May	Treaty with Russia and the Netherlands concerning Russian-Dutch loan	London
20 May	Territorial treaty between King of Sardinia and Austria, Britain, France, Prussia and Russia (accession: Switzerland, 20 May)	Vienna
20 May	Convention with France concerning occupation of Martinique	Barbados
22 May	Convention with Sardinia for fortification of Genoa	Turin
31 May	Treaty between the Netherlands and Austria, Prussia, Britain and Russia concerning Kingdom of the Netherlands	Vienna
6 June	Treaty of subsidy with Württemberg	Brussels
7 June	Treaty of subsidy with Bavaria	Brussels

Date Signed	Subject	Place Signed
9 June	Act of the Congress of Vienna, signed by Britain, Austria, France, Portugal, Prussia, Russia and Sweden (accessions: the Netherlands, 20 Oct; Two Sicilies, 1 Feb 1816; Sardinia, 15 Oct 1816; Spain, 7 June 1817; Parma, 25 Jan 1818; Hesse-Darmstadt, 1 Mar 1818; Saxony, 10 Mar 1818; Württemberg, 14 Apr 1818; Denmark, 20 Apr 1818; Tuscany, 22 Apr 1818; Hesse-Cassel, 11 Jan 1819; Bavaria, 7 May 1820)	Vienna
3 July	Convention between Prussian, English and French commanders for suspension of hostilities	St Cloud
3 July	Convention of commerce with USA	London
2 Aug	Convention with Austria, Prussia and Russia concerning custody of Napoleon	Paris
10 Aug	Capitulation of island of Guadeloupe, signed by Britain and France	Guadeloupe
12 Aug	Convention with the Netherlands concerning colonies of Demerara, Essequibo and Berbice	London
18 Sep	Accession of Britain to territorial treaty between Saxony and Prussia of 18 May	Paris
3 Nov	Protocol of conference with Austria, Prussia and Russia to regulate disposition of territories ceded by France	Paris
5 Nov	Treaty with Austria, Prussia and Russia concerning Ionian Islands (accessions: France, 27 Sep 1816; Turkey, 24 Apr 1819)	Paris
20 Nov	Treaty of alliance and friendship with Austria, Prussia and Russia	Paris
20 Nov	Definitive treaty with Austria, Prussia, Russia and France (accessions: Hesse-Cassel, 15 Oct 1816; Spain, 8 June 1817; Bavaria, 20 Dec 1817; Parma, 30 Jan 1818; Hesse-Darmstadt, 1 Mar 1818; Saxony, 21 Mar 1818; Sardinia, 9 Apr 1818; Denmark, 21 Apr 1818; Tuscany, 24 Apr 1818; Württemberg, 14 Aug 1818; the Netherlands, 8 Feb 1822)	Paris
20 Nov	Convention between Britain, Austria, Prussia and Russia, and France concerning French indemnity	Paris
20 Nov	Convention with Austria, Prussia, Russia and France concerning occupation of a military line in France by an allied army	Paris
20 Nov	Convention between Britain, Austria, Prussia and Russia, and France concerning claims of subjects of allied powers upon France	Paris
20 Nov	Act signed with Austria, France, Prussia and Russia guaranteeing Swiss neutrality	Paris
20 Nov	Protocol signed with Austria, Prussia and Russia respecting the 700 million francs France is to pay allied powers	Paris
20 Nov	Convention with France concerning claims of British subjects	Paris
1816		
3 Apr	Treaty with Algiers concerning Ionian Islands	Algiers

Date Signed	Subject	Place Signed
17 Apr	Declaration of Bey of Tunis concerning abolition of Christian slavery	Bardo
17 Apr	Treaty with Tunis concerning Ionian Islands	Bardo
29 Apr	Declaration of Bey of Tripoli concerning abolition of Christian slavery	Tripoli
29 Apr	Treaty with Tripoli concerning Ionian Islands	Tripoli
20 May	Additional article with Algiers concerning Hanover	Algiers
30 June	Treaty with Hesse touching its renunciations and possessions	Frankfurt
28 Aug	Declaration of Bey of Algiers concerning abolition of Christian slavery	Algiers
26 Sep	Convention of commerce and navigation with King of the Two Sicilies	London
16 Nov	Treaty with the Netherlands concerning Luxembourg, etc.	Frankfurt
1817		
28/29 Apr	Arrangement with USA concerning naval forces on American Lakes	Washington
17 May	Convention with Turkish commissaries	Joannina
28 July	Additional convention with Portugal for prevention of slave trade (separate Article, 11 Sep; Additional Articles, 15 Mar 1823)	London
23 Sep	Treaty with Spain for abolition of slave trade (Additional Articles, 10 Dec 1822)	Madrid
19 Oct	Declaration of Bey of Tunis that Tunisian ships shall not cruise in English Channel (similar declaration by Bey of Tripoli, 8 Mar 1818)	Bardo
1818		
25 Apr	Convention between Britain, Austria, Prussia and Russia, and France for final liquidation of private claims upon French government (accessions: Hesse-Darmstadt, 5 May; Tuscany, 1 June; Saxony, 6 June; Bavaria, 12 June; Württemberg, 15 June; Sardinia, 30 June; Swiss Confederation, 2 July; Baden, 22 July; the Netherlands, 30 July; Parma, 3 Aug; Hesse-Cassel, 26 Aug; Denmark, 17 Sep): Additional Articles, 4 July 1818	Paris
4 May	Treaty with Netherlands for preventing subjects engaging in slave trade (Additional Articles, 31 Dec 1822 and 25 Jan 1823)	The Hague
6 Oct	Convention with Post Office of the Netherlands	The Hague
9 Oct	Convention with France for evacuation of French territory by Allied troops (accessions: Parma, 12 Nov; Switzerland, 12 Nov; Sardinia, 22 Mar 1819; Baden, 28 Aug 1819; Bavaria, 7 May 1820; Spain, 6 July 1820; Tuscany, 2 Dec 1820)	Aix-la-Chapelle
20 Oct	Convention of commerce with USA	London
1819		
2 Feb	Definitive arrangement with France relative to liquidation of French indemnity, signed by Britain, Austria, Prussia, Russia and France	Paris

Date Signed	Subject	Place Signed
10 July	Treaty with Austria, Prussia, Russia and Baden	Frankfurt
20 July	General treaty of territorial commission assembled at Frankfurt, signed by Britain, Austria, Prussia, Russia (accessions: Baden, 4 Aug 1820; Parma, 15 Aug 1820; Tuscany, 10 Nov 1820; Saxony, 18 Dec 1820; Sardinia, 30 Dec 1820)	Frankfurt
1820		
15 May	Final Act of ministerial conferences held at Vienna to complete and consolidate organisation of German Confederation	Vienna
1822		
18 June	Decision of British and American commissioners concerning boundaries	Utica
12 July	Convention with Russia (as mediator) and USA concerning slave trade	St Petersburg
22 Nov	Declaration of Congress of Verona concerning a solution to slave trade, signed by Britain, Austria, France, Prussia and Russia	Verona
1823		
12 Mar	Convention with Spain for settlement of English claims against Spain	Madrid
17 Nov	Convention with Emperor of Austria for definitive settlement of Austrian loan	Vienna
1824		
1 Jan	Declaration of Bey of Tunis concerning slave trade	Tunis
7 Jan	Declaration of Bey of Tunis concerning administration of justice to British and Sardinian subjects	Tunis
19 Jan	Explanatory articles to treaty of peace with Morocco of 14 June 1801	Fez
17 Mar	Treaty of commerce and exchange with the Netherlands	London
2 Apr	Convention of commerce with Prussia	London
16 June	Convention of commerce with Denmark	London
24 Apr/16 July	Declaration with Sweden and Norway concerning navigation and trade	
26 July	Declarations of Bey of Algiers on renewal of peace with Britain	Algiers
6 Nov	Treaty with King of Sweden and Norway for preventing slave trade	Stockholm
1825		
2 Feb	Treaty of amity, commerce and navigation with United Provinces of Rio de la Plata	Buenos Aires
9 Apr	Convention with Russia concerning north-west coast of America, and Pacific Ocean	St Petersburg
18 Apr	Treaty of amity, commerce and navigation with Colombia	Bogota
1826		
26 Jan	Convention of commerce and navigation with France	London
18 Mar	Convention of commerce and navigation with Sweden and Norway	London

Date Signed	Subject	Place Signed
4 Apr	Protocol of conference with Russia concerning British mediation between Ottoman Porte and the Greeks	St Petersburg
13 Apr	Declaration of Bey of Tunis concerning treatment of British subjects and vessels	Tunis
20 June	Treaty with King of Siam	Bangkok
13 Nov	Convention with USA	London
23 Nov	Treaty of commerce and navigation with Ava (Burma)	Ra-ta-na-para
23 Nov	Convention with Brazil for abolition of African slave trade	London
26 Dec	Treaty of amity, commerce and navigation with Mexico	London
1827		
19 Jan	Convention with Portugal for maintaining corps of British troops sent to Portugal (Additional Article, 13 Mar)	Brighthelm-stone
6 July	Treaty with France and Russia for pacification of Greece	London
6 Aug	Convention of commerce with USA	London
6 Aug	Convention with USA concerning north-west coast of America	London
17 Aug	Treaty of amity and commerce with Brazil	Rio de Janeiro
29 Sep	Convention with USA concerning boundaries	London
1828		
6 Aug	Convention with Pasha of Egypt, concerning Morea	Alexandria
28 Oct	Convention of claims with Spain	London
1829		
5 May	Agreement with Brazil concerning British claims	Rio de Janeiro
21 Dec	Convention of commerce and navigation with Emperor of Austria	London
1830		
3 Feb	Protocol of conference with France and Russia concerning Greek independence	London
19 July	Convention with Buenos Aires concerning British claims	Buenos Aires

SOURCES: *British Diplomatic Representatives 1689–1789*, ed. D. B. Horn (London: Royal Historical Society, 1932). *British Diplomatic Representatives 1789–1852*, ed. S. T. Bindoff, E. F. Malcolm Smith and C. K. Webster (London: Royal Historical Society, 1934).

Principal British Diplomatic Representatives, 1760–1830

Abbreviations of Diplomatic Rank: Amb: Ambassador; Env: Envoy; Ex: Extraordinary; in Ch of Aff: In Charge of Affairs; Mil: Military; Min: Minister; Miss: Mission; Plen: Plenipotentiary; Res: Resident; Sec: Secretary; Spec: Special.

Bavaria

Onslow Burrish	1746–58	Min
Fulke Greville	1764–70	Env Ex
Lewis de Visme, AM	1769–74	Min Plen
Hugh Elliot	1774–6	Min Plen
Morton Eden	1776–9	Min Plen
Hon. John Trevor	1780–3	Min Plen
Thomas Walpole	1784–8	Min Plen
	1788–96	Env Ex & Plen
Hon. Arthur Paget	1798–9	Env Ex
William Wickham	1800	Plen
Francis Drake	1800–2	Env Ex
	1802–4	Env Ex & Min Plen

Diplomatic relations suspended 1804–14

George Rose	1814–15	Env Ex & Min Plen
Hon. Frederick Lamb	1815–20	Env Ex & Min Plen
Brook (Sir Brook 1822) Taylor	1820–8	Env Ex & Min Plen
B Erskine	1828–43	Env Ex & Min Plen

Denmark

Dudley Cosby	1763–5	Min Res
Robert Gunning	1766	Min Res
	1766–71	Env Ex
Col Sir Robert Keith, KB	1771–2	Env Ex
Ralph Woodford	1772–3	Env Ex
Daniel de Laval	1774–8	Min Res
	1778–9	Env Ex
Morton Eden	1779–83	Env Ex
Hugh Elliot	1783–9	Env Ex
Daniel Hailes	1792–4	Env Ex
Ld Robert Fitzgerald	1796–9	Env Ex
B Whitworth	1800	Plen on Ex Miss
Nicholas Vansittart	1801	Plen on Spec Miss

Diplomatic relations suspended 1801–2

B St Helens	1801–2	Plen
Robert Liston	1803–4	Env Ex & Min Plen on Ex Miss
Benjamin Garlike	1805–7	Env Ex & Min Plen
Brook Taylor	1807	Env Ex & Min Plen
Francis Jackson	1807	Env Ex & Min Plen
Anthony Merry	1807	Env Ex & Min Plen

Diplomatic relations suspended 1807–14

Maj.-Gen. Hon. Alexander Hope and Edward Thornton	1813	Plens
Edward Thornton	1813–14	Plen
Augustus (Rt Hon. 1822) John Foster	1814	Spec Miss
	1814–24	Env Ex & Min Plen
Rt Hon. Henry (Sir Henry 1831) Wynn	1825–53	Env Ex & Min Plen

Holy Roman Empire

Vt Stormont	1763–72	Amb Ex & Plen
Lt-Gen. Rt Hon. Sir Robert Murray Keith	1772–92	Env Ex & Plen
Sir Morton Eden	1793–4 & 1794–9	Env Ex & Plen
Thomas Grenville and Earl Spencer	1794	Ex Miss
George Hammond	1797	Ex Miss
B Minto	1799–1801	Env Ex & Min Plen
William Wickham	1800–1	Plen
Hon. Arthur (Rt Hon. Sir Arthur 1804) Paget	1801–6	Env Ex & Min Plen

The Empire ceased to exist in 1806, the Emperor thereafter styling himself Emperor of Austria.

Robert Adair	1806–8	Min Plen
E of Pembroke	1807	Plen on Spec Miss
Charles Stuart	1809	Spec Miss
Benjamin Bathurst	1809	Ex Miss

Diplomatic relations suspended 1809–13

E of Aberdeen	1813–14	Amb Ex & Plen
Lt-Gen. Rt Hon. Charles William Stewart (Vane 1819), B Stewart (M of Londonderry 1822)	1814–22	Amb Ex & Plen
Sir Henry Wellesley (B Cowley 1828)	1823–31	Amb Ex & Plen

Flanders

Sir James Porter	1763–5	Min Plen
William Gordon (Bt 1775)	1765–77	Min Plen
Alleyne Fitzherbert	1777–82	Min Res
	1782–3	Min Plen
Vt Torrington	1783–9	Min Plen
E of Elgin	1792–3	Env Ex

Diplomatic relations suspended Feb–July 1793 during French occupation of Brussels

E of Elgin	1793–4	Env Ex

Diplomatic relations suspended 1794–1814 when Southern Netherlands were annexed to France. From 1814 to 1830 the Southern Netherlands formed part of the Kingdom of the United Netherlands.

France

Hans Stanley	1761	Min
D of Bedford	1762–3	Amb Ex & Plen
E of Hertford	1763–5	Amb Ex & Plen
D of Richmond	1765–6	Amb Ex & Plen
E of Rochford	1766–8	Amb Ex & Plen
Earl Harcourt	1768–72	Amb Ex & Plen
Vt Stormont	1772–8	Amb Ex & Plen
Thomas Grenville	1782	Min
Alleyne Fitzherbert	1782–3	Min Plen
D of Manchester	1783–4	Amb Ex & Plen
D of Dorset	1784–90	Amb Ex & Plen
William Eden	1786–8	Env Ex & Plen
William Wyndham Grenville	1787–8	No special rank
Earl Gower	1790–2	Amb Ex & Plen

Diplomatic relations suspended 1792–1801

B Malmesbury	1796 & 1797	Plen
B Whitworth	1802–3	Amb Ex & Plen

Diplomatic relations suspended 1803–14

E of Yarmouth	1806	Plen
E of Lauderdale	1806	Plen
Rt Hon. Sir Charles Stuart (B. Stuart de Rothesay 1828)	1814	Env Ex & Min Plen
D of Wellington	1814–15	Amb Ex & Plen
Rt Hon. Sir Charles Stuart (B. Stuart de Rothesay 1828)	1815–24	Amb Ex & Plen
Vt Granville	1824–8	Amb Ex & Plen
B Stuart de Rothesay	1828–31	Amb Ex & Plen

The Netherlands

Sir Joseph Yorke	1751–61	Min Plen
Sir Joseph Yorke KB	1761–80	Amb Ex & Plen
Sir James Harris, KB (B Malmesbury 1788)	1784–8	Env Ex & Plen
	1788–9	Amb Ex & Plen
Rt Hon. Alleyne Fitzherbert	1789–90	Env Ex & Min Plen
B Auckland	1790–3	Amb Ex & Plen
B Malmesbury	1794	Ex Miss
Rt Hon. Alleyne Fitzherbert, Baron St Helens	1794–5	Amb Ex & Plen

Diplomatic relations suspended 1795–1802

Robert Liston	1802–3	Env Ex & Min Plen

Diplomatic relations suspended 1803–13

E of Clancarty	1813–14	Amb Ex & Plen
Brook Taylor	1814	Spec Miss
Rt Hon. Charles Stuart	1815	Amb Ex & Plen
E of Clancarty	1817–24	Amb Ex & Plen
Vt Granville	1824	Amb Ex & Plen
Rt Hon. Sir Charles Bagot	1824–32	Amb Ex & Plen

Ottoman Empire see Turkey

Poland

Thomas Wroughton	1762–9	Res
	1769–78	Min Plen
John Osborn	1771	Env Ex
Richard Oakes	1778	Res, or Min Plen
Vt Dalrymple	1782–4	Min Plen
Charles Whitworth	1785–8	Min Plen
Daniel Hailes	1788–92	Env Ex
Col William Gardiner	1792–5	Min Plen

Portugal

E of Kinoull	1760	Amb Ex & Plen
Hon. Edward Hay	1762–7	Env Ex & Plen
William Henry Lyttleton	1761–71	Env Ex & Plen
Hon. Robert Walpole	1771–1800	Env Ex & Plen

William Fawkener	1786–7	Env Ex & Plen
John Frere	1800–2	Env Ex & Min Plen
Lord Robert Fitzgerald	1802–6	Env Ex & Min Plen
E of Rosslyn, E of St Vincent and Gen. John Simcoe	1806	Plens on Ex Miss
Rt Hon. John Villiers	1808–10	Min Plen on Spec Miss
Charles (Rt Hon. Sir Charles 1812) Stuart	1810–14	Env Ex & Min Plen
Thomas Sydenham	1814	Env Ex & Min Plen
Rt Hon. George Canning	1814–15	Amb Ex & Plen
Rt Hon. Sir Edward Thornton	1823	Amb Ex
	1823–4	Env Ex & Min Plen
Rt Hon. Sir William à Court, Bt (B Heytesbury 1828)	1824–8	Amb Ex & Plen
Rt Hon. Sir Charles Stuart	1825	Amb on Spec Miss
Rt Hon. Sir Frederick Lamb	1828	Amb Ex & Plen

Representatives to the Portuguese Court while resident in Brazil, 1808–21:

Vt Strangford	1808–15	Env Ex & Min Plen
Rt Hon. Edward Thornton	1819	Amb Ex
	1819–21	Env Ex & Min Plen

Prussia

Maj.-Gen. Joseph Yorke	1758	Min Plen
Andrew Mitchell	1760–4	Min Plen
Sir Andrew Mitchell, KB	1766–71	Env Ex & Plen
James Harris	1772–6	Env Ex
Hugh Elliot	1777–82	Env Ex
Sir John Stepney, Bt	1782–4	Env Ex
Joseph Ewart	1784–5	In Ch of Aff
	1785–8	Sec
	1788–91	Env Ex & Min Plen
Vt Dalrymple	1785–7	Env Ex & Plen
Sir Morton Eden	1791–3	Env Ex & Min Plen
B Malmesbury	1793–4	Ex Miss
Ld Henry Spencer	1795	Env Ex & Min Plen
E of Elgin	1795–8	Env Ex & Min Plen
George Hammond	1796	Ex Miss
Ld Granville Gower	1798	Spec Miss
Rt Hon. Thomas Grenville	1798	Ex Miss
E of Carysfort	1800–1	Env Ex & Min Plen
Francis Jackson	1802–6	Env Ex & Min Plen
B Harrowby	1805–6	Ex Miss

Diplomatic relations suspended 1806–7

Vt Morpeth	1806	Plen
B Hutchinson	1806	Plen
Benjamin Garlike	1807	Min

Diplomatic relations suspended 1807–13

Maj.-Gen. (Lt-Gen. 1814) Sir Charles Stewart	1813–14	Env Ex & Min Plen
George (Rt Hon. 1818, Rt Hon. Sir George 1819) Henry Rose	1815–23	Env Ex & Min Plen

E of Clanwilliam	1823–8	Env Ex & Min Plen
Sir (Rt Hon. Sir 1829) Brook Taylor	1828–30	Env Ex & Min Plen

Russia

Thomas Wroughton	1759–61	Consul-General
	1762	Min Res
E of Buckinghamshire	1762–5	Amb Ex
Samuel Swallow	1762–76	Consul-General
Sir George Macartney	1764–7	Env Ex
B Cathcart	1768–72	Amb Ex
Sir Robert Gunning (KB 1773)	1772–5	Env Ex & Plen
Walter Shairp	1776–87	Consul-General
Sir James Harris (KB 1779)	1777–83	Env Ex & Plen
Alleyne Fitzherbert	1783–7	Env Ex & Plen
John Cayley	1787	Consul-General
Charles (Sir Charles 1793) Whitworth (B Whitworth 1800)	1788–1800	Env Ex & Min Plen
William Fawkener	1791	Env Ex & Min Plen on Spec Miss

Diplomatic relations suspended

B St Helens	1801–2	Amb Ex & Plen
Adm. Rt Hon. Sir John Borlase Warren, Bt	1802–4	Amb Ex & Plen
Ld Granville Gower	1804–6 and 1807	Amb Ex & Plen
M of Douglas and Clydesdale	1807	Amb Ex & Plen on Spec Miss

Diplomatic relations suspended 1807–12

Edward Thornton	1812	Plen
Vt (Earl 1814) Cathcart	1812–19	Amb Ex & Plen
Rt Hon. Sir Charles Bagot	1820–4	Amb Ex & Plen
Rt Hon. Stratford Canning	1825	Spec Miss
Vt Strangford	1825–6	Amb Ex & Plen
D of Wellington	1826	Spec Miss
D of Devonshire	1826	Amb Ex on Spec Miss
M of Hertford	1827	Spec (Garter) Miss
B Heytesbury	1828–30	Amb Ex & Plen

Sardinia and Savoy

James Stewart MacKenzie	1760–1	Env Ex & Plen
George Pitt	1761–4	Env Ex
	1764–8	Env Ex & Plen
Sir William Lynch, MP	1768–70	Env Ex
	1770–9	Env Ex & Plen
B Cardiff	1779–83	Env Ex & Plen
Hon. John Trevor	1783–9	Env Ex
	1789–99	Env Ex & Min Plen

Diplomatic relations suspended 1798–9

Thomas Jackson	1799–1806	Min Plen

No diplomatic representation 1806–8

Hon. (Rt Hon. 1824) William Hill Noel-Hill 1824)	1808–24	Env Ex & Min Plen
Augustus (Sir Augustus 1831), Foster	1825–40	Env Ex & Min Plen

Saxony

Philip Stanhope, MP	1764–8	Env Ex
Robert Keith	1769–71	Env Ex
John Coburn	1771–5	Env Ex
Sir John Stepney, Bt, MP	1776–82	Env Ex
Morton Eden	1783–9	Env Ex
	1789–91	Env Ex & Min Plen
Hugh Elliot	1792–1802	Env Ex & Min Plen
Henry Wynn	1803–6	Env Ex

Diplomatic relations suspended 1806–16

John Morier	1816–24	Env Ex
George Chad	1824–8	Min Plen
Edward Ward	1828–31	Min Plen

Sicily and Naples

Sir James Gray, Bt (KB 1761)	1759–65	Env Ex & Plen
Sir (Rt Hon. Sir 1791) William Hamilton, FRS, FSA (KB 1772)	1767–1800	Env Ex & Plen
Hon. Arthur Paget	1800–1	Env Ex & Min Plen
William Drummond	1801–3	Env Ex & Min Plen
Hugh Elliot	1803–6	Env Ex & Min Plen
Lt-Gen. Hon. Henry Fox	1806–7	Env Ex & Min Plen
William Drummond	1807–8	Env Ex & Min Plen
B Amherst	1809–11	Env Ex & Min Plen
Lt-Gen. Ld William Bentinck	1811–14	Env Ex & Min Plen
William à Court (Rt Hon. Sir William à Court, Bt 1817)	1814–22	Env Ex & Min Plen
William Hamilton	1822–5	Env Ex & Min Plen
Rt Hon. William Noel-Hill	1825–32	Env Ex & Min Plen

Spain

E of Bristol	1758–61	Amb Ex & Plen

Diplomatic relations suspended 1761—3

E of Rochford	1763–6	Amb Ex & Plen
Sir James Gray, Bt	1767–9	Amb Ex & Plen
James Harris, MP	1768–71	Sec
	1771–2	Min Plen
B Grantham	1771–9	Amb Ex & Plen

Diplomatic relations suspended 1779–83

Richard Cumberland	1780–1	No special rank
Robert Liston	1783–8	Min Plen
E of Chesterfield	1784–5	Amb Ex & Plen
B Auckland	1788–90	Amb Ex & Plen

Rt Hon. Alleyne Fitzherbert (B St Helens 1791)	1790–4	Amb Ex & Plen
E of Bute	1795–6	Amb Ex & Plen

Diplomatic relations suspended 1796–1802

John Hookham Frere	1802–4	Env Ex & Plen

Diplomatic relations suspended 1804–8

Charles Stuart	1808–9	Spec Miss
John Hookham Frere	1808–9	Env Ex & Min Plen
M of Wellesley	1809	Amb Ex & Plen
Rt Hon. Henry (Sir Henry 1812)	1810–11	Env Ex & Min Plen
Wellesley	1811–21	Amb Ex & Plen
Rt Hon. Sir William à Court, Bt	1822–4	Env Ex & Min Plen
Rt Hon. Frederick Lamb	1825–7	Env Ex & Min Plen
George Bosanquet	1827–30	Chargé d'Affaires

Sweden
Diplomatic relations suspended 1748–63

Lt-Col Robert Campbell	1757	Min Res
Sir John Goodricke, Bt	1758–64	Min Res
	1764–73	Env Ex
Lewis de Visme, AM	1773–6	Env Ex
Sir Thomas Wroughton (KB 1780)	1778–87	Env Ex
	1787	Env Ex & Plen
Robert Liston	1789–92	Env Ex & Min Plen
Ld Henry Spencer	1793–4	Env Ex
Daniel Hailes	1797–1800	Env Ex

Diplomatic relations suspended 1801–2

B St Helens	1801–2	Plen
Charles Arbuthnot	1802–3	Env Ex
Hon. Henry Pierrepont	1804–7	Env Ex & Min Plen
Alexander Straton	1807	Env Ex & Min Plen
Rt Hon. Henry Pierrepont	1807	Ex Miss
Edward Thornton	1808	Env Ex & Min Plen
Anthony Merry	1808–9	Env Ex & Min Plen

Diplomatic relations suspended 1810–12

Edward (Rt Hon. Edward 1816) Thornton	1811 and 1812	Plen
	1812–17	Env Ex & Min Plen
Maj.-Gen. Hon. Alexander Hope	1813	Plen on confidential mil miss
Vt Strangford	1817–20	Env Ex & Min Plen
Rt Hon. William Vesey-Fitzgerald	1820–2	Env Ex & Min Plen
Rt Hon. Sir Benjamin Bloomfield (B Bloomfield 1825)	1823–33	Env Ex & Min Plen

Switzerland

Arthur Villettes	1749–62	Min
Robert Colebrooke	1762–5	Min

Col Pictet (Count of Pictet)	1763–7	Min to Republic of Geneva
William Norton	1765–83	Min
Isaac Pictet (son of Col Pictet)	1772–4	In Ch of Aff at Geneva
Lord Robert Fitzgerald	1792–5	Min Plen
William Wickham	1794–5	Spec Miss
	1795	Chargé d'Affaires
	1795–7	Min Plen

Diplomatic relations suspended 1797–1814

Stratford Canning	1814–19	Env Ex & Min Plen
Henry Wynn	1822–3	Env Ex & Min Plen
Charles Vaughan	1823–5	Min Plen
Hon. Algernon Percy	1826–32	Min Plen

Turkey

James Porter	1746–62	Amb
Hon. Henry Grenville	1761–5	Amb
John Murray	1766–75	Amb
Sir Robert Ainslie	1776–94	Amb
Robert Liston	1794–5	Amb
Adm. Sir William Sidney Smith	1798–9	Plen
E of Elgin	1799–1803	Amb Ex & Plen
William Drummond	1803	Amb Ex & Plen
Rt Hon. Charles Arbuthnot	1805–7	Amb Ex & Plen

Diplomatic relations suspended 1807–8

Rt Hon. Sir Arthur Paget	1807	Amb Ex & Plen on Spec Miss
Robert Adair	1808–9	Plen
	1809–10	Amb Ex & Plen
Rt Hon. Robert (Sir Robert 1816) Liston	1812–20	Amb Ex & Plen
Vt Strangford	1821–4	Amb Ex & Plen
Rt Hon. Stratford Canning	1826–7	Amb Ex & Plen
Rt Hon. Robert (Sir Robert 1829) Gordon	1829–31	Amb Ex & Plen

United Provinces see The Netherlands

United States of America

Richard Oswald	1782–3	Commissioner
David Hartley, MP	1783–4	Min Plen
George Hammond	1791–5	Min Plen
Robert Liston	1796–1800	Env Ex & Min Plen
Anthony Merry	1803–6	Env Ex & Min Plen
Hon. David Erskine	1806–9	Env Ex & Min Plen
George Rose	1807–8	Spec Miss
Francis Jackson	1809–10	Env Ex & Min Plen
Augustus Foster	1811–12	Env Ex & Min Plen

Diplomatic relations suspended 1812–14

B Gambier, Henry Goulburn and William Adams	1814	Plens
Rt Hon. Charles Bagot	1816–19	Env Ex & Min Plen

Rt Hon. Stratford Canning   1820–3   Env Ex & Min Plen
Charles (Sir Charles 1833) Vaughan   1825–35   Env Ex & Min Plen

International Conferences and Congresses, 1800–30

1801–2	Congress of Amiens	
	M Cornwallis	Plen
1814	Congress of Châtillon-sur-Seine	
	Vt Castlereagh	Plen on Ex Miss
	Vt Cathcart	Plen
	E of Aberdeen	Plen
	Maj.-Gen. Sir Charles William Stewart	Plen
1814	First Conference of Paris	
	Vt Castlereagh	Plen
	Vt Cathcart	Plen
	E of Aberdeen	Plen
	Lt. Gen. Sir Charles William Stewart	Plen
1814–15	Congress of Vienna	
	Vt Castlereagh	First Plen 1814–15
	D of Wellington	First Plen 1815
	E of Clancarty	Plen
	Earl Cathcart	Plen
	Lt. Gen. Rt Hon. Charles William Stuart,	Plen
	B Stewart	
1815	Second Conference of Paris	
	Vt Castlereagh	Plen
	D of Wellington	Plen
1816–19	Territorial Commission of Frankfort	
	E of Clancarty	Plen
1818	Conference of Aix-la-Chapelle	
	Vt Castlereagh	Plen
	D of Wellington	Plen
1822	Conference of Verona	
	D of Wellington	Plen on Ex Miss

7   The Armed Forces

Outlines of British Campaigns, 1755–1830

I   The Seven Years War
II   War of American Independence
III   Expeditions and Naval Operations, 1793–1814
IV   Peninsular War
V   Waterloo Campaign
VI   War of 1812
VII   Greek War of Independence
VIII India

I   The Seven Years War, 1756–63

(a) Europe

1756   29 Aug. Frederick the Great's invasion of Saxony began the conflict in Europe (Britain and France had been at war since May 1756).

1757   July. A French army invaded Hanover. Cumberland was defeated at HASTENBECK,* and signed the Convention of Kloster-Seven 8 Sep, disbanding his army.

5 Nov. Frederick the Great's victory at Rossbach. The Convention was repudiated, and Ferdinand of Brunswick was given command of the allied army.

1758   Apr. British subsidies to Frederick by the Treaty of London. Ferdinand launched an offensive against the French, pushing them across the Rhine 27 Mar, and defeating them at Krefeld 23 June. The French replied by invading Hesse.

1759   13 Apr. Ferdinand defeated by Broglie at BERGEN.

1 Aug. Ferdinand defeated the French at MINDEN; they retreated from Hesse.

1760   Broglie was victorious at Korbach 10 July, but this was offset by Ferdinand's victory at WARBURG 31 July. Hanover was saved, but a diversion on the Lower Rhine was defeated by the French at KLOSTER KAMP 16 Oct.

1761   Ferdinand's advance from Westphalia was defeated by Broglie

---

* Where the name of a battle is given in capital letters, further details can be found in the section 'Principal Battles, 1755–1830', pp. 92–5.

near Grünberg 21 Mar. A French counter-thrust was defeated at
VELLINGHAUSEN 15 July.

5 Oct. Pitt resigned, and Bute refused to renew the subsidy treaty
with Frederick.

1762 5 Jan. Death of Empress Elizabeth of Russia.

5 May. Treaty of St Petersburg – peace between Prussia and
Russia.

22 May. Peace between Prussia and Sweden.

1763 15 Feb. Treaty of Hubertusburg signed by Prussia, Austria and
Saxony, restoring the *status quo ante bellum.*

(b) North America

1755 9 July. Braddock's expedition to attack Fort Duquesne was destroyed at the MONONGAHELA RIVER.

1756 Aug. Montcalm captured Forts Oswego and George, and built
Fort Ticonderoga.

1757 June–Sep. British expedition to attack Louisburg led by Lord
Loudoun failed.

1758 A fourfold attack on the French planned.

July. Fort Duquesne and Louisburg captured by Amherst; but
Abercromby's attack on Fort Ticonderoga failed.

Sep. Forts Frontenac, Oswego and Duquesne taken from the
French.

1759 July. Fort Niagara fell to British expedition.

Aug. Ticonderoga and Champlain captured.

June-Sep. Attack on Quebec by Wolfe and Saunders. The French
led by Montcalm were defeated in a battle before QUEBEC 13
Sep, after Wolfe had scaled the Heights of Abraham. Quebec
surrendered 18 Sep.

1760 8 Sep. Marquis de Vaudreuil surrendered Montreal, and with it
French Canada.

(c) Naval and minor operations

1755 8 June. Boscawen captured two French ships carrying reinforcements to Canada, although the rest escaped. There was a general attack on French shipping.

1756 28 June. Minorca fell to the French. Admiral Byng, who had failed
to relieve it after an inconclusive naval battle 20 May, was
executed.

1757 Sep. Failure of a raid on Rochefort.

1758 Feb. Commodore Holmes captured Emden. Attacks on the French
coast: Cherbourg taken in June, but expedition against St Malo
repulsed in Sep.

All French factories on the West African coast captured.

1759 May. Guadeloupe taken from the French.

18 Aug. Boscawen defeated the French Mediterranean fleet off Lagos.

20 Nov. Hawke destroyed the Brest squadron in battle of QUIBERON BAY.

1760 Feb. French expedition to Ireland surrendered at Kinsale.

1761 June. Dominica and Belle Ile captured from the French.

1762 4 Jan. England declared war on Spain, and seized Havana in Aug and Manila in Oct. A British army led by Lord Tyrawley helped the Portuguese to resist a Spanish invasion. Rodney forced the surrender of Martinique, Grenada, St Vincent and St Lucia. St John's, Newfoundland, was lost to the French.

(d) Treaty of Paris 10 Feb 1763

Signed by Britain, France, Spain and Portugal. Principal points: France ceded to Britain Canada, Nova Scotia, Cape Breton and all lands east of the Mississippi, except New Orleans; she retained fishing rights on the Newfoundland banks.

England restored to France the islands of Guadeloupe, Martinique, St Lucia and Maria Galante. France evacuated territories of Hanover, Hesse, Brunswick and Prussia. Minorca exchanged for Belle Ile. Britain restored Havana to Spain, in exchange for Florida. Spain had been compensated for this in the secret Treaty of San Ildefonso, 3 Nov 1762, by receiving from France, New Orleans and all Louisiana west of the Mississippi. Spain recovered Manila, and evacuated Portugal and Portuguese colonies.

In Africa Britain kept Senegal and restored Gorée to France.

II   War of American Independence 1775–1783

1775 19 Apr. Detachment of 700 British troops sent from Boston by General Gage to destroy stores of the Massachusetts Militia at Concord. The force was opposed at Lexington, where the first shots of the war were fired, and harassed on the return march from Concord to Boston, suffering 273 casualties. Boston was besieged.

31 May. American troops before Boston adopted by the Second Continental Congress as the Continental Army, and George Washington appointed commander-in-chief 15 June.

17 June. After receiving reinforcements, Gage attacked the American entrenchments on Breed's Hill (battle of BUNKER HILL), suffering heavy losses in carrying them at the third attempt. Gage replaced by Howe.

Attack on Canada

May. Arnold and Ethan Allen seized Fort Ticonderoga and lesser posts on Lake Champlain. Montreal was taken in Nov, but an attack on Quebec failed in Dec. The following year Carleton, the British governor, retook Montreal and forced the Americans back to Ticonderoga.

1776 4 Mar. Washington occupied Dorchester Heights commanding Boston Harbour. British forces evacuated to Halifax 17 Mar.

4 July. Declaration of Independence.

July. Howe arrived off New York from Halifax with 30,000 men, and landed on Staten Island. He defeated Putnam in the battle of Long Island 27 Aug, and occupied New York 15 Sep.

Washington, defeated in a skirmish at White Plains 28 Oct, retreated across New Jersey, and crossed the Delaware into Pennsylvania 8 Dec.

26 Dec. Washington crossed the Delaware by night, and attacked a force of Hessians at TRENTON, taking 900 prisoners. As he withdrew he defeated the British at the battle of Princeton 3 Jan 1777.

1777 British plan to divide the rebel states by the line of the Hudson, with Burgoyne advancing from Canada, in cooperation with St Leger from Lake Ontario and Howe from New York.

Burgoyne moved south with 8,200 men, and occupied Ticonderoga 5 July.

16 Aug. Colonel Baum was sent to seize stores, but was defeated at BENNINGTON.

19 Sep. Burgoyne suffered heavy losses in a battle at FREEMAN'S FARM (see SARATOGA CAMPAIGN). He was now confronted by a greatly superior force under Gates.

Meanwhile, St Leger had retreated after failing to take Fort Stanwix, and Clinton moved north from New York too late to influence the campaign.

7 Oct. Attempting to break out, Burgoyne was defeated at BEMIS HEIGHTS (see SARATOGA CAMPAIGN), and began peace negotiations. He surrendered with 5,700 men at Saratoga 17 Oct.

July. Howe sailed from New York to Chesapeake Bay with 18,000 men, defeated the Americans at BRANDYWINE CREEK 11 Sep, and occupied Philadelphia 27 Sep.

4 Oct. Howe defeated Washington's attempt to mount a surprise attack on camp at GERMANTOWN. Washington's army spent a hard winter at Valley Forge.

1778 6 Feb. Treaties of commerce and alliance between France and the United States. War between France and Britain 17 June.

18 June. Clinton, who had succeeded Howe as commander-in-chief, began the evacuation of Philadelphia, which was successfully carried out, despite a defeat by Washington at Monmouth 28 June.

Clinton now sent an army to overrun the southern states, hoping for loyalist assistance. Savannah was occupied 29 Dec.

In the West Indies, the French captured Dominica 8 Sep, but British forces took St Lucia 13 Nov.

At sea an inconclusive engagement took place between Keppel and D'Orvilliers off Ushant 27 July. John Paul Jones successfully attacked British shipping in the Irish Sea.

1779   21 June. Spain entered the war. Gibraltar was besieged June 1779–Feb 1783.

In the West Indies, D'Estaing took St Vincent in June and Grenada 4 July, and defeated Admiral Byron off Grenada 6 July.

Aug. A Franco-Spanish fleet entered the Channel, but withdrew.

Sep–Oct. Assaults on Savannah by French and American troops beaten off.

1780   8 Jan. Rodney defeated a Spanish fleet and relieved Gibraltar.

Feb. Clinton landed with 12,000 men to attack Charleston, which fell 12 May. Clinton returned to New York, leaving the pacification of South Carolina to Cornwallis, who defeated Gates at CAMDEN 16 Aug.

Aug. Armed neutrality formed by Russia, Sweden and Denmark to resist British seizure of enemy goods in neutral ships. Later joined by Prussia, Austria, Portugal, the Netherlands, and the Kingdom of the Two Sicilies.

7 Oct. British raiding force under Colonel Ferguson defeated at King's Mountain.

20 Dec. Britain declared war on Holland. Warren Hastings seized Dutch settlements of Negapatam and Trincomali, but an attempt on the Cape of Good Hope failed in 1781.

1781   17 Jan. British cavalry under Tarleton defeated by Morgan at COWPENS.

15 Mar. Cornwallis defeated Greene at Guilford, but suffered heavy losses.

July–Aug. Franco-Spanish occupation of Minorca. Port Mahan fell 5 Feb 1782.

Aug. Cornwallis established himself at Yorktown. He was besieged there by Washington and Rochambeau, and the French fleet under de Grasse, and forced to surrender 19 Oct. Clinton's relieving force arrived too late on 24 Oct.

In the West Indies Rodney captured the Dutch islands of St Eustatius and St Martin in Feb. In June the French took Tobago, and in Oct St Eustatius.

1782   Feb. French take St Kitts and Nevis.

12 Apr. Rodney's naval victory in the battle of THE SAINTS.

30 Nov. Preliminary peace between Britain and the United States.

1783   3 Sep. Treaty of Versailles. Signed by Britain, France and the

United States. Britain signed a separate treaty with Holland 20 May 1784.

Britain recognised the independence of the United States, and guaranteed her fishing rights in the Newfoundland fisheries.

France kept St Lucia and Tobago. She returned Britain's other West Indian islands and Gambia, in return for her Indian stations, Senegal and Goree, and the right to a share in the Newfoundland fisheries.

Spain retained Minorca and West Florida, and received East Florida.

Holland received back her colonies apart from Negapatam.

III Expeditions and Naval Operations, 1793–1814

1793
1 Feb. France, already at war with Austria, Prussia and Piedmont, declared war on Britain and Holland, and on Spain 7 Mar.

Aug. Admiral Hood occupied Toulon after a Royalist uprising. French successes on land forced him to evacuate 19 Dec.

Dec. Expedition of 12,000 men arrived too late to aid Royalist rebels in La Vendée.

1793–95
Campaign in the Low Countries.

Duke of York sent to Low Countries at head of force of British, Dutch, Hanoverians and Hessians. He was defeated at Hondschoote in Sep 1793, and Tourcoing in May 1794.

July 1794. French reoccupied Brussels. Austrians retreated towards the Rhine, and British fell back into Holland.

Apr 1795. British army evacuated from Bremen after the French had overrun Holland.

1793–98
Campaign in the West Indies.

Nov 1793. 7,000 men under Grey sailed with a squadron under Jervis to the West Indies.

By 1796 military action, particularly involving slave revolts, and disease had resulted in 40,000 dead and 40,000 incapacitated.

1797 Trinidad captured.

Oct 1798. Campaign ended with evacuation of San Domingo.

1794
1 June. Howe defeated French fleet off USHANT, but food convoy allowed to reach Brest safely.

Aug. British forces occupied Corsica.

1795
June. Emigrés landed from British ships at Quiberon Bay. They were defeated by Hoche 16–20 July, and a small British force was evacuated 20–21 July.

Nov. An expedition of 2,500 sailed to La Vendée, but did not disembark.

1797   14 Feb. Jervis defeated Spanish fleet at CAPE ST VINCENT.

11 Oct. Duncan defeated Dutch fleet at CAMPERDOWN.

1798   June. Irish rebels defeated at Vinegar Hill. A force of 1,200 French under General Humbert landed in Killala Bay 22 Aug, but Cornwallis forced their surrender 8 Sep.

1 Aug. Nelson destroyed French fleet at the battle of the NILE.

Nov. British captured Minorca.

1798–1800 British supported uprising by Maltese against the French, who surrendered 5 Sep 1800.

1799   Expedition to Den Helder.

27 Aug. British troops under Abercromby landed in Holland; the Dutch navy in the Texel surrendered. Russo-British force, now under the Duke of York, planned to advance on Amsterdam, but was checked in battle of BERGEN-OP-ZOOM 19 Sep. Further attacks 2 Oct (Battle of ALKMAAR) and 6 Oct made little progress.

18 Oct. By the Convention of Alkmaar the allies agreed to evacuate Holland.

1801   Campaign against the French in Egypt.

8 Mar. British troops under Abercromby landed at Aboukir Bay. Attack on ALEXANDRIA failed 13 Mar, but a French counterattack was beated off 21 Mar, though Abercromby was fatally wounded. His successor, Hutchinson, advanced on Cairo, which the French agreed to evacuate in June.

French forces remaining in Alexandria surrendered 31 Aug.

2 Apr. 1801 Nelson, second-in-command to Sir Hyde Parker, defeated Danes in battle of COPENHAGEN.

1805   21 Oct. Nelson defeated Franco-Spanish fleet in the battle of TRAFALGAR.

1806   Jan. Expedition of 6,000 men under General Sir David Baird captured the Cape of Good Hope from the Dutch.

1806–7   Expeditions to South America.

June 1806. Home Popham, who had escorted Baird to Cape Town, took 1,500 men under Beresford to attack Buenos Aires. Beresford forced to surrender in Aug 1806. In 1807 General Whitelocke occupied Montevideo, and then moved against Buenos Aires, but had to withdraw.

1807   2–7 Sep. Danish fleet captured in second battle of Copenhagen.

1809   July. Walcheren Expedition – 40,000 men under Chatham sailed for the Scheldt estuary to take Antwerp. They were delayed by resistance of Flushing, which surrendered 16 Aug. There were heavy losses when fever broke out. Half the force returned to England in Sep; the rest remained to garrison Walcheren, but were evacuated in Dec.

1810   Mauritius and Réunion captured.

1811   Java captured.

1813   Graham sent to Holland with 6,000 men to support an Orangeist revolt. But the Prussians failed to take part in an intended attack on Antwerp, and after an unsuccessful attack on Bergen-op-Zoom, Graham's force remained largely inactive until the end of the war.

IV Peninsular War, 1808–1814

1807   Oct. French declared war on Portugal. Junot entered Lisbon 30 Nov.

1808   Mar. French invasion of Spain. Joseph Bonaparte proclaimed King.

May. National rising in Spain. Dupont capitulated with 20,000 men to Spanish forces at Baylen 19 July.

1 Aug. British army under Wellesley landed in Portugal. French defeated at ROLIÇA 17 Aug, and VIMEIRO 21 Aug.

30 Aug. Convention of Cintra signed, allowing Junot to evacuate Portugal. Sir John Moore given command of British army, which advanced into Spain.

4 Dec. Napoleon entered Madrid. British retreated to the coast at Corunna.

1809   16 Jan. Battle of CORUNNA – Soult's attack was beaten off and the army evacuated, but Moore was killed.

22 Apr. Wellesley landed with British army at Lisbon, forced Soult to withdraw from Oporto, and defeated the French at TALAVERA 28 July.

1810   10 July. French took Ciudad Rodrigo, and invaded Portugal.

27 Sep. Wellington defeated Masséna at BUSACO RIDGE, then took shelter behind fortified lines of the Torres Vedras.

1811   Mar. Masséna forced to retreat from Portugal. Wellington pursued him, besieged Almeida, and defeated a relieving army at FUENTES DE OÑORO 3–5 May. Almeida fell 10 May.

16 May. As he moved to relieve Badajoz, Soult was defeated at ALBUERA by Beresford.

1812   Wellington took the offensive, capturing CIUDAD RODRIGO in Jan, and BADAJOZ in Apr. 22 July, Wellington defeated Marmont at SALAMANCA. 12 Aug Wellington entered Madrid. However he failed to take Burgos, and fell back to Ciudad Rodrigo.

1813   Wellington again advanced, and defeated the French at VIT-
ORIA 21 June. He drove Soult across the PYRENEES 25 July–
1 Aug, and invaded France.

1814   Wellington defeated Soult at ORTHEZ 27 Feb, and
TOULOUSE 10 Apr.

18 Apr. Hostilities suspended after Napoleon's abdication.

V   Waterloo Campaign 1815

1815   1 Mar. Napoleon landed in France and entered Paris 20 Mar.

25 Mar. Austria, England, Prussia and Russia concluded a new
alliance against Napoleon.

15 June. French army captured Charleroi.

16 June. Napoleon attacked Blücher's Prussians at LIGNY, while
Ney engaged the Anglo-Dutch army at QUATRE BRAS.

Ney recalled d'Erlon's army corps, which he had sent to help
Napoleon, but it failed to return in time; both allied armies were
able to conduct orderly retreats.

17 June. Grouchy sent to prevent Blücher joining Wellington, but
Blücher had retreated towards Wavre and not Liége as
Napoleon believed.

18 June. Battle of WATERLOO – French attacks failed to drive
Wellington from his defensive positions, and the arrival of
Blücher in the later afternoon ensured the total defeat of the
French.

22 June. Napoleon abdicated, and the allies entered Paris 7 July.

VI   War of 1812

1812   19 June. Maritime grievances caused the United States to declare
war on Britain.

A plan for a three-fold attack on Canada failed, and British under
General Brock forced the surrender of Detroit 16 Aug.

1813   24 Apr. American expedition captured and burnt York (Toronto).

10 Sep. Americans under Commodore Perry won battle of Lake
Erie. Americans advanced, recaptured Detroit 29 Sep, and
defeated General Proctor at the battle of the Thames 5 Oct.

18 Dec. British took Fort Niagara.

1814   July. Americans advanced across the Niagara River, took Fort
Erie, and won battle of Chippewa 5 July. But after battle of
Lundy's Lane 25 July they fell back on Fort Erie, which they
later abandoned in Nov.

Aug. British veterans under Ross landed forty miles from
Washington, defeated the Americans at BLADENSBURG 24
Aug, and captured and burnt parts of the capital.

11 Sep. American naval force won battle of Plattsburg, halting a British invasion by way of Lake Champlain.

13 Sep. British attack on Baltimore repulsed.

24 Dec. War concluded by the treaty of Ghent, largely restoring the pre-war situation.

1815 8 Jan. Before news of the peace reached him, Pakenham was killed leading an unsuccessful British attack on NEW ORLEANS.

VII Greek War of Independence, 1821–30

British naval intervention 1827

1827 6 July. Treaty of London – France, Russia and England threatened action in support of the Greeks, unless the Turks agreed to an armistice.

16 Aug. Note sent to Turks demanding an armistice.

8 Sep. Egyptian fleet landed reinforcements at Navarino.

20 Oct. Battle of NAVARINO – Egyptian fleet destroyed by action of British, French and Russian squadrons.

1828 26 Apr. Russia declared war on Turkey.

VIII India

1756 20 June. Surajah Dowlah, Nawab of Bengal, captured Calcutta, and imprisoned 146 Europeans in the 'Black Hole', where 123 died.

1757 2 Jan. Robert Clive and Admiral Watson recaptured Calcutta.

23 June. Clive routed Surajah Dowlah at PLASSEY.

1758 French force under Comte de Lally-Tollendal reached Pondicherry, and captured Fort St David in June.

Dec 1758–Feb 1759. Lally unsuccessfully besieged Madras.

1760 22 Jan. Eyre Coote defeated Lally at WANDIWASH.

1761 15 Jan. Lally's surrender at Pondicherry marked the end of the French bid for power in India.

1764 23 Oct. Mutiny in Bengal army crushed by Major Munro at BUXAR.

1766–9 First Mysore War – ended when Hyder Ali concluded a defensive alliance with East India Company.

1779–82 First Maratha War. Gwalior stormed by Captain Popham in 1780. Peace by the Treaty of Salbai.

1780–84 Second Mysore War.

1780 Hyder Ali invaded the Carnatic, but was defeated by Coote at PORTO NOVO in June, Pollilur in Aug, and Sholingarh in Sep.

Aug 1782. French under Admiral de Suffren captured Trincomalee, and sent aid to Hyder Ali.

1784. Ali's son, Tippoo Sahib, made peace by the Treaty of Mangaloore.

1789–92 Third Mysore War.
Tippoo Sahib attacked the ruler of Travancore, an ally of Britain. Cornwallis invaded Mysore, stormed the capital Bangaloore, and besieged Tippoo in Seringapatam. Tippoo made peace in Mar 1792.

1795–6 Ceylon captured from the Dutch.

1799 Fourth Mysore War.
After a small French force had landed in Mysore, Lord Wellesley declared war, and Tippoo Sahib was killed when Seringapatam was stormed in May 1799.

1803–5 Second Maratha War.
1803. Arthur Wellesley defeated Sindhia of Gwalior at ASSAYE 23 Sep, and ARGAUM 29 Nov. General Lake stormed Aligarh 4 Sep, and defeated Marathas at Delhi 16 Sep, and Laswari 1 Nov. Sindhia submitted 20 Dec. Further uprisings by Marathas suppressed 1804–5.

1814 Nov. Britain invaded Nepal. The Gurkhas were forced to make peace in 1816.

1817–18 Third Maratha War.
Attacks by Marathas and bands of marauding robbers called Pindaris.
21 Dec 1817. Sir Thomas Hyslop crushed the army of Maratha leader, Holkar, at Mahidput.
1818. Lord Rawdon-Hastings hunted down the Pindaris; the ruler of the Marathas, the Peshwa, surrendered 2 June.

1823–6 First Burmese War.
5 Mar 1823. British declared war on Burma after Burmese invasion of India.
May 1824. Rangoon occupied.
2 Apr 1825. British victory at battle of Danubyu. Campbell occupied Prome 25 Apr.
24 Feb 1826. Peace by the Treaty of Yandabo.

Ships Taken or Destroyed by the Naval and Marine Forces of Great Britain

Force	In the French War, ending 1802					In the French War, ending 1814					
	French	Dutch	Spanish	Other Nations	Total	French	Spanish	Danish	Russian	American	Total
Of the line	45	25	11	2	83	70	27	23	4	0	124
Fifties	2	1	0	0	3	7	0	1	0	1	9
Frigates	133	31	20	7	191	77	36	24	6	5	148
Sloops, etc.	161	32	55	16	264	188	64	16	7	13	288
Total	341	89	86	25	541	342	127	64	17	19	569

SOURCE: Haydn, *Book of Dates* (London, 1857).

Principal Battles, 1755–1830
I Land

Battle	Date	Campaign	Combatants	Strength of Armies	Commanders	Casualties
ALBUERA	16 May 1811	Peninsular War	British, Portuguese, Spanish French	35,000 24,000	Marshal Beresford Marshal Soult	6,000 8,000
ALEXANDRIA	13 Mar 1801	War of the Second Coalition – British Expedition to Egypt	French British	6,000 10,000	General Friant General Abercromby	500 1,300
ALEXANDRIA	21 Mar 1801	War of the Second Coalition – British Expedition to Egypt	British French	10,000 11,000	General Abercromby General Ménou	1,400 2,000
ALKMAAR	2 Oct 1799	War of the Second Coalition – British Expedition to Holland	British, Russians French, Dutch	30,000 30,000	Duke of York General Brune	2,000 2,000
ARGAUM	29 Nov 1803	Second Maratha War	British Marathas	15,000 30,000	Arthur Wellesley Sindhia of Gwalior	360 –
ASSAYE	23 Sep 1803	Second Maratha War	British Marathas	7,000 30,000	Arthur Wellesley Sindhia of Gwalior	1,600 6,000
BADAJOZ, SIEGE OF	16 Mar–6 Apr 1812	Peninsular War	British, Portuguese French, Hessians, Spanish	60,000 5,000	Wellington General Phillipon	4,700 –
BARROSA	5 Mar 1811	Peninsular War	British, Portuguese, Spanish French	4,500 9,000	General Graham Marshal Victor	1,200 2,000
BENNINGTON	16 Aug 1777	War of American Independence	Americans Hessians	2,500 1,400	General Stark Lt.-Col Baum	70 207
BERGEN	13 Apr 1759	Seven Years' War – Germany	French Allies	30,000 24,000	Duc de Broglie Ferdinand of Brunswick	1,800 2,500
BERGEN-OP-ZOOM	19 Sep 1799	War of the Second Coalition – British Expedition to Holland	French, Dutch British, Russians	18,000 20,000	General Vandamme Duke of York	3,000 4,000

Battle	Date	War	Nationality	Strength	Commander	Casualties
BLADENSBURG	24 Aug 1814	War of 1812	British	4,000	General Ross	250
			Americans	6,000	General Winder	80
BRANDYWINE CREEK	11 Sep 1777	War of American Independence	British	15,000	General Howe	600
			Americans	10,500	George Washington	1,000
BUNKER HILL	17 June 1775	War of American Independence	British	2,500	General Howe	1,050
			Americans	1,600	Colonel Prescott	450
BUSACO RIDGE	27 Sep 1810	Peninsular War	British, Portuguese	51,300	Wellington	1,250
			French	66,000	Marshal Masséna	4,600
BUXAR	23 Oct 1764	Conquest of Bengal	British	7,000	Major Munro	850
			Indian Armies	40,000	Surajah Dowlah	4,000
CAMDEN	16 Aug 1780	War of American Independence	British	2,200	Earl Cornwallis	320
			Americans	3,000	General Gates	750
CASTELLA	13 Apr 1813	Peninsular War	British, Portuguese, Spanish	17,000	General Murray	600
			French	15,000	Marshal Suchet	800
CIUDAD RODRIGO, SIEGE OF	8–19 Jan 1812	Peninsular War	British, Portuguese Spanish	35,000	Wellington	1,100
			French	2,000	M. Reynaud	500 casualties and 1,500 survivors surrendered
CORUNNA	16 Jan 1809	Peninsular War	British	14,000	General Moore	800
			French	16,000	Marshal Soult	2,000
COWPENS	17 Jan 1781	War of American Independence	Americans	1,000	General Morgan	72
			British	1,000	Colonel Tarleton	329
FUENTES DE OÑORO	3–5 May 1811	Peninsular War	British, Portuguese	37,600	Wellington	1,450
			French	48,300	Marshal Masséna	2,260
GERMANTOWN	4 Oct 1777	War of American Independence	British	9,000	General Howe	520
			Americans	11,000	George Washington	670
HASTENBECK	26 July 1757	Seven Years War – Germany	French	60,000	Marshal d'Estrées	2,350
			Allies	36,000	Duke of Cumberland	1,300
KLOSTER KAMP	23 June 1758	Seven Years War – Germany	Allies	7,500	Erbprinz of Hesse-Kassel	1,600
			French	7,000	Marquis de Castries	3,000
MAIDA	4 July 1806	War of the Third Coalition – Southern Italy	British	5,100	General Stuart	330
			French	6,500	General Reynier	2,200

Battle	Date	Campaign	Combatants	Strength of Armies	Commanders	Casualties
MINDEN	1 Aug 1759	Seven Years War – Germany	Allies French	42,500 54,000	Ferdinand of Brunswick Marquis de Contades	2,700 4,900
MONONGAHELA RIVER	9 July 1755	Anglo-French Struggle for North America	French, Indians British, Virginians	900 1,400	Captains Beaujeu and Dumas General Braddock	65 900
NEW ORLEANS	8 Jan 1815	War of 1812	Americans British	4,500 5,300	General Jackson General Pakenham	21 2,036
NIVE	9–13 Dec 1813	Peninsular War – Southern France	British, Portuguese, Spanish French	60,000 60,000	Wellington Marshal Soult	5,000 8,000
NIVELLE	10 Nov 1813	Peninsular War – Southern France	British, Portuguese, Spanish French	80,000 63,000	Wellington Marshal Soult	2,700 4,300
ORTHEZ	27 Feb 1814	Peninsular War – Southern France	British Portuguese, Spanish French	44,000 36,000	Wellington Marshal Soult	2,000 4,000
PLASSEY	23 June 1757	Seven Years War – India	British Bengal	3,000 60,000	Robert Clive Surajah Dowlah	65 500
PYRENEES	25 July – 1 Aug 1818	Peninsular War	British, Portuguese, Spanish French	40,000 53,000	Wellington Marshal Soult	7,000 13,500
QUATRE BRAS	16 June 1815	Waterloo Campaign	British French	36,000 25,000	Wellington Marshal Ney	4,700 4,300
QUEBEC	13 Sep 1759	Seven Years War – Canada	British French	5,000 4,500	General Wolfe Marquis de Montcalm	660 1,400
ROLIÇA	17 Aug 1808	Peninsular War	British French	14,000 4,400	Sir Arthur Wellesley Comte de Laborde	480 600
SALAMANCA	22 July 1812	Peninsular War	British, Portuguese, Spanish French	48,500 50,000	Wellington Marshal Marmont	4,800 14,000

SARATOGA CAMPAIGN:

Battle	Date	War	Nationality	Strength	Commander	Casualties
(i) FREEMAN'S FARM	19 Sep 1777	War of American Independence	Americans	3,000	General Gates	320
			British	2,000	General Burgoyne	600
(ii) BEMIS HEIGHTS	7 Oct 1777	War of American Independence	Americans	11,000	General Gates	150
			British	1,600	General Burgoyne	600
	17 Oct 1777	Burgoyne surrendered with 5,700 men at Saratoga.				
TALAVERA	28 July 1809	Peninsular War	British	20,600	Sir Arthur Wellesley	5,400
			Spanish	34,800	Gregorio de la Cuesta	1,200
			French	46,000	Marshals Jourdan and Victor	7,300
TOULOUSE	10 Apr 1814	Peninsular War – Southern France	British, Portuguese, Spanish	50,000	Wellington	4,600
			French	42,000	Marshal Soult	3,200
TRENTON	25 Dec 1776	War of American Independence	Americans	2,400	Washington	5
			British (German mercenaries)	1,400	Colonel Johann Rall	30 (900 captured)
TRINCOMALEE	26 Sep 1767	First Mysore War	British	12,000	Colonel Smith	150
			Hyderabad and Mysore	60,000	Hyder Ali	4,000
VELLINGHAUSEN	15–16 July 1761	Seven Years War – Germany	Allies	65,000	Ferdinand of Brunswick	1,400
			French	92,000	Prince de Soubise and the Duc de Broglie	5,000
VIMEIRO	21 Aug 1808	Peninsular War	British	17,000	Sir Arthur Wellesley	720
			French	13,000	Marshal Junot	2,000
VITORIA	21 June 1813	Peninsular War	British, Portuguese, Spanish	79,000	Wellington	4,900
			French	66,000	King Joseph and Marshal Jourdan	5,200
WANDIWASH	22 Jan 1760	Seven Years War – India	British	4,400	Colonel Coote	190 out of 1,900 Europeans
			French	3,600	Comte de Lally-Tollendal	600 out of 2,300 Europeans
WARBURG	31 July 1760	Seven Years War – Germany	Allies	—	Ferdinand of Brunswick	1,200
			French	35,000	Chevalier du Muy	2,000

Battle	Date	Campaign	Combatants	Strength of Armies	Commanders	Casualties
WATERLOO	18 June 1815	Waterloo Campaign	British	24,000	Wellington	15,000
			Dutch, Belgians, Germans	44,000		
			Prussians	50,000	Blücher	7,000
			French	72,000	Napoleon	26,000

II Sea

Battle	Date	Campaign	Combatants	Number of Ships Engaged	Commanders	Ships Lost	Casualties
CAMPERDOWN	11 Oct 1797	French Revolutionary Wars	British	16	Admiral Duncan	0	1,000
			Dutch	16	Admiral de Winter	9	1,100
CAPE SAINT VINCENT	14 Feb 1797	French Revolutionary Wars	British	15	Sir John Jervis	0	300
			Spanish	27	Don Juan de Langara	4	800
COPENHAGEN	2 Apr 1801	French Revolutionary Wars	British	18	Admirals Parker and Nelson	6	1,000
			Danes	17	Olfert Fischer	17	1,700
NAVARINO	20 Oct 1827	War of Greek Independence	British, French, Russians	27	Admirals Codrington, de Rigny, and Heiden	0	200
			Turks, Egyptians	89	Ibrahim Pasha	60	8,000
NILE	1 Aug 1798	War of the Second Coalition	British	14	Admiral Nelson	0	1,000
			French	13	Admiral Brueys	11	10,000
QUIBERON BAY	20 Nov 1759	Seven Years War	British	23	Admiral Hawke	2	300
			French	21	Marshal de Conflans	5	2,500
THE SAINTS	12 Apr 1782	War of American Independence	British	36	Admiral Rodney	0	1,100
			French	34	Comte de Grasse	9	3,000
TRAFALGAR	21 Oct 1805	War of the Third Coalition	British	27	Lord Nelson	0	1,700
			French	33	Admiral Villeneuve	20	6,900
USHANT	1 June 1794	French Revolutionary Wars	British	25	Lord Howe	0	1,000
			French	26	Admiral Villaret-Joyeuse	7	3,000

Strength and Cost of the Army, 1755–1830

		Total Supplies Granted for the Army (£)	Subsidy and Pay of Foreign Troops (£)	Numbers of Men Voted	Numbers of Officers and Men in Army according to Mutiny Act
1755		1,139,548	52,000	31,422	34,263
1756		2,174,540	468,946	47,488	49,749
1757		2,516,119	355,639	68,791	53,777
1758		4,173,890	1,475,897	88,370	52,543
1759		4,882,444	1,968,178	91,446	57,294
1760		6,926,490	1,844,487	99,044	64,971
1761		8,615,293	2,091,659	105,221	67,776
1762		7,810,539	1,023,583	120,633	17,536
1763		4,877,139	321,907	120,419	17,532
1764		2,781,652	422,995	31,773	17,421
1765		2,313,343	60,344	31,654	17,306
1766		2,060,414	50,000	31,752	16,754
1767		1,585,573	–	31,701	17,253
1768		1,472,484	–	31,700	17,142
1769		1,358,056	–	31,589	17,666
1770		1,547,931	45,565	30,949	23,432
1771		1,810,320	–	43,546	17,547
1772		1,514,656	–	30,641	17,070
1773		1,516,402	–	30,641	18,024
1774		1,534,721	–	30,641	18,024
1775		1,597,051	–	30,641	21,930
1776		3,500,367	560,455	50,234	20,752
1777		3,815,393	642,431	80,669	90,734
1778		4,833,667	624,157	82,995	20,057
1779		6,013,082	654,677	115,863	30,346
1780		6,796,502	2,418,806	122,677	35,005
1781		7,815,540	658,043	128,549	39,666
1782		7,817,767	724,120	131,989	49,455
1783		5,676,650	656,550	124,254	54,678
1784		4,158,073	182,772	30,680	17,483
1785		2,286,263	120,280	29,557	17,483
1786		2,042,730	–	33,544	18,053
1787		1,876,287	–	35,544	17,634
1788		2,081,905	–	32,117	17,634
1789		1,917,063	–	38,592	17,697
1790		1,874,075	–	38,784	17,448
1791	GB	1,961,326	36,094	39,377	17,448
	Ireland	512,093		15,502	
1792	GB	1,814,800	–	36,476	17,013
	Ireland	557,512		15,532	
1793	GB	3,968,559	455,852	131,181	17,013
	Ireland	919,616		20,232	

Year		Total Supplies Granted for the Army (£)	Subsidy and Pay of Foreign Troops (£)	Numbers of Men Voted	Numbers of Officers and Men in Army according to Mutiny Act
1794	GB	6,636,560	1,169,323	183,157	27,289
	Ireland	1,481,210		20,232	
1795	GB	11,674,359	1,197,226	301,081	60,244
	Ireland	1,421,705		23,478	
1796	GB	11,907,399	200,000	217,575	119,380 (Mar)
	Ireland	1,479,148		22,246	49,219 (Dec)
1797	GB	15,988,089	500,000	207,447	60,765
	Ireland	2,701,839		40,901	
1798	GB	12,852,815	–	225,264	48,609
	Ireland	2,751,355		32,854	
1799	GB	12,600,609	825,000	225,343	52,051
	Ireland	4,174,583		35,515	
1800	GB	14,462,262	3,114,162	Not stated	80,275
	Ireland	3,745,148			
1801		16,352,057	300,000	205,414	85,940
1802		12,871,338	–	279,855 (6 mths) / 110,945 (6 mths)	84,445(Mar) / 70,299(June)
1803		12,786,619	–	197,827	66,574
1804		19,108,859	–	291,019	129,039
1805		18,581,127	–	284,305	135,121
1806		18,507,519	–	303,831	134,473
1807		20,055,947	180,000	309,065	121,529(Mar) / 113,795(June)
1808		20,839,189	1,400,000	331,777	124,063
1809		22,444,770	1,300,000	339,408	133,922
1810		21,717,080	1,380,000	340,835	98,780
1811		23,687,005	2,400,000	340,321	84,801
1812		27,574,757	2,400,000	342,273	245,996
1813		36,689,335	3,600,000	354,510	227,442
1814		37,276,850	4,300,000	362,125	236,497
1815		46,699,092	7,451,056	246,988	204,386(Mar) / 190,767(June)
1816		12,344,344	300,000	133,505	176,675
1817		11,442,977	–	92,606	121,035
1818		10,035,290	1,125,682	90,647	133,640
1819		9,782,470	1,000,000	80,841	80,841
1820		9,443,244	–	92,586	92,586
1821		8,736,092	–	93,262	81,468

	Total Supplies Granted for the Army (£)	Subsidy and Pay of Foreign Troops (£)	Numbers of Men Voted	Numbers of Officers and Men in Army according to Mutiny Act
1822	7,755,042	–	71,779	71,790
1823	7,294,458	–	72,140	72,140
1824	7,403,288	–	76,700	76,700
1825	7,818,205	–	86,893	86,893
1826	7,711,629	–	86,764	87,240
1827	8,153,229	–	86,803	87,359
1828	8,009,314	–	90,519	91,075
1829	7,734,993	–	91,075	89,723
1830	7,403,651	–	88,848	88,848

SOURCE: *Parliamentary Papers, 1868–69*, Vol. XXXV, pp. 697–703; Clode, C. M., *The Military Forces of the Crown* (London, 1869), Vol. I, pp. 398–9.

The British Army and the American War of Independence

Strength of the British Army: April 1775–March 1782*

	Apr 1775	Mar 1776	Aug 1777	Oct 1778	July 1779	Sep 1780	Sep 1781	Mar 1782
British Isles	12,700	16,347	18,446	62,422	67,421	78,437	78,061	78,969
Gibraltar	3,064	3,188	3,141	5,031	4,930	5,786	5,560	5,336
East Indies	–	–	–	1,099	1,009	1,245	1,099	1,062
West Indies	1,983	1,937	3,315	1,751	8,119	11,153	10,087	8,756
North America	6,991	14,374	23,694	52,561	47,624	44,554	47,301	47,223
Elsewhere	2,325	9,284	2,274	2,309	2,588	6,077	7,173	10,961
Total	27,063	45,130	57,637	112,239	131,691	147,152	149,282	150,310

* These figures include all effective officers and other ranks in Regular, Provincial and German units.
SOURCE: Philip Katcher, *King George's Army 1775–1783* (Osprey, 1973).

Loans and Subsidies to Foreign States during the Wars of 1793–1814

	£	£		£	£
1793			1794		
Hanover	492,650		Prussia	1,226,495	
Hesse-Cassel	190,623		Sardinia	200,000	
Sardinia	150,000		Hesse-Cassel	437,105	
		833,273	Hesse-Darmstadt	102,073	
			Baden	25,196	
			Hanover	559,376	
					2,550,245

	£	£
1795		
Germany, Imperial Loan (35 Geo. III, c.93)	4,600,000	
Baden	1,794	
Brunswick	97,722	
Hesse-Cassel	317,492	
Hesse-Darmstadt	79,605	
Hanover	478,348	
Sardinia	150,000	
		5,724,961
1796		
Hesse-Darmstadt	20,076	
Brunswick	12,794	
		32,870
1797		
Hesse-Darmstadt	57,015	
Brunswick	7,571	
Germany, Imperial Loan (37 Geo. III, c.59)	1,620,000	
		1,684,586
1798		
Brunswick	7,000	
Portugal	120,013	
		127,013
1799		
Prince of Orange	20,000	
Hesse-Darmstadt	4,812	
Russia	825,000	
		849,812
1800		
Germany	1,066,666	
German Princes	500,000	
Bavaria	501,017	
Russia	545,494	
		2,613,177
1801		
Portugal	200,114	
Sardinia	40,000	
Hesse-Cassel	100,000	
Germany	150,000	
German Princes	200,000	
		690,114

	£	£
1802		
Hesse-Cassel	33,451	
Sardinia	52,000	
Russia	200,000	
		285,451
1803		
Hanover	117,628	
Russia	63,000	
Portugal	31,647	
		212,275
1804		
Sweden	20,119	
Hesse-Cassel	83,304	
		103,423
1805		
Hanover		35,341
1806		
Hanover	76,865	
Hesse-Cassel	18,982	
Germany	500,000	
		595,847
1807		
Hanover	19,899	
Russia	614,183	
Hesse-Cassel	45,000	
Prussia	180,000	
		859,082
1808		
Spain	1,497,873	
Sweden	1,100,000	
Sicily	300,000	
		2,897,873
1809		
Spain	529,039	
Portugal	600,000	
Sweden	300,000	
Sicily	300,000	
Austria	850,000	
		2,579,039
1810		
Hesse-Cassel	45,150	
Spain	402,875	
Portugal	1,237,518	
Sicily	425,000	
		2,110,543

	£	£			£	£
1811			**1814**			
Spain	220,690		Spain		450,000	
Portugal	1,832,168		Portugal		1,500,000	
Sicily	275,000		Sicily		316,667	
Portuguese sufferers	39,555		Sweden		800,000	
			Russia		2,169,982	
		2,367,413	Prussia		1,319,129	
1812			Austria		1,064,882	
Spain	1,000,000		France (advanced to			
Portugal	2,167,832		Louis XVIII to			
Portuguese sufferers	60,445		enable him to			
Sicily	400,000		return to France)		200,000	
Sweden	278,292		Hanover		500,000	
Morocco	1,952		Denmark		121,918	
		3,908,521				8,442,578
1813						
Spain	1,000,000					46,289,459
Portugal	1,644,063					
Sicily	600,000					
Sweden	1,320,000					
Russia	657,500					
Russian sufferers	200,000					
Prussia	650,040					
Prince of Orange	200,000					
Austria	500,000					
Morocco	14,419					
		6,786,022				

SOURCE: G. R. Porter, *The Progress of the Nation*, Vol. II (London, 1838) pp. 335–8.

Annual Parliamentary Votes for the Navy, 1755–1830

	Total Naval Supplies Granted (£)	Numbers of Seamen and Marines Voted	Numbers Borne (inc Marines on Shore)		Total Naval Supplies Granted (£)	Numbers of Seamen and Marines Voted	Numbers Borne (inc Marines on Shore)
1755	1,714,289	22,000*	33,612	1766	2,722,283	20,287	16,817
1756	3,349,021	50,000*	52,809	1767	1,869,321	20,287	15,755
1757	3,503,939	66,419	63,259	1768	1,526,357	20,287	15,511
1758	3,874,421	74,845	70,694	1769	1,924,669	20,287	16,730
1759	5,236,263	84,845	84,464	1770	1,622,067	20,287	19,768
1760	5,609,708	88,355	86,626	1771	3,082,500	40,000	31,310
1761	5,594,790	88,355	80,954	1772	2,070,665	25,000	26,299
1762	5,954,252	89,061	84,797	1773	1,885,573	20,000	21,688
1763	5,128,977	34,287	38,350	1774	2,104,917	20,000	19,928
1764	2,094,800	20,287	20,603	1775	1,684,060	18,000	19,846
1765	2,945,966	20,287	19,226	1776	3,227,056	28,000	31,084

	Total Naval Supplies Granted (£)	Numbers of Seaman and Marines Voted	Numbers Borne (inc Marines on Shore)		Total Naval Supplies Granted (£)	Numbers of Seamen and Marines Voted	Numbers Borne (inc Marines on Shore)
1777	4,210,306	45,000	52,836	1804	12,350,606	100,000	99,372
1778	5,001,896	60,000	72,258	1805	15,035,630	120,000	114,012
1779	4,589,069	70,000	87,767	1806	15,864,341	120,000	122,860
1780	7,003,284	85,000	97,898	1807	17,400,337	130,000	130,917
1781	8,936,277	90,000	99,362	1808	18,317,548	130,000	139,605
1782	8,063,206	100,000	105,443	1809	19,578,467	130,000	144,387
1783	6,483,833	110,000	65,677	1810	19,829,434	145,000	146,312
1784	3,153,869	26,000	28,878	1811	20,935,894	145,000	144,762
1785	2,551,308	18,000	22,183	1812	20,442,149	145,000	144,844
1786	2,434,327	18,000	17,257	1813	21,212,012	140,000	147,047
1787	2,286,000	18,000	19,444	1814	19,312,071	116,923	126,414
1788	2,411,407	18,000	19,740	1815	19,032,700	85,384	78,891
1789	2,328,570	20,000	20,396	1816	10,114,346	33,000	35,196
1790	2,433,637	20,000	39,526	1817	7,645,422	19,000	22,944
1791	4,008,405	24,000	34,907	1818	6,547,809	20,000	23,026
1792	1,985,482	16,000	17,361	1819	6,527,781	20,000	23,230
1793	3,971,915	45,000	59,042	1820	6,691,345	23,000	23,985
1794	5,325,332	85,000	83,891	1821	6,383,686	22,000	24,937
1795	6,315,523	100,000	99,608	1822	5,480,325	21,000	23,806
1796	7,552,552	110,000	112,382	1823	5,442,540	25,000	26,314
1797	13,033,673	120,000	120,046	1824	5,762,893	29,000	30,502
1798	13,449,389	120,000	119,592	1825	5,983,127	29,000	31,456
1799	13,654,013	120,000	120,409	1826	6,135,004	30,000	32,519
1800	13,619,080	111,538	123,527	1827	6,125,850	30,000	33,106
1801	15,857,037	131,538	131,959	1828	5,995,965	30,000	32,818
1802	13,833,574	94,461	77,765	1829	5,878,795	30,000	32,458
1803	10,211,378	100,000	67,148	1830	5,594,955	29,000	31,160

* No marines voted in these years.

SOURCE: *Parliamentary Papers 1868–69*, Vol. XXXV, pp. 693–5.

Military Office-holders

Commanders-in-Chief 1756–1830

1757–59	Vt (Earl) Ligonier
1759–66	office vacant
1766–69	M of Granby
1769–78	office vacant
1778–82	Ld Amherst
1782–93	Hon. Henry Seymour Conway
1793–95	Ld Amherst
1795–09	D of York
1809–11	Sir David Dundas
1811–27	D of York
1827–28	D of Wellington
1828–42	Vt Hill

Field Marshals created during the period 1756–1830

1757	Sir Robert Rich
	Vt Molesworth
	Vt (Earl) Ligonier
1763	Ld Tyrawley
1793	Hon. Henry Seymour Conway
	D of Gloucester
	Sir Geoffrey Howard
1795	D of York
1796	D of Argyll
	Ld Amherst
	Ld Howard de Walden
	Studholme Hodgson
	Marquis Townshend
	Ld Frederick Cavendish
	D of Richmond
1805	D of Kent
1813	D of Wellington
	D of Cumberland
	D of Cambridge
1816	D of Gloucester
	Leopold, D of Saxe-Coburg (later King of the Belgians)
1821	M of Drogheda
	Earl Harcourt
1830	Sir Alured Clarke
	Sir Samuel Hulse

Biographical Details of Major Commanders, 1755–1830

Abercromby, Sir Ralph (1734–1801)
Cornet in 3rd Dragoon Guards 1756. Served in Germany in Seven Years War as ADC to General Sir William Pitt. MP for Clackmannanshire 1774–80 and 1796–8. Opposed American war. Maj.-Gen. 1793. Served in Flanders 1793–5. Knighted 1795. Commanded expedition to West Indies 1795–7. Commanded forces in Ireland 1797–8, but conflict with Irish government led to his resignation, and he was appointed to Scottish Command. Second-in-command of expedition to Holland 1799. Given command of forces in Mediterranean 1800. Led expedition to Egypt, where he was wounded in the battle of 21 Mar 1801, and died 28 Mar.

Amherst, Jeffrey Amherst, B (1717–97)
Ensign in the Guards 1731. ADC to Ligonier and Cumberland in War of Austrian Succession. Maj.-Gen. 1758, and given command of expedition against French in Canada. Chief command in America Sep 1758 after capture of Louisburg, and led attack on Ticonderoga 1759. Governor-General of British North America 1760–3. Privy Councillor and Lt-Gen.

of the Ordnance 1772. C-in-C of the army 1772–95 (except 1782–83). Baron 1776. General 1778. Field-Marshal 1796.

Anson, George Anson, B (1697–1762)
Entered navy 1712. Captain 1724. Given command of Pacific squadron, and carried out circumnavigation 1740–4. Rear-Admiral 1744. Promoted to Board of Admiralty 1745. Vice-Admiral, and command of Channel Fleet 1746. Defeated French off Cape Finisterre May 1747, and created Baron. First Lord of the Admiralty 1751–6 and 1757–62, carrying out important administrative reforms. Admiral of the Fleet 1761.

Beresford, William Carr Beresford, Vt (1768–1854)
Ensign in 6th Foot 1785. Served at Toulon 1793, Corsica 1794, India 1800, Egypt 1801–3 and Cape of Good Hope 1806. In 1806 he led the raid on Buenos Aires, where he was captured but later escaped. Occupied Madeira 1807. Recalled to British army in Portugal and made commandant of Lisbon. Maj.-Gen. 1808. Lt.-Gen. 1812. Took part in retreat to Corunna. C-in-C of the Portuguese army 1809–19. Commanded corps in Estremadura Jan–May 1811, defeating French at Albuera, and Centre Corps of army Oct 1813–Apr 1814. MP for Waterford 1811–14. Baron 1814. Viscount 1823. General 1825. Master-General of the Ordnance 1828–30.

Boscawen, Edward (1711–61)
Entered navy 1726. Took part in attacks on Porto Bello 1739 and Cartagena 1741. MP for Truro 1741. Fought in battle off Cape Finisterre May 1747. Made C-in-C of forces in East Indies 1747. Vice-Admiral 1755. Second-in-command of fleet under Hawke 1757. Admiral 1758, and cooperated with Amherst and Wolfe in capture of Louisburg. Privy Councillor, and command of Mediterranean fleet 1759. In the battle of 18 Aug off Lagos he disrupted French plans for invading Britain. General of Marines 1760.

Braddock, Edward (1695–1755)
Ensign in Coldstream Guards 1710. Served in Holland at siege of Bergen-op-Zoom 1747. Maj.-Gen. 1754, and appointed to command in North America. He mounted an expedition to attack Fort Duquesne, but his force was destroyed in an ambush after crossing the Monongahela 9 July 1755. He himself was wounded, and died 13 July.

Burgoyne, John (1723–92)
Cornet in 13th Light Dragoons 1740. Took part in raids on Cherbourg 1758, and St Malo 1759. Raised a light cavalry regiment and commanded it in Portugal 1762. MP for Midhurst 1761, and for Preston 1768. Maj.-Gen. 1772. Sent to Boston 1774, then to Canada as second-in-command to

Carleton. Led an expedition from Canada 1777, but was forced to surrender his whole force at Saratoga 17 Oct. C-in-C in Ireland 1782–3.

Clinton, Sir Henry (1738–95)

Born in Newfoundland where his father was Governor, and served in New York Militia. Lieutenant in Coldstream Guards 1751. ADC to Prince of Brunswick in Seven Years War. MP for Boroughbridge 1772, Newark 1774, and Launceston 1790. Maj.-Gen. 1772. Sent to America 1775, and fought at Bunker Hill. Lt.-Gen. 1776. Returned to America as second-in-command to Howe, whom he succeeded in 1778. Knighted in 1777. Resigned 1781, after Cornwallis' surrender at Yorktown. General 1793. Governor of Gibraltar 1794.

Clive, Robert Clive, B (1725–74)

Sent to Madras in service of East India Company 1743. Fought a duel and twice attempted suicide. Taken prisoner when Madras fell in 1746, but escaped to Fort St David. In Sep 1751 he seized Arcot to distract Chanda Sahib from the siege of Trichinopoly, and followed this with victories at Arni and Covrepauk. In England 1753–5. Returning to Madras, he led the expedition which retook Calcutta Jan 1757, and defeated Surajah Dowlah at Plassey in June. Governor of Bengal 1757–60. Returned to England 1760. Baron in Irish peerage 1762. Knighted 1764. MP for Shrewsbury 1761–74. During his second period as Governor and C-in-C of Bengal 1765–7 he carried out important administrative reforms. Acquitted of corruption in India before Parliamentary Committees 1772–73. Committed suicide 22 Nov 1774.

Coote, Sir Eyre (1726–83)

Entered army at an early age, and served in Germany in War of Austrian Succession and against Jacobites 1745. In India 1754–62. Played important part in victory at Plassey 1757. Defeated French at Wandiwash 1760. In the following year he captured Pondicherry, and was given command of East India Company forces in Bengal. MP for Leicester 1768. Made C-in-C in Madras Presidency 1769, but quarrelled with the Governor and returned to England 1770. Knighted 1771. Maj.-Gen. 1775. Lt.-Gen. 1777. Returned to India as C-in-C 1779, and defeated Hyder Ali. Died at Madras 28 Apr 1783.

Cornwallis, Charles Cornwallis, M of (1738–1805)

Ensign in Grenadier Guards 1756, and served as ADC to Granby in Germany. MP for family borough of Eye 1760. Constable of the Tower 1770. Maj.-Gen. 1775. Lt.-Gen. 1777. Sent to America 1776, and made second-in-command of the forces there 1778. Defeated Americans at Camden 1780 and Guilford 1781, but forced to surrender at Yorktown 19 Oct 1781. Governor-General and C-in-C in India 1786–93; carried out reforms, and defeated Tippoo Sahib in the Third Mysore War. Marquess 1792. Master-General of the Ordnance 1795–1801. Again appointed Governor-General and C-in-C 1799, but it was not necessary for him to take up his duties. Viceroy and C-in-C in Ireland 1798–1801. Negotiated Peace of Amiens as Plenipotentiary to France 1802. Again appointed Governor-General and C-in-C in India; left England Mar 1805, but died in India 5 Oct.

Craufurd, Robert (1764–1812)
Ensign in 25th Regiment 1799. Served under Cornwallis in India 1790–2. Deputy quartermaster-general in Ireland 1798. MP for East Retford 1799–1806. Served as English military commissioner at Suvarov's head-quarters, and on the staff in expedition to Holland 1799. Took part in attack on Buenos Aires 1807. Sent to Peninsula 1807, where he commanded the Light Division Feb 1810–Feb 1811 and Apr 1811–Jan 1812. Maj.-Gen. 1811. Killed at Ciudad Rodrigo 24 Jan 1812.

Cumberland, William Augustus, D of (1721–65)
Second surviving son of George II. Colonel of Coldstream Guards 1740. Maj.-Gen. 1742. Lt.-Gen. 1743. Wounded at Dettingen 1743. C-in-C of the allied army 1745; defeated at Fontenoy. Recalled to put down the Jacobite Rebellion; defeated the rebels at Culloden 1746 and earned the nickname 'Butcher'. Returned to Flanders 1747, and defeated by Saxe at Lauffeld. On outbreak of Seven Years War he was defeated at Hastenbeck July 1757, and signed the Convention of Kloster-Seven for the evacuation of Hanover. As a result he resigned in disgrace Oct 1757.

Gage, Thomas (1721–87)
Lieutenant in 48th Foot 1741. Fought in Flanders in War of Austrian Succession, and at Culloden. Sent to America 1754, and wounded in Braddock's expedition 1755. Organised a Light Infantry Regiment (80th) 1758, and commanded light infantry in attack on Ticonderoga. Governor of Montreal 1760. Maj.-Gen. 1761. Lt.-Gen. 1770. C-in-C in North America 1763–72. Governor of Massachusetts Bay 1774. Sent force to seize arms at Concord, and fought battle of Bunker Hill 1775. Appointed C-in-C in North America Aug 1775, but resigned Oct. General 1782.

Granby, John Manners, M of (1721–70)
Eldest son of Duke of Rutland. MP for Grantham 1741–54, and Cambridgeshire 1754–70. Colonel of a regiment raised in 1745 to suppress Jacobites; served as a volunteer on Cumberland's staff. Served in Flanders 1747. Maj.-Gen. 1755. Colonel of Royal Horse Guards 1758. Lt.-Gen. 1759. Succeeded Sackville in command of British forces 1759, and defeated French at Warburg 1760. Master-General of the Ordnance 1763. C-in-C of the army 1766–70.

Hawke, Edward Hawke, B (1705–81)
Entered navy 1720. Captain 1734. Took part in action at Toulon 1744.
Rear-Admiral and second-in-command of Channel Fleet 1747, commanding it from Sep due to Sir Peter Warren's ill-health. He defeated
French off Cape Finisterre Oct 1747, and was knighted. MP for Portsmouth 1747–76. Vice-Admiral 1748. Succeeded to Warren's command
1748–52. Command of Western Squadron 1755. Sent to relieve Byng in
the Mediterranean 1756. Admiral 1757, and led naval force in unsuccessful expedition to Rochefort. Command of Western Squadron 1759; defeated French at Quiberon Bay 20 Nov. First Lord of the Admiralty
1766–71. Admiral and C-in-C of the Fleet 1768. Baron 1776.

Hill, Rowland Hill, Vt (1772–1842)
Ensign in 38th Foot 1790. Saw action at Toulon 1793, and Egypt 1801.
Maj.-Gen. 1805. Sent to Portugal in command of a brigade 1808; fought at
Roliça and Vimeiro, and took part in retreat to Corunna. Commanded
Second Division in Peninsula June 1809–Jan 1811, and May 1811–Mar
1813. Lt.-Gen. 1812. MP for Shrewsbury 1812–14. Commanded Right
Wing of army Mar 1813–Apr 1814. Baron 1814. Commanded Second
Corps in Waterloo campaign. Second-in-command of army of occupation
in France until 1818. General 1825. General Commanding-in-Chief 1828.
Resigned and created viscount 1842.

Hood, Samuel Hood, Vt (1724–1816)
Entered navy 1741. Post Captain 1756. Saw active service in Austrian
Succession and Seven Years Wars. Commissioner of Portsmouth dock-
yard and Governor of the Naval Academy 1778. Rear-Admiral 1780, and
sent to West Indies as second-in-command under Rodney. Baron in Irish
peerage 1782. MP for Westminster, defeating Fox 1784. C-in-C at Portsmouth 1787–8. Vice-Admiral 1787. A Lord of the Admiralty 1788. C-in-C
in Mediterranean 1793–4, directing operations at Toulon. Admiral 1794.
Viscount 1796. Governor of Greenwich Hospital 1796–1816.

Howe, Richard Howe, Earl (1726–99)
Entered navy 1739. Post Captain 1746. MP for Dartmouth 1757–82.
Succeeded as viscount in Irish peerage 1758. Commanded ships in raids
on French coast 1758, and played important part in battle of Quiberon
Bay 1759. A Lord of the Admiralty 1763–5. Treasurer of Navy 1765–70.
Rear-Admiral 1770. Vice-Admiral 1775. Command of North America
station 1776–8. Admiral, viscount and command of Channel Fleet Apr
1782; relieved Gibraltar in autumn. First Lord of the Admiralty Jan–Apr
1783, and Dec 1783–Aug 1788. Baron and Earl 1788. Command of
Channel Fleet May–Dec 1790, and 1793–7; defeated French off Ushant
1794. Admiral of the Fleet and General of Marines 1796. Helped pacify
mutineers at Spithead 1797.

Howe, William Howe, Vt (1729–1814)

Cornet in Cumberland's Light Dragoons 1746. MP for Nottingham 1758–80. Commanded 58th Foot Regiment at siege of Louisburg 1758, and leading a newly formed light infantry battalion, took part in capture of Quebec 1759 and Montreal 1760. Maj.-Gen. 1772. Lt.-Gen. 1775. Sent to Boston as second-in-command and led left wing in battle of Bunker Hill. Succeeded Gage in supreme command Oct 1775. Resigned 1778. Lt.-Gen. of the Ordnance 1782–1803. General 1793. Held home commands 1793 and 1795. Succeeded to viscountcy on death of his brother, Admiral Lord Howe, 1799. Governor of Plymouth 1805.

Keith, George Keith Elphinstone, Vt (1746–1823)

Entered navy 1761. Captain 1775. Saw action in American War. MP for Dumbartonshire 1780, and for Stirlingshire 1790. Served under Hood at Toulon 1793. Rear-Admiral 1794. Vice-Admiral 1795. Commanded expedition to Cape Town 1795. Baron in Irish peerage 1797. Second-in-command in Channel 1797–8. Sent to Mediterranean as second-in-command to St Vincent 1798 and succeeded him 1799. Admiral 1801. Commanded North Sea station 1803–7, and Channel Fleet 1812–15. Viscount 1814.

Ligonier, John Ligonier, Earl (1680–1770)

Born at Castres in France of Huguenot parents who took refuge in Ireland 1697. Served under Marlborough 1702–11. Lt-Governor of Fort St Philip, Minorca, 1712. Colonel of 7th Dragoon Guards 1720. Maj.-Gen. 1739. Lt.-Gen. 1743. Staff officer to George II; commanded Second Division at Dettingen and the Foot at Fontenoy. C-in-C in Netherlands 1746–7. MP for Bath 1748. Lt.-Gen. of the Ordnance 1748–56. Viscount in Irish peerage 1757. C-in-C of the army 1757–9, and military adviser to Pitt. Master-General of the Ordnance 1759–62. Baron 1763. Field-Marshal and Earl 1766.

Lynedoch, Thomas Graham, B (1748–1843)

Volunteer under Hood at Toulon 1793. Lt.-Col. on raising 90th Foot 1794. MP for Perthshire 1794–1807. British Military Commissioner with Austrian Army in Italy 1796. Took part in capture of Minorca 1798, and siege of Valetta 1800. With Moore in Swedish expedition 1808, and retreat to Corunna. Maj.-Gen. 1809. Commanded brigade in Walcheren expedition 1809. Lt.-Gen. 1810. Commanded Cadiz garrison 1810–11, and defeated French at Barrosa Mar 1811. Commanded 1st Division July 1811–July 1812, and May–Oct 1813. Appointed in Nov 1813 to command British troops cooperating with Russians in Holland. Baron 1814. General 1821.

Moore, Sir John (1761–1809)

Ensign in 51st Foot 1776, and saw action in Nova Scotia during American

War. MP for Linlithgow, Selkirk and Peebles 1784–90. Served in Corsica 1794–5, West Indies 1796–7, Ireland 1797–9, Holland 1799, and the Mediterranean and Egypt 1800–1. Maj.-Gen. 1798. Trained troops at Shorncliffe 1803–6. Knighted 1804. Lt-Gen. 1805. Sent to Sicily 1806, and succeeded General Henry Fox in Mediterranean command 1807. Led abortive expedition to Sweden 1808. To Peninsula 1808, and succeeded to command after Convention of Cintra. Advanced into Spain, but forced to retreat to Corunna, where he was fatally wounded as his army evacuated 16 Jan 1809.

Nelson, Horatio Nelson, Vt (1758–1805)
Entered navy 1770. Served in Arctic expedition 1773, and afterwards in the East Indies. Post Captain 1779. Led naval force against San Juan 1780. West Indian station 1784. Sent to Mediterranean under Hood 1793; engaged in occupation of Corsica 1794, where he lost the sight of his right eye. Took part in battle of Cape St Vincent, and promoted rear-admiral Feb 1797. Led unsuccessful attack on Santa Cruz July 1797, and lost his right arm. Returned to fleet off Cadiz 1798. Failed to intercept French expedition to Egypt, but destroyed French fleet in the battle of the Nile, and was made a baron. Became involved with Lady Hamilton, wife of English ambassador to Naples; stayed at Naples despite Keith's order to take fleet to Minorca. Resigned his command and returned overland with the Hamiltons 1800. Vice-Admiral 1801. Appointed second-in-command of expedition to the Baltic, and destroyed Danish fleet at Copenhagen. Created a viscount and succeeded Sir Hyde Parker as C-in-C. Appointed to Mediterranean command 1803. Villeneuve eluded his blockade of Toulon in spring 1805, but Nelson defeated the Franco-Spanish fleet at Trafalgar 21 Oct, though he himself was killed.

Pakenham, Sir Edward (1778–1815)
Second son of Baron Longford. Ensign 92nd Foot 1794. Served in Ireland during rebellion of 1798. Maj.-Gen. 1812. Sent to Peninsula, where he commanded 3rd Division June 1812–Jan 1813, and 6th Division Jan–June 1813 and July–Aug 1813. Sent to America after death of General Ross, and killed leading attack on New Orleans 8 Jan 1815.

Rodney, George Brydges Rodney, B (1718–92)
Entered navy 1732. Post Captain 1742. Took part in Hawke's victory off Cape Finisterre Oct 1747. Governor and C-in-C of Newfoundland 1749–52. MP for Saltash 1751, and for Northampton 1768. Served in expedition against Rochefort 1757, and at capture of Louisburg 1758. Rear-Admiral 1759. Raided transport ships on French coast 1759–60. C-in-C of Leeward Islands station 1761–3. Vice-Admiral 1762. Baronet 1764. Governor of Greenwich Hospital 1765–70. Jamaica command 1771–4. Admiral 1778. C-in-C of Leeward Islands 1779–82. Ordered to

relieve Gibraltar on his way to the West Indies, he defeated the Spanish and captured a convoy Jan 1780. Defeated French at the battle of The Saints 1782, and created a baron.

Sackville, George Sackville, Vt (1716–85)

Known from 1720–70 as Lord George Sackville, and from 1770–82 as Lord George Germain. Third son of Duke of Dorset. Captain in 6th Dragoon Guards 1737. Distinguished service in War of Austrian Succession; wounded at Fontenoy. MP for Dover 1741–61, Kent 1761–8, and East Grinstead 1768–82. Involved in Irish affairs 1750–6. Maj.-Gen. 1755. Lt.-Gen. of the Ordnance 1757–9. Took part in attack on St Malo 1758. Given command of British contingent in Germany Oct 1758. Court-martialled for refusing to charge at Minden 1759. Colonial Secretary 1775–82. Viscount 1782.

St Vincent, John Jervis, E of (1735–1823)

Entered navy 1749. Distinguished service at Quebec 1759. Post Captain 1760. Engaged in home waters and reliefs of Gibraltar during American War. MP for Launceston 1783, Yarmouth 1784, and Wycombe 1790. Rear-Admiral 1787. Vice-Admiral 1793. C-in-C of expedition to West Indies 1793. Admiral 1795. Command of Mediterranean fleet 1797; defeated Spanish off Cape St Vincent, and created an earl. Resigned through ill-health 1799, but took command of Channel Fleet the following year. First Lord of the Admiralty 1801–4. Resumed Channel command 1806–7. Retired 1810. Admiral of the Fleet 1821.

Saumarez, James Saumarez, B de (1757–1836)

Entered navy 1770. Distinguished himself at the battle of The Saints 1782. Knighted for capturing French frigate La Réunion 1793. Fought in battles of L'Orient 1795 and Cape St Vincent 1797; second-in-command at the Nile 1798. Rear-Admiral and baronet 1801. Given order to blockade Cadiz, where he defeated Franco-Spanish fleet 12 July 1801. Vice-Admiral and second-in-command of fleet off Brest 1807. Command of Baltic Fleet 1808–13. Admiral 1814. C-in-C at Plymouth 1824–7. Baron 1831.

Wellington, Arthur Wellesley, D of (1769–1852)

Fifth son of Earl of Mornington. Ensign in 73rd Highlanders 1787. Served in Flanders 1794–5. Sent to India 1796, and took part in Mysore and Maratha Wars; won victories at Assaye and Argaum 1803. Maj.-Gen. 1802. Irish Secretary 1807. Took part in expedition against Copenhagen 1807. Sent to Peninsula 1808; defeated Junot at Vimeiro, but came home in Oct after Convention of Cintra. Returned to Portugal Apr 1809, defeated French at Talavera in July, and was created viscount in Sep. Defended Lisbon behind lines of the Torres Vedras 1810. Advanced into

Spain 1812, capturing Ciudad Rodrigo and Badajoz. Earl Feb 1812. Defeated Marmont at Salamanca July 1812. Marquis Oct 1812. Defeated French at Vitoria June 1813. Field-Marshal 1813. Invaded France, and defeated Soult at Orthez Feb, and Toulouse Apr 1814. Duke May 1814. Commanded army which defeated Napoleon at Waterloo 18 June 1815. Commanded army of occupation until 1818. Master-General of the Ordnance 1818. C-in-C of the army Jan–Apr 1827. Prime Minister Jan 1828–Nov 1830. Foreign Secretary under Peel 1834–5. Accepted a seat in the Cabinet 1841. C-in-C 1842. Died 14 Sep 1852.

Wolfe, James (1727–59)
Second Lieutenant in Marines 1741. Transferred as Ensign to 12th Foot 1742. Fought at Dettingen 1743, against Jacobites at Falkirk and Culloden 1745–46, and was wounded at Lauffeld 1747. Garrison duty in Scotland and England 1749–57. Quartermaster-general in attack on Rochefort 1757. Served under Amherst in expedition against Cape Breton 1758, and was largely responsible for capture of Louisburg. Given command as a Major-General of expedition against Quebec; killed in battle of Heights of Abraham 13 Sep 1759 which led to the capture of the city.

York, Frederick Augustus, D of (1763–1827)
Second son of George III. Gazetted a Colonel 1780. Lt.-Gen. and Colonel of Coldstream Guards 1784. Given command of British army in Flanders 1793. Field-Marshal 1795. C-in-C of the army 1798. Commanded expedition to Holland 1799. Forced to resign as C-in-C in 1809 because of corruption over military appointments by his mistress; acquitted of receiving bribes by House of Commons and reinstated in 1811. Concerned with administrative reforms, soldiers' welfare and education in the army.

Bibliography

I   Army
Barnett, Correlli, *Britain and Her Army* (London, 1970)
Fortescue, Sir John, *A History of the British Army* (London, 1899–1923)
Fuller, J. F. C., *Sir John Moore's System of Training* (London, 1924)
—— *British Light Infantry in the Eighteenth Century* (London, 1925)
Glover, Michael, *Wellington's Peninsular Victories* (London, 1963)
—— *Wellington as Military Commander* (London, 1968)
—— *The Peninsular War 1807–1814* (London, 1974)
Glover, Richard, *Peninsular Preparation: the Reform of the British Army 1795–1809* (CUP, 1963)
Longford, Elizabeth, *Wellington: The Years of the Sword* (London, 1969)
—— *Wellington: Pillar of State* (London, 1972)

Mackesy, Piers *The War in the Mediterranean 1803–1810* (London, 1957)
—— *The War for America 1775–1783* (London, 1964)
—— *The Strategy of Overthrow 1798–1799* (London, 1974)
Savory, Sir Reginald, *His Britannic Majesty's Army in Germany During the Seven Years' War* (OUP, 1966)
Sheppard, E. W., *A Short History of the British Army* (London, 1950)
Weller, Jac, *Wellington in the Peninsula* (London, 1962)
—— *Wellington at Waterloo* (London, 1967)
—— *Wellington in India* (London, 1972)
Young, Peter, and Lawford, J. P., *History of the British Army* (London, 1970)

II Navy
Baugh, D. A., *British Naval Administration in the Age of Waterloo* (Princeton UP, 1965)
Corbett, Sir Julian, *England in the Seven Years' War* (2 vols) (London, 1907)
Lewis, M. A., *The Navy of Britain, an Historical Portrait* (London, 1948)
—— *Social History of the Royal Navy, 1793–1815* (London,1960)
Mahan, A. T., *The Influence of Sea Power on History 1660–1783* (London, 1890)
—— *The Influence of Sea Power upon the French Revolution and Empire, 1793–1815* (2 vols) (London, 1892)
—— *Sea Power in its Relation to the War of 1812* (London, 1905)
Marcus, G., *A Naval History of England:* Vol. I: *The Formative Centuries* (London, 1961), Vol. II: *The Age of Nelson* (London, 1971)
Richmond, Sir Herbert, *The Navy in India 1763–1783* (London, 1931)
—— *Statesmen and Sea Power* (OUP, 1946)

A detailed bibliography may be found in *A Guide to the Sources of British Military History*, ed. Robin Higham (London, 1972).

8 The Empire and India

Main Territories under British Rule by 1830

Territory	Original Entry into British Rule and Status in 1830	Territory	Original Entry into British Rule and Status in 1830
Antigua	Colony (1663)	Jamaica	Colony (seized 1655 and ceded 1670)
Ascension	Admiralty administered territory (1815)	Malta	Ceded colony (1814)
Australia	First settled 1788	Mauritius	Ceded colony (1814)
Bahamas	First settled 1646: colony (1783)	Montserrat	First settled (1642) as colony
Barbados	First settled 1627: colony (1662)	Newfoundland	Settlement began 1623
		Norfolk Island	Settled 1788
Bermuda	First settled 1609: colony (1684)	Pitcairn	Settled 1790
British Guiana	Ceded colony (1814)	St Christopher (St Kitts) and Nevis	Colony (1625)
British Honduras	First settled 1638		
Canada	Ceded colonies from 1714 onwards	St Helena	Administered by E. India Co. 1673
Cape of Good Hope	Ceded colony (1814)	St Lucia	Ceded colony (1814)
		St Vincent	Ceded colony (1763)
Cayman, Turks and Caicos Islands	Ceded (1670)	Seychelles	Dependency of Mauritius (1810)
		Sierra Leone	Colony (1808)
Ceylon	Ceded colony (1802)	Singapore	Under Indian Government, 1824
Dominica	Colony (1763)		
Gambia	Settlement began 1618	Trinidad and Tobago	Ceded (1802 and 1814)
Gibraltar	Ceded colony (1713)		
Gold Coast	Settlement began 1750	Tristan da Cunha	British settlement (1815)
Grenada	Ceded colony (1763)		
India	Settlement began 1601	Virgin Islands	Colonies (1666)
Ireland	Union with Great Britain (1801)	Windward Isles	Colonies (1763 and 1814)

The American Colonies

Events leading up to the American War of Independence

1763 Peace of Paris signed (10 Feb). Britain gains Canada, Florida, Louisiana east of the Mississippi, Cape Breton, and islands of the St Lawrence.
Proclamation establishing the Alleghenies as temporary boundary line beyond which colonies could not expand.

1765   Stamp Act passed (22 Mar), imposing a stamp duty on legal transactions in America to pay for colonial defence.
Beginning of campaign in Britain and American colonies against the Act.

1766   Petitioning movement of British merchants against the Stamp Act. Appointment of parliamentary inquiry into merchant grievances.
Passing of Declaratory Act, confirming sovereign right to tax the colonies. Stamp Act repealed.

1767   New York Assembly formally refuses to enforce the Mutiny Act. Massachusetts grants indemnity for all offences committed during Stamp Act disturbances.
Townshend introduces duties on paper, paint, glass, lead and tea imported into America (passed 2 June) to pay for colonial defence and establish a civil list within the colonies.
Boston enters a non-importation agreement against the duties.

1768   Massachusetts House of Representatives petitions against taxation without representation and circularises other colonies urging common action against the import duties.
Attacks upon customs officials and American Board of Customs forced to leave Boston.
Troops sent to New England.

1769   Cabinet decides to abolish all Townshend duties except those on tea (1 May).

1770   Townshend's Revenue Act amended leaving duties only on tea.
Boston 'Massacre' (5 Mar). British soldiers kill five people in a mob attacking a customs house.

1771   South Carolina assembly suspended for grant of £1,500 to the Supporters of the Bill of Rights Society in London.
Quarrels with assemblies of North Carolina and Georgia.

1772   Revenue cutter *Gaspee* boarded and burnt (10 June).
Committees of Correspondence formed to publicise grievances and coordinate colonial resistance.

1773   Tea Act passed. All duties on tea re-exported by East India Company to be remitted and direct export to America.
American resistance to landing of East India tea. In 'Boston Tea Party' (16 Dec), three shiploads of tea dumped in Boston Harbour.

1774   Fuller's motion to repeal duty on tea defeated by 182 votes to 49.
Coercive measures taken against American colonies. Boston Port Act closes Boston to shipping until compensation paid to East India Company and customs officers mistreated by the mob. Massachusetts Government Act deprives colony of the right to elect councillors and gives the Governor power to appoint and dismiss all civil officers except judges of the supreme court; also substitutes nominated jurors for elected ones and restricts town meetings. Administration of Justice Act provides for removal of

trials to Britain or other colonies. Quartering Act provides for requisition of quarters for troops. Quebec Act provides for government of province of Quebec by an appointed Governor and Council. Toleration extended to Roman Catholics and provision made for payment of tithes by Roman Catholic communicants. French and English legal codes merged. Jurisdiction of Governor of Quebec extended along western edge of Pennsylvania to the Ohio and Mississippi. Continental Congress meets at Philadelphia. Considers and rejects a federal structure of government in North America controlling all aspects of administration but still subordinate to the British parliament and Crown.

Congress decides on the 'Suffolk Resolves' for defiance of Coercive Acts, withholding of taxes until all privileges restored to Massachusetts, and defensive military preparations in the event of arrest of leaders.

1775   North's 'conciliatory propositions' put before the Commons.
        Chatham Conciliation Bill defeated.
        Burke's conciliation proposals defeated (22 Mar).
        Governor Gage receives instruction to put down rebellion; British troops sent to seize rebel supplies at Concord, engage American forces at Lexington (18 Apr).

1776   Second Continental Congress meets at Philadelphia (10 May).
        Declaration of Independence (4 July).

The Original Thirteen American Colonies
(in order in which they ratified the American Constitution)

State	Date of Ratification	First Permanent Settlement
Delaware	7 Dec 1787	1683
Pennsylvania	12 Dec 1787	1682
New Jersey	18 Dec 1787	1664
Georgia	2 Jan 1788	1733
Connecticut	9 Jan 1788	1635
Massachusetts	6 Feb 1788	1620
Maryland	28 Apr 1788	1634
South Carolina	23 May 1788	1670
New Hampshire	21 June 1788	1623
Virginia	25 June 1788	1607
New York	26 July 1788	1614
North Carolina	21 Nov 1789	1650
Rhode Island	29 May 1790	1636

Major Events in Irish History

1768   Octennial Act for Irish Parliaments.
1769   Defeat of government bills for augmentation of army, defeat of

             supply bill, attacks on pension list, and introduction of militia bill. Supply bill and army augmentation passed; parliament prorogued until 1771.

1771   Act to extend leases to Roman Catholics reclaiming bog-land.

1773   Defeat of measure to tax absentee proprietors.

1774   Act to provide form of oath of allegiance acceptable to Roman Catholics.

1775   Measures passed to open trade to Irish merchants and encouragement given to linen manufacture.

1775–6   Attacks on government policy towards American colonies and defeat of government money bills.

1776   First Volunteer companies formed in Wexford.

1777   New Irish parliament meets for business and attacks state of trade and financial administration.

             First Volunteer company in Belfast.

1778   Censure motion on state of Irish finances passed.

             Act passed to allow Catholics to take leases on land for life or up to 999 years; also to inherit or bequeath land on same terms as Protestants.

1778–9   Widespread Volunteer movement to repel French invasion and assert Irish rights.

1779   Demands for further easing of restrictions on Irish trade pressed in the English House of Commons.

             Widespread agitation for removal of trade restrictions.

             Demonstration of armed volunteers in Dublin (4 Nov).

             Attack by English politicians in House of Commons over Irish trade issue. Acts forbidding the export of wool, woollen goods, and glass from Ireland repealed.

1780   Irish permitted to trade with British settlements in Africa and America on same terms as rest of British Isles. Prohibitions on import of gold and silver from Great Britain repealed. Irish allowed to import foreign hops and Turkey Company opened to Irish merchants. Protestant dissenters released from having to take the Sacrament in the Church of Ireland. Grattan's motion (19 Apr) that 'the King's most excellent majesty, and the lords and commons of Ireland, are the only power competent to enact laws to bind Ireland' adjourned by 136 votes to 97. Irish magistrates refuse to operate Mutiny Act and Mutiny Bill prepared in Irish parliament passed. Perpetual Mutiny Act passed by British parliament.

1782   Convention of Ulster Volunteers at Dungannon (15 Feb) declare Poynings' Law 'unconstitutional and a grievance'; demand a measure of religious equality; control of the Mutiny Act; and same security of tenure for Irish as for English judges.

Grattan's motion for Irish independence defeated by 137 votes to 68 (22 Feb).

Resolution for independence passed unanimously (16 Apr). 'The Constitution of 1782':

Repeal of legislative authority of British parliament and passing of Yelverton's Act to end the power of the chief governor and council of Ireland to originate or alter bills; only bills enacted by Irish parliament to be transmitted to the King. Perpetual Mutiny Act replaced by biennial act and Irish judges granted same tenure as English.

Catholic relief acts passed concerning land, education, the residence of bishops and clergy, and registration of priests, but not granting full political rights.

1783   Renunciation Act (23 Geo. III, c.28) confirmed the complete legislative and judicial independence of Ireland.

National Volunteer Convention at Dublin chaired by Henry Flood agrees plan 'for the more equal representation of the people in parliament'. Irish parliament refuses Flood leave to bring in reform bill by 157 votes to 77 (30 Nov).

1783–4 Appeals for protective legislation for Irish manufactures raised in Irish parliament but rejected.

1784   First power-driven machinery established in Ireland.

Bounties given to export of cotton. Foster's Corn Law providing bounties for export of grain.

1785   Proposals for commercial union between Ireland and England abandoned.

1790   Whig Club founded by Grattan and others to press for parliamentary reform.

1791   Society of United Irishmen founded in Belfast by Theobald Wolfe Tone and others for religious equality and radical reform of parliament. Similar societies set up in many other Irish towns and cities.

1792   Catholic relief bill removing disabilities attaching to marriages between Catholics and Protestants; Catholics admitted to the legal profession and restrictions on education removed. Provisions for granting political rights defeated.

Catholic Convention in Dublin (3 Dec) and petitions for further concessions.

1793   Catholic Relief Act. Roman Catholics admitted to parliamentary and municipal franchise on same terms as Protestants; granted right to bear arms; hold most civil and military offices; still to remain subject to exclusion from parliament.

Arms act passed to restrict imports of arms and ammunition.

Convention Act prevents calling of further representative assemblies.

1794   Earl Fitzwilliam becomes viceroy of Ireland (Aug).
         Catholic Committee begins campaign for further relief meas-
         ures.
1795   Fitzwilliam commits government to Catholic relief.
         Cabinet instructs him to oppose. Recalled (23 Feb).
         Grattan's bill to admit Catholics to parliament rejected (May).
         Wolfe Tone leaves for America.
         First 'Orange Society' founded after sectarian fighting in
         Armagh (Sep). Outrages against Catholic peasantry.
1796   Insurrection Act passed, providing government with repressive
         powers to deal with disturbed areas.
         Suspension of Habeas Corpus. Creation of Protestant
         Yeomanry. Arming of United Irishmen.
         French expedition accompanied by Wolfe Tone fails to land at
         Bantry Bay (Dec).
1797   Military repression of United Irish organisation in Ulster by
         General Lake (from Mar). Followed by suppression of United
         Irishmen in other provinces.
         Grattan's reform bill fails to pass parliament.
1798   Leaders of United Irishmen seized in Dublin (Mar).
         Capture of Lord Edward Fitzgerald (19 May).
         Outbreak of rebellion (26 May). Attack on New Ross fails (5
         June). Capture of Vinegar Hill (21 June) and defeat of Wexford
         rising. Ulster rising: attack on Antrim repulsed (7 June); defeat
         of Ulster rebels at Ballynahinch (13 June).
         Landing of General Humbert at Killala Bay (22 Aug).
         Surrenders at Ballinamuch (8 Sep). Recapture of Killala (23
         Sep) ends Connaught rising.
         Failure of Hardy's expedition to Lough Swilly and capture of
         Wolfe Tone (12 Oct).
         Vt Castlereagh becomes Chief Secretary of Ireland (Nov).
1799   Defeat of government address to Irish parliament requesting
         them to consider scheme of union with England by 111 votes to
         106.
         Act establishing virtual martial law in Ireland.
1800   Motion pledging the continuing independence of the Irish par-
         liament defeated by 138 votes to 96 (16 Jan).
         Proposals for legislative union betweeen England and Ireland
         approved by 158 votes to 115 (6 Feb).
         Terms of union accepted by both houses (28 Mar).
         Act of Union receives royal assent (1 Aug). By provisions of act
         (39 and 40 Geo. III, c.67) Ireland merged with Great Britain in
         one Kingdom, to be known as 'The United Kingdom of Great
         Britain and Ireland'.
         Succession to the crown to be governed by same provisions as

the union between England and Scotland. Irish parliament ceases to exist. 32 Irish peers (28 temporal peers elected for life and 4 spiritual lords in rotation) to sit in the House of Lords. 100 members (64 county, 35 borough and 1 university) to sit in the House of Commons.

Church of England and Church of Ireland united. Commercial union (with some qualification) established. Financial systems to remain distinct, subject to review. Ireland to provide two-seventeenths of United Kingdom expenditure.

Separate act provides for £1,400,000 from Irish revenues to compensate Irish parliamentary officials and borough patrons. Last meeting of Irish parliament (2 Aug).

1803	Emmett's 'rising' suppressed (23 July). Emmett and 21 others executed.
1808	Grattan's motion for Catholic Emancipation defeated in the Commons by 281 votes to 128.
1810	Catholic Committee set up to campaign for Catholic Emancipation. Reconstituted in 1811 as the Catholic Board.
1812	Motion to consider Catholic claims passed by 225 votes to 106.
1813	Emancipation bill defeated in committee.
1814	Catholic Board dissolved by government order.
1817	Irish and British exchequers united because of increase of Irish national debt.
	Partial failure of potato crop.
1819	Catholic Emancipation bill defeated in the Commons.
1821	Catholic Emancipation defeated in the House of Lords.
1823	Catholic Association founded by O'Connell to campaign for political and other rights.
1824	Catholic Association opened to associate members at 1d. per week, the 'Catholic rent'.
1825	O'Connell unsuccessfully prosecuted for incitement to rebellion. Catholic Association suppressed but refounded under new name.
	Sir Francis Burdett introduces relief bill, allied to raising country franchise from 40s to £10 and payment of Catholic clergy from public funds. Rejected in the House of Lords.
1826	Catholic Association secures return of members pledged to Emancipation in Louth, Monaghan, Waterford, and Westmeath.
1828	Election of O'Connell for Co. Clare.
1829	Catholic Emancipation Act (10 Geo. IV, c.7). Roman Catholics made eligible for all offices of state except regent, lord lieutenant, and lord chancellor. No oath of supremacy required to sit in either house of parliament.
	Catholic Association and similar organisations suppressed.

£10 franchise replaces 40s franchise in counties.

1830   Beginning of anti-tithe campaign.

1832   Irish Reform Act receives royal assent (7 Aug).

Holders of Important Office concerned with India

Presidents of the Board of Control
These are listed on pp. 29–30

Chairmen and Deputy Chairmen of the East India Company, 1783–1830*

1783	Sir Henry Fletcher, Nathaniel Smith
1783	(Nov) Nathaniel Smith, William Devaynes
1784	Nathaniel Smith, William Devaynes
1785	William Devaynes, Nathaniel Smith
1786	John Michie, John Motteux
1787	John Motteux, Nathaniel Smith
1788	Nathaniel Smith, John Michie
1788	(Dec) William Devaynes, *vice* Michie, deceased
1789	William Devaynes, Stephen Lushington
1790	Stephen Lushington, William Devaynes
1791	John Smith Burgess, Francis Baring
1792	Francis Baring, John Smith Burgess
1793	William Devaynes, Thomas Cheap
1794	William Devaynes, John Hunter
1795	Stephen Lushington, David Scott
1796	David Scott, Hugh Inglis
1797	Hugh Inglis, Jacob Bosanquet
1798	Jacob Bosanquet, Stephen Lushington
1799	Stephen Lushington, Hugh Inglis
1800	Hugh Inglis, David Scott
1801	David Scott, Charles Mills
1801	(Sep) Scott resigned. Charles Mills, John Roberts
1802	John Roberts, Jacob Bosanquet
1803	Jacob Bosanquet, John Roberts
1804	William Elphinstone, Charles Grant
1805	Charles Grant, George Smith
1806	William Elphinstone, Edward Parry
1807	Edward Parry, Charles Grant
1808	Edward Parry, Charles Grant
1809	Charles Grant, William Astell
1810	William Astell, Jacob Bosanquet
1811	Jacob Bosanquet, Hugh Inglis
1812	Hugh Inglis, Robert Thornton
1813	Robert Thornton, William Elphinstone
1814	William Elphinstone, John Inglis
1815	Charles Grant, Thomas Reid
1816	Thomas Reid, John Bebb
1817	John Bebb, James Pattison
1818	James Pattison, Campbell Marjoribanks

* The election took place in Apr each year.

1819   Campbell Marjoribanks, George Robinson
1820   George Robinson, Thomas Reid
1821   Thomas Reid, James Pattison
1822   James Pattison, William Wigram
1823   William Wigram, William Astell
1824   William Astell, Campbell Marjoribanks
1825   Campbell Marjoribanks, George Robinson
1826   George Robinson, Hugh Lindsay
1827   Hugh Lindsay, James Pattison
1828   William Astell, John Loch
1829   John Loch, William Astell
1830   William Astell, Robert Campbell

Secretaries of the Board of Control, 1784–1830
(holding office with the Government)

8 Sep 1784	C. W. Boughton-Rouse	6 Jan 1810	Sir Patrick Murray
10 May 1791	Henry Beaufoy	14 Mar 1812	John Bruce
3 July 1793	William Broderick	20 Aug 1812	Thomas Courtenay
19 Nov 1803	Benjamin Hobhouse	2 May 1829	George Banks
22 May 1804	George Holford	16 Feb 1830	J. S. Wortley
14 Feb 1806	Thomas Creevey	18 Dec 1830	Dudley, Lord Sandon
8 Feb 1807	George Holford		

Assistant Secretaries (permanent)

1784	William Broderick	1817	John Wright
1795	William Cabell	1828	Benjamin Jones
1800	John Meheux		

Secretaries of the East India Company, 1784–1830
1784   Thomas Morton (Asst. William Ramsay)
1792   William Ramsay (Asst. James Cobb)
1814   James Cobb (Asst. James Dart)
1817   James Dart (Asst. Peter Auber)
1829   Peter Auber (Asst. William Carter)

SOURCE: C. N. Philips, *The East India Company*

Colonial Governors

Antigua

1752	Sir George Thomas	1795	Maj.-Gen. Leigh
1766	James Verchild	1796	John Thomas
1768	William Woodley	1799	Robert Thompson
1771	Sir Ralph Payne	1799	William Woodley
1776	William H. Burt	1801	Lord Lavington
1781	Sir Thomas Shirley	1809	James Tyson
1788	John Nugent	1809	John Julius
1790	Sir Thomas Shirley	1810	Hugh Elliott
1791	John Nugent	1813	John Julius
1792	William Woodley	1814	Lt-Gen. Sir James Leith
1793	John Stanley	1815	Henry Rawlins

1816	Maj.-Gen. Ramsay		1793	Sir John Shore
1819	Maj.-Gen. Sir B. Durban		1798	E of Mornington
1826–34	Sir Patrick Ross		1805	Marquis Cornwallis
			1805	Sir George H. Barlow

Bahamas

			1807	Lord Minto
1759	William Shirley		1813	E of Moira
1767	Thomas Shirley		1823	Ld Amherst
1774	Montford Browne		1828–35	Ld William Cavendish-Bentinck
1779	John Maxwell			
1787	E of Dunmore			

Bermuda

1796	John Forbes		1745	William Popple
1797	W. Dowdeswell		1764	G. J. Bruere
1801	John Hackett		1780	George Bruere
1804	Charles Cameron		1782	William Browne
1820	Gen. M. Grant		1788	Henry Hamilton
1829–33	Sir J. C. Smyth		1794	James Craufurd
			1796	William Campbell

Barbados

			1797	George Beckwith
1756	Charles Pinfold		1805	Francis Gore
1766	Samuel Rous		1806	John Hodgson
1768	William Spry		1811	Sir J. Cockburn
1771	Samuel Rous		1819	Sir William Lumley
1772	Hon. Edward Hay		1825–31	Sir H. Turner
1773	John Dotin			

Bombay

1780	James Cunninghame			
1783	John Dotin		1760	Charles Crommelin
1784	David Parry		1767	Thomas Hodges
1793	William Bishop		1771	William Hornby
1794	George Poyntz Rickets		1784	Rawson Hart Boddam
1800	William Bishop		1788	Maj.-Gen. William Medows
1801	Ld Seaforth		1790	Maj.-Gen. Sir Robert Aber-
1806	John Spooner			cromby
1810–14	Sir George Beckwith		1792	George Dick (acting)
1815	Sir James Leith		1795	Jonathan Duncan
1817	Lord Combermere		1811	George Brown (acting)
1820	John Braithwaite Skeete		1812	Sir Evan Nepean
1821	Samuel Hinds		1819	Hon. Mountstuart Elphinstone
1821	Sir Henry Warde		1827	Maj.-Gen. Sir John Malcolm
1827	John Braithwaite Skeete		1830–31	Lt.-Gen. Sir Thomas Sidney
1829–31	Sir James Lyon			Beckwith

Bengal

British Honduras

1760	John Z. Holwell			(*Superintendents*)
1760	Henry Vansittart		1786	Col Edward Marcus Despard
1764	John Spencer		1790	Col Peter Hunter
1765	Ld Clive		1790–7	by annually elected magistrate
1767	Harry Verelst		1797	Col Thomas Barrow
1769	John Cartier		1800	Gen. Sir Richard Basset
1772	Warren Hastings		1805	Lt-Col. Alexander Hamilton
			1809	Lt-Col. John Nugent Smyth
	(*Governors-General*)		1814	Maj. George Arthur
1774	Warren Hastings		1822	Maj.-Gen. Allan Hampden
1785	Sir John Macpherson			Pye
1786	Earl Cornwallis		1823	Maj.-Gen. Edward Codd

1829	Maj. Alexander McDonald (acting)	1776	(no British governor)
1830–37	Lt.-Col. Francis Cockburn	1779	James Wright

Canada

See Lower Canada, Upper Canada, Quebec, etc.

Cape of Good Hope

1795	J. H. Craig
1797	Earl Macartney
1798	Sir Francis Dundas (Lt.-Gov.)
1799	Sir George Young
1801	Sir Francis Dundas
1803–6	under Batavian Government
1806	Sir David Baird
1807	E of Caledon
1811	Sir John Francis Cradock
1813	Hon. Robert Meade (Lt.-Gov.)
1814	Ld Charles Henry Somerset
1826	Richard Bourke (Lt.-Gov.)
1828–34	Hon. Sir Galbraith Lowry Cole

Ceylon
(Military Governors)

1796	James Stuart
1796	Welborne Ellis Doyle
1797	Pierre-Frédéric de Meuron
1798	Frederick North
1805	Thomas Maitland
1812	Robert Brownrigg
1822	Edward Paget
1824	Edward Barnes
1831	Robert Wilmot-Horton

Connecticut

1754	Thomas Fitch
1766	William Pitkin
1769	Jonathan Trumbull

Florida East

1764	James Grant
1771	James Moultrie
1773	Patrick Tonyn

Florida West

1763	George Johnstone
1767	Montfort Browne
1769	John Eliot
1769	Elias Durnford
1770	Peter Chester

Georgia

1757	Henry Ellis
1760	James Wright

Gibraltar

1758	William, Earl Home
1761	John Parslow
1762	Edward Cornwallis
1770	Robert Boyd
1775	B Heathfield
1790	Robert Boyd
1794	Henry Clinton
1795	Charles O'Hara
1802	Thomas Trigge
1802	D of Strathearn and Kent
1802	Charles Barnet
1804	Henry Edward Fox
1806	Hew Whitefoord Dalrymple
1806	Gordon Drummond
1809	John Francis Cradock
1810	Colin Campbell
1814	George Don
1820	E of Chatham
1835	Alexander George Woodford

Grenada

1764	Brig.-Gen. Robert Melville
1768	Ulysses Fitzmaurice
1770	Brig.-Gen. Robert Melville
1771	Frederick Corsar
1771	Ulysses Fitzmaurice
1771	Brig.-Gen. W. Leybourne
1775	Frederick Corsar
1775	William Young
1776	Sir George Macartney
1784	Lt.-Gen. Edward Matthew
1785	William Lucas
1787	Samuel Williams
1788	James Campbell
1789	Samuel Williams
1788	James Campbell
1789	Samuel Williams
1793	Ninian Home
1795	Kenneth McKenzie
1795	Samuel Williams
1796	Alexander Houston
1797	Col Charles Green
1798	Samuel Mitchell
1801	Rev. Samuel Dent
1804	Abraham Charles Adye
1805	Brig.-Gen. F. Maitland
1807	John Harvey
1808–9	A. C. Adye
1810	Maj.-Gen. F. Maitland
1810	A. C. Adye

1812	Col R. Ainslie
1813	John Harvey
1813	Maj.-Gen. Sir Charles Shipley
1815	George Paterson
1816	Maj.-Gen. Phineas Riall
1817	Andrew Houston
1821	Maj.-Gen. Phineas Riall
1821–25	George Paterson
1826–31	Sir James Campbell

Hudson's Bay Company

1750	Atwell Lake
1760	William Baker
1770	Bibye Lake, jr
1782	Samuel Wegg
1799	James Winter Lake
1807	William Mainwaring
1812	Joseph Berens
1822	John Henry Pelly

Jamaica

1758	George Haldane
1762	W. H. Littleton
1767	Sir W. Trelawney
1773	Sir B. Keith
1777	Maj.-Gen. Dalling
1782	Maj.-Gen. Campbell
1790	E of Effingham
1795	E of Balcarras
1801	Lt.-Gen. Nugent
1806	Lt.-Gen. Sir G. Coote
1808	D of Manchester
1829–32	E of Belmore

Lower Canada

1791	B Dorchester
1796	Robert Prescott
1799	Robert Shore Milnes
1805	Thomas Dunn
1807	James Henry Craig
1811	George Prevost
1815	Gordon Drummond
1816	John Coape Sherbrooke
1818	D of Richmond
1820	E of Dalhousie
1828	James Kempt White

Madras

1775	George Pigot
1763	Robert Palk
1767	Charles Bourchier
1770	Josias Dupre
1773	Alexander Wynch
1775	Ld Pigot

1776	George Stratton
1777	John Whitehill (acting)
1778–80	Sir Thomas Rumbold
1781	Ld Macartney
1785	Alexander Davidson (acting)
1786	Maj.-Gen. Sir Archibald Campbell
1789	John Holland (acting)
1790	Maj.-Gen. William Medows
1792	Sir Charles Oakeley
1794	Ld Hobart
1798	Ld Clive
1803	Ld William Cavendish-Bentinck
1807	Sir George Hilaro Barlow
1813	Lt.-Gen. Hon. John Abercromby (acting)
1814	Rt Hon. Hugh Elliot
1820	Maj.-Gen. Sir Thomas Munro
1827–32	Stephen Rumbold Lushington

Malta

(Chief Commissioners)

1799	Alexander John Ball
1801	Henry Pigot
1801	Charles Cameron
1802	Alexander John Ball
1810	Hildebrand Oakes

(Governors)

1813	Thomas Maitland
1824	E of Moira
1827	Frederick Cavendish Ponsonby

Maryland

1753–69	Horatio Sharpe
1769–76	Robert Eden

Massachusetts

1757	Thomas Downal
1760	Thomas Hutchinson
1760	Francis Bernard
1769	Thomas Hutchinson
1774	Thomas Gage

Mauritius

1810	Robert Townsend Farquhar
1811	Henry Warde
1811	Robert Townsend Farquhar
1817	Gage John Hall
1818	John Dalrymple
1819	Ralph Darling
1820	Robert Townsend Farquhar
1823	Galbraith Lowry Cole
1828	Charles Colville

Minorca

1756–63	under France
1763	Richard Lyttelton
1766	George Howard
1768	John Mostyn
1779	James Murray
1782	under Spain
1798	Charles Stuart
1801	Henry Edward Fox

New Brunswick
(Lt.-Governors)

1786	Guy Carleton
1787	E. Winslow
1788	Lt-Col Johnston
1809	Gen. M. Hunter
1811	Gen. W. Balfour
1812	Gen. George Stracey Smyth
1823	Ward Chipman
1824	J. M. Bliss
1825–31	Gen. Sir H. Douglas

Newfoundland

1760	Capt. James Webb
1761	Capt. Groves
1764	Capt. Hugh Palliser
1769	Capt. Hon. John Byron
1772	Commodore Molyneux (Ld Shuldham)
1775	Commodore Robert Duff
1776	Admiral John Montagu
1779	Admiral Richard Edwardes
1782	Admiral John Campbell
1786	Admiral John Elliott
1789	Admiral Mark Milbanke
1794	Admiral Sir James Wallace
1797	Admiral William Waldegrave (Ld Radstock)
1800	Admiral Charles Pole
1802	Admiral James Gambier
1804	Admiral Sir Erasmus Gower
1807	Admiral John Holloway
1810	Admiral Sir John Duckworth
1813	Admiral Sir Richard Keats
1816	Admiral Francis Pickmore
1818	Admiral Sir Charles Hamilton
1825–34	Capt. Sir Thomas Cochrane

New Hampshire

1741	Benning Wentworth
1767	John Wentworth

New Jersey

1758	Francis Bernard
1760	Thomas Boone
1761	Josiah Hardy
1763	William Franklin

New South Wales

1788	Arthur Phillip
1792	Francis Grose
1794	William Paterson
1795	John Hunter
1800	Philip Gidley King
1806	William Bligh
1808	Joseph Foveaux
1809	William Paterson
1809	Lachlan Macquarie
1821	Thomas Makdougall Brisbane
1825	Ralph Darling
1831	Richard Bourke

North Carolina

1754	Arthur Dobbs
1765	William Tryon
1771	James Hasell
1771	Josiah Martin

Northern Australia
(Commandants)

Melville Island (Fort Dundas)

1824	Maurice Barlow
1826	John Campbell
1828	Humphrey Robert Hartley

Raffles Bay (Fort Wellington)

1827	James Stirling
1827	Henry Smyth
1828	George Sleeman
1828	Collet Barker

Nova Scotia
(Lt.-Governors)

1756	A. Moulton
1760	J. Belcher
1764	M. Wilmot
1766	M. Franklin
1773	F. Legge
1776	M. Arbuthnot
1778	R. Hughes
1781	Sir A. S. Hammond
1782	J. Park
1783	P. Fanning
1791	R. Bulkeley
1792	J. Wentworth
1808	Sir G. Prevost

1811	Sir J. Sherbrooke
1811	Gen. Darroch
1816	Gen. Smyth
1819	E of Dalhousie
1820	Sir J. Kempt
1826–36	M. Wallace

Penang

1786	Francis Light
1794	Philip Mannington
1795	Forbes Ross McDonald
1799	George Leith
1804	Robert Townsend Farquhar
1805	Philip Dundas
1807	Norman Macalister
1810	Charles Andrew Bruce
1810	William Edward Phillips
1812	William Petrie
1816	William Edward Phillips
1817	John Alexander Bannerman
1819	William Edward Phillips
1824	Robert Fullerton

Pennsylvania

1759	James Hamilton
1763	John Penn
1771	James Hamilton
1771	Richard Penn
1773	John Penn

Persian Gulf

(*Chief Political Residents*)

1822	John Macleod
1823	Ephraim Gerrish Stannus
1827	David Wilson
1831	David Alexander Blane

Prince Edward Island

(*Lt.-Governors*)

1770	Walter Paterson
1786	Lt.-Gen. Edmund Fanning
1805	Col Joseph Debarres
1813	Charles Douglas Smith
1822–31	Col John Ready

Quebec

1760	B Amherst
1763	James Murray
1768	Guy Carleton
1778	Frederick Haldimand
1786	B Dorchester

Rhode Island

1758	Stephen Hopkins

1762	Samuel Ward
1763	Stephen Hopkins
1765	Samuel Ward
1767	Stephen Hopkins
1768	Josias Lyndon
1769	Joseph Wanton

South Carolina

1756	William Henry Lyttelton
1760	William Bull
1761	Thomas Boone
1764	William Bull, jr
1766	Charles Greville Montagu
1769	William Bull, jr
1771	Charles Greville Montagu
1774	William Bull, jr
1775	William Campbell

Tobago

1764	Browne
1768	General Robert Melville
1770	Stewart
1771	William Leybourne
1771	Maj. Young
1781	Ferguson
1784	Dillon
1794	Ricketts
1795	Lindsay
1796	Delaney
1800	Masters
1800	Robley
1802	Sahuhie
1802	Magento
1803	Buthtir
1803	Picton
1803	McDonald
1803	Johnston
1804	Halkett
1805	Campbell
1805	Mitchell
1806	Balfour
1807	Sir William Young
1815	Balfour
1816	Campbell
1816	Sir F. P. Robinson
1819	Cumine
1820	Robley
1823	Nichol
1826	Brasnell
1827	Piggott
1828–33	Maj.-Gen. Blackwell

Trinidad

1797	Sir Ralph Abercrombie

1798	J. Harvey ⎫		**Upper Canada**
	Col Fullerton ⎪		(*Lt.-Governors*)
	Lt.-Col Thomas ⎬ *Commissioners*	1791	John Graves Simcoe
	Picton ⎭	1796	Peter Russell
1801	Col Sir F. Picton	1799	Peter Hunter
1803	Brig.-Gen. Sir Thomas Hislop	1805	Alexander Grant
1810	Lt.-Col Tolly (acting)	1806	Francis Gore
1811	Col Munroe	1817	Samuel Smith
1813	Sir R. J. Woodford	1818	Peregrine Maitland
1821	Lt.-Col A. W. Young (acting)	1829	John Colborne
1823	Sir R. J. Woodford	1836	Francis Bond Head
1828	Col Farquharson (acting)	1838	George Arthur
1829–33	Maj.-Gen. Sir Lewis Grant		

9 Radicalism, Trade Unions and Political Reform

Trade Unions

Chronology of Trade Union Developments

1762   Liverpool seamen's strike.
1765   Colliers' strike in the North-East over the yearly 'bond'.
        Successful campaign of Spitalfields' weavers against import of
        French silks (5 Geo. III, c.48).
1767–8 Series of industrial disputes amongst the London trades, includ-
        ing Spitalfields weavers, coal-heavers, seamen, hatters, tailors,
        watermen, sawyers and coopers.
1768   Seamen's strike in the North-East.
1773   Spitalfields Act (13 Geo. III, c.68) obtained to regulate wages of
        Spitalfields weavers.
1775   Liverpool sailors' strike.
1778–9 Framework knitters campaign for a minimum wage act rejected
        by Parliament. Some machine-breaking in Lancashire.
1792–3 Widespread strikes reported in both London and the provinces,
        especially amongst East Coast seamen, Lancashire miners, and
        Liverpool shipyard workers.
1793   Friendly Societies Act (33 Geo. III, c.54) gives societies legal
        status and protection for their funds.
1797   Unlawful Oaths Act (37 Geo. III, c.123) makes secret oath-
        taking illegal. Used to restrict trade union organisation.
1799   Combination Act (39 Geo. III, c.86). See pp. 129–30.
        Association of Lancashire weavers formed.
1800   Combination Act (39 and 40 Geo. III, c.106). See p. 130.
1801   Extensive strike of shipwrights in government dockyards.
1802   Shipwrights' strike in Thames civilian yards organised by John
        Gast.
        Petition of South-Western clothiers against gig-mills.
        Stoppage of work and machine-breaking.
1803   First annual suspension of woollen statutes. Strike of Tyne
        keelmen.
1805   Woollen workers petition for regulation of wool trade.

1807	Cotton weavers petition for minimum wage bill.
1808	Manchester cotton weavers' strike.
1809	Repeal of protective legislation in the woollen industry. Tyne keelmen's strike.
1810	London printers prosecuted for conspiracy. Lancashire spinners' strike.
1811	Beginning of Luddite campaign in Nottinghamshire.
1812	Scottish weavers' strike. Framework-knitters bill to regulate the trade rejected in the House of Lords.
1813	Wage clauses of 5 Eliz. c.4 empowering judges to fix wage rates repealed by 53 Geo. III, c.40. Robert Owen publishes *A New View of Society*.
1814	Apprenticeship regulations of 5 Eliz. c.4 abolished by 54 Geo. III, c.96.
1815	Seamen's strike in North-East England.
1816	New Lanark mill opened. Strikes in several districts, especially amongst iron-workers and colliers.
1818	Weavers' and spinners' strikes in Lancashire. Attempts to form a 'General Union of Trades'.
1819	Keelmen's strike on Tyneside.
1820	Scottish weavers' strike.
1821	Robert Owen's *Report to the County of Lanark*. The London Co-operative and Economical Society formed.
1824	Act to repeal the Laws relative to the Combination of Workmen (5 Geo. IV, c.95). See pp. 131–2.
1825	Act revising the Law affecting Combinations (6 Geo. III, c.129). Widespread strikes in England and Scotland. John Gast and others establish *Trades Newspaper*.
1828	*The Co-operator* journal founded and the British Association for Promoting Co-operative Knowledge.
1829	General Union of Spinners formed under the initiative of John Doherty.
1830	Strike of Northumberland and Durham Colliers' Union under leadership of Thomas Hepburn.

The Combination Acts

Combination Act 1799
Unintended result of petition of master millwrights of London for a bill to outlaw combination of journeymen millwrights and regulate their wages.

Suggested by Wilberforce, promoted by Pitt.

Provisions
Summary prosecution before a single magistrate on credible evidence of one or more witnesses.

Maximum sentence 3 months in gaol or 2 months in House of Correction with hard labour.

Illegal to:

(1) Combine with another to improve conditions or raise wages;

(2) try to induce another to leave his work (e.g. strike);

(3) refuse to work with another (e.g. boycott a non-member of a combination);

(4) attend a meeting with purpose of improving wages and conditions, persuade another to attend one, raise money for one;

(5) contribute to expenses of a person tried under the Act; and

(6) hold money for a combination and refuse to answer questions about it.

Petitions against 1799 Act

Objected to:

(1) vagueness of language used to describe offences under Act;

(2) summary jurisdiction: held to deprive citizens of right to trial by jury;

(3) bias in favour of employers, many of whom were magistrates;

(4) possibility of trial before a man's own employer;

(5) compulsion to answer questions about money possibly held for a combination: incriminate oneself or face automatic sentence under Act; and

(6) difficulties placed in way of man sentenced under Act to raise money for appeal: if appeal successful, financial supporters not liable under Act; but if appeal unsuccessful, supporters automatically offenders against it.

Combination Act 1800

Playwright Sheridan put workers' case in House of Commons. 1799 Act repealed, replaced by 1800 Act.

Changes

(1) 2 magistrates instead of 1 to try cases;

(2) Employer-magistrates prohibited from trying cases of men in their own trade;

(3) Arbitration provision to deal with disputes (rarely invoked); and

(4) Masters prohibited from combining to reduce wages, increase hours or worsen conditions (no reported cases).

Offences otherwise as in 1799 Act. Thus, the Combination Acts of 1799 and 1800 contained no new legal principle. The Acts were intended to provide a general speedy remedy against combinations which were already illegal on numerous grounds (see following section).

The Repeal of the Combination Acts
Movement for reform headed by Francis Place, master tailor of Charing Cross, former journeyman breeches-maker. Joseph Hume, radical MP, led the movement within Parliament. On 12 Feb 1824, Hume moved resolutions in House of Commons for committee to consider laws on: (1) emigration of artisans; (2) exportation of machiners; and (3) combinations of workmen.

Combination Act 1824
Provisions
(1) Previous statutes relating to combinations, including Act of 1800, almost entirely repealed.
(2) Combinations – (*a*) to get increase or fix wages; (*b*) to lessen or alter hours; (*c*) to reduce amount of work; (*d*) to induce another to depart from employment before end of time for which hired, or (*e*) to quit or return his work before end of time for which hired, or (*f*) to refuse to enter into employment; or (*g*) to regulate production or management methods – not to be liable to indictment or prosecution for conspiracy or other crime under common or statute law.
   A similar provision applied to combinations of masters.
(3) Violence to persons or property, or threats or intimidation, which achieved purposes 2(*a*) to (*g*), made an offence, whether committed by an individual or by a combination; penalty was imprisonment and being 'kept to hard labour' for up to two months.
(4) Administration by summary trial before two magistrates; master, or fathers or sons of masters, engaged in any trade or manufacture being excluded from administering this law.
   Purpose of Act was to make peaceful negotiation lawful, but to outlaw the use of violence, etc., to coerce an agreement (not particularly well drafted for this).
   Large strikes of 1825, accompanied by violence, rioting and even murder, made Parliament reconsider, leading to the Combination Act of 1825.

Combination Act 1825
Parliamentary Committee set up to inquire into working of 1824 Act. Chaired by Wallace, Master of Mint; Hume also on Committee, and he with Place managed to reduce severity of 1825 Act. Trade union committees set up all over country to agitate against re-enactment of Combination Laws.

Provisions
(1) Combination Act of 1824 repealed.
(2) Act exempted from prosecution only those combinations of workmen or masters which met together solely to agree what wages or hours of

employment to require or demand. Combinations for any other objects unlawful. The effect of this provision was to allow collective bargaining only over wages and hours; strikes or lock-outs to alter *these* terms not in practice regarded as unlawful, though the Act did not confer a *right* to strike or lock-out (no such provision being known to English law until the Industrial Relations Act of 1971).

(3) A series of offences introduced, each punishable by imprisonment with or without hard labour for up to three months: the use of

(*a*) *violence*, construed by judges to mean the infliction of bodily harm or any act of injury to property, with the intention to coerce another;

(*b*) *threats*, construed as creating fear in a person's mind that some evil might befall him, with a coercive result;

(*c*) *intimidation*, i.e. fear created by actions rather than words (as in *b*) with the effect of coercing another;

(*d*) *molestation*, vaguely meaning interference with another – e.g. as by picketing; and

(*e*) *obstruction*, e.g. of right of free passage into or out of work, along a highway, etc. Also applied to picketing,

in order to force someone to

(*a*) leave his employment;

(*b*) refuse to take employment;

(*c*) join a club or association;

(*d*) contribute to a fund;

(*e*) obey rules, for example, of a combination;

(*f*) change his method of manufacture; or

(*g*) limit the number of his apprentices, and so on.

The overall effect of the statute was to enforce a narrow definition of the lawful activities of a trade union, confining these to peaceful collective bargaining over wages and hours only. Combination to negotiate outside these limits was liable at law not only as contravening the terms of the statute, but as criminal conspiracy at common law 'in restraint of trade'. In addition, many of the methods which a union might employ in furtherance of its objectives were liable to prosecution as intimidation, etc., crimes which were exceedingly ill-defined

Political Reform

The Parliamentary Reform Movement, 1760–1829

1763   Arrest of John Wilkes for issue No. 45 of the *North Briton*. General warrants declared illegal.

1768   Wilkes elected for Middlesex and refused seat in House of Commons. Anti-bribery bill introduced in House of Commons.

1769 Formation of Society of the Supporters of the Bill of Rights.
1770 Publication of Edmund Burke's *Thoughts on the Present Discontents* demanding limited reform and an end to corruption. William Dowdeswell introduces a bill for the disfranchisement of revenue officers.

Grenville's Election Act (10 Geo, III, c.16) allowed election petitions to be heard by select committee instead of in front of the whole house. Made perpetual in 1774.
1771 John Sawbridge's motion for leave to introduce a bill for shorter parliaments defeated by 105 votes to 54.

Printers' Case effectively left newspapers free to report debates in parliament.

Franchise of borough of New Shoreham widened (11 Geo. III, c.55).
1774 Bill introduced to permit several polling places in each county.
1775 Beginning of American War of Independence.
1776 Publication of Major Cartwright's *Take Your Choice* outlines radical reform programme.

Wilkes seeks leave to bring bill before parliament for 'a just and equal Representation of the People of England in Parliament'.
1778 Bill introduced to exclude government contractors from Parliament. Second bill introduced 1779. Both defeated by postponement.
1779 First meeting of Yorkshire reformers.
1780 Yorkshire petition presented to House of Commons.

Convention of county associations in London.

Bills for disfranchisement of revenue officers and exclusion of placemen from House of Commons defeated.

Dunning's resolution that the influence of the Crown 'had increased, was increasing and ought to be diminished' carried.

Burke's bills to reform civil establishment defeated.

Duke of Richmond's proposals for universal suffrage, annual election and equal electoral districts refused a hearing in House of Lords.

Society for Constitutional Information founded.
1782 Bill introduced by Lord Mahon to curtail election expenses.

Bill introduced for more effectual representation in Ireland.

Bills introduced to lower Scottish county franchise and abolish wadset voting.

Voting rights at Cricklade extended (22 Geo. III, c.31).

Revenue officers disfranchised (22 Geo. III, c.41); Government contractors disqualified from sitting in House of Commons (22 Geo. III, c.45). Civil Establishment Act (22 Geo. III, c.82).

Rejection of Pitt's motion for a committee on parliamentary reform by 161 votes to 141.

Thatched House Tavern meeting in London proposes petitioning movement for 'a substantial Reform of the Commons' House of Parliament'.

1783 Pitt's proposals for the addition of at least 100 county members, gradual disfranchisement of corrupt boroughs, increased representation for London, and the prevention of bribery defeated by 293 votes to 149.

Debates on reform of Irish representation. Leave to introduce reform bill defeated by 158 votes to 49.

1784 Edinburgh convention for reform of Scottish representation.

Yorkshire Association ceases to meet after petitioning in January.

1785 Pitt's proposals to redistribute seats from 36 'decayed' boroughs to the counties and to enfranchise county copyholders defeated by 248 votes to 174.

Henry Flood's reform bill for Ireland defeated by 112 votes to 60.

Further convention of Scottish reformers in Edinburgh.

1786 Attempt to raise issue of Scottish representation defeated in the Commons.

1787 Further move for inquiry into Scottish representation defeated.

1788 Scottish petitioning movement for reform (46 petitions).

Lord Mahon's Act for registration of county voters (28 Geo. III, c.36).

Meetings of Revolution Societies to celebrate the 'Glorious Revolution'.

1789 Lord Mahon's Act suspended and repealed before coming into operation (29 Geo. III, c.13 and 29 Geo. III, c.18).

Meeting of London Revolution Society addressed by Dr Richard Price, welcoming the French Revolution and calling for reform in the civil and religious establishment.

1790 Flood's motion to create 100 extra county members and remove seats from smaller boroughs withdrawn for lack of support.

Edmund Burke publishes *Reflections on the Revolution in France*.

1791 Publication of Thomas Paine's *Rights of Man, Part One*.

Formation of reform societies in Manchester and Sheffield.

1792 Formation of London Corresponding Society and the Society of the Friends of the People.

Publication of *Rights of Man, Part Two*.

Charles Grey states intention of raising reform motion in the Commons during the next session.

Motion for reform of the Scottish burghs defeated by 69 votes to 27.

Address of London Corresponding Society demanding annual elections and 'an equal Representation of the Whole Body of the People'.

1793 Charles Grey's motion to refer reform to committee defeated by 282 votes to 41.

British Convention meets in Edinburgh and dissolved by authorities.

1794   Mass meeting of London Corresponding Society at Chalk Farm, London, and preparations for a new Convention.

1795   Mass meetings of London Corresponding Society at St George's fields and Copenhagen Fields.

1796   Missionary tours of LCS members to Kent and Birmingham.

1797   Rejection of Charles Grey's motion for leave to bring a motion for reform by 256 votes to 91.

1800   Grey's motion to amend Act of Union by disfranchising forty of the smallest English boroughs and reduce the number of proposed Irish MPs at Westminster defeated by 176 votes to 34.

1804   Franchise at Aylesbury extended to three neighbouring hundreds (44 Geo. III, c.60).

1806   George Tierney's bill to prohibit conveyance of voters to poll by candidates defeated by 42 votes to 17.

1807   Election of Sir Francis Burdett and Lord Cochrane as radical candidates for Westminster.

1809   Anti-bribery act sponsored by John Christian Curwen passed preventing corrupt agreements to obtain seats (49 Geo. III, c.118).
        Burdett's motion for limiting duration of parliaments and extending franchise to householders defeated by 74 votes to 54.

1810   Thomas Brand's proposals for extending county franchise to copyholders, borough franchise to householders paying parochial rates, triennial parliaments, redistribution of seats from decayed boroughs with compensation to patrons, and exclusion of place-holders defeated by 234 votes to 115.

1811   Formation of the Union for Parliamentary Reform.

1812   London Hampden Club constituted.
        Defeat of Brand's motion to extend county vote to copyholders and abolish the right of nomination by 215 votes to 88.

1816   Widespread distress and agitation for reform.
        Cobbett produces first cheap edition of the *Political Register*.
        Spa Fields meetings in London.

1817   Convention of reformers at Crown and Anchor Tavern, London, to prepare reform campaign.
        Burdett's motion for a select committee on reform defeated by 265 votes to 77.
        March of the 'Blanketeers' and Pentrich 'Rising'.

1818   Sir Robert Heron's motion for triennial parliaments defeated by 117 votes to 42.
        Burdett's motions for annual parliaments, manhood suffrage, secret ballot and equal electoral districts defeated by 106 votes to nil.

1819   Series of reform meetings in the North and Midlands.
        Reform meeting in St Peter's Fields, Manchester (Peterloo) dispersed.
1821   Seats of Grampound transferred to Yorkshire (1 and 2 Geo. IV, c.47).
        Lord Durham's bill advocating triennial Parliaments, equal electoral districts, and ratepayer franchise defeated by 55 votes to 43.
1822   Lord John Russell's motion to remove one hundred members from smallest boroughs and redistribute them to counties and unenfranchised towns defeated by 269 votes to 164.
        Group of leading Whigs resolve that reform a matter of urgent necessity and organise county meetings.
1823   Defeat of Russell's reform proposals and Hamilton's resolutions on state of Scottish county representation defeated by 117 votes to 152.
1826   Russell's reform motion defeated by 247 votes to 124.
1827   Bill to redistribute seats of Penryn to Manchester and Birmingham rejected by Lords.
1828   Polling limited in boroughs to eight days and providing for several polling places where necessary (9 Geo. IV, c.59).
1829   Catholic Emancipation passed (10 Geo. IV, c.7); act to raise Irish county franchise to £10 freeholders.
        Lord Blandford's motion for reform defeated by 160 votes to 57.
        Formation of Birmingham Political Union.

The Reform Crisis, 1830–2

1830
26 June   Death of George IV.
24 July   Parliament dissolved.
July–Sep   General Election.
 2 Nov   Wellington declares against reform.
16 Nov   Resignation of Wellington. Grey called to form a government.

1831
 1 Mar   Reform Bill introduced in Commons.
23 Mar   Reform Bill passes second reading.
20 Apr   Government defeated on Gascoyne's amendment.
23 Apr   Parliament dissolved.
Apr–June   General Election.
24 June   Reform Bill reintroduced in Commons.

7 July	Bill receives second reading.
22 Sep	Bill passes third reading by 345 votes to 236.
8 Oct	Reform Bill defeated in the Lords.
8–10 Oct	Derby and Nottingham riots.
29–31 Oct	Bristol riots.
12 Dec	New reform bill introduced in Commons.
18 Dec	Reform Bill passes second reading.

1832

15 Jan	William IV agrees to creation of peers in order to obtain passage of reform.
22 Mar	Reform Bill passes third reading by 355 votes to 239.
14 Apr	Reform Bill passes second reading in Lords by 184 votes to 175.
7 May	Government defeated on Lyndhurst's motion.
9 May	Resignation of cabinet after King refuses to create peers.
9–15 May	'May days'.
15 May	Wellington advises King to recall Grey.
18 May	Grey receives assurances from the King that peers will be created as necessary.
4 June	Reform Bill receives third reading in Lords by 106 votes to 22.
7 June	Reform Bill receives Royal Assent.

Major Reform Societies and Clubs

The Society of the Supporters of the Bill of Rights

Formed Feb 1769 under the aegis of the Rev. John Horne (Horne Tooke) to support Wilkes. It provided the organisation for the reform movement in the capital and was joined by several metropolitan MPs. Although weakened by a split when Horne Tooke set up the Constitutional Society in 1771, it provided the model for later political societies.

The Yorkshire Association

Grew out of Yorkshire meeting of Dec 1779 when committee set up 'to prepare a Plan of Association on legal and constitutional grounds to support that laudable reform and such other measures as may conduce to restore the Freedom of Parliament'. It aimed at the shortening of parliaments and a more equal representation of the people, votes being withheld from any parliamentary candidate who declined to pledge himself to these reforms. Other counties formed similar associations, which met at a Convention of Representatives in Mar 1780.

The Association advocated the promotion of economical reform, the addition of a hundred more county members, and triennial parliaments. Ceased activity after failure of Pitt's plan of reform in Apr 1785.

The Society for Promoting Constitutional Information

Formed in Apr 1780 on the initiative of Major Cartwright to disseminate political information. Founder members included John Jebb, Thomas Brand Hollis and Richard Brinsley Sheridan. Members elected by ballot with a subscription of not less than a guinea. Later members included Thomas Paine and John Horne Tooke. Active in reform campaigns of 1780–5 and also supported various philanthropic schemes. Revived after 1789, sending a congratulatory address to French National Convention in Nov 1792 and delegates to the British Convention at Edinburgh in Oct 1793. Papers seized and six members arrested on charges of High Treason in May 1794.

London Revolution Society

Most important of several 'Revolution Societies' which met annually to celebrate the 'Glorious Revolution' of 1688. Organised with a committee and officers, the Society had no fixed constitution other than support of 'Whig' constitutional principles. Members included prominent London dissenters, such as Dr Richard Price, and leading Whig reformers. Its meeting on 4 Nov 1789 initiated the debate on the French Revolution when Price preached on the text of 'The Love of our Country', welcoming the French Revolution and urging repeal of the Test Acts and parliamentary reform in Britain. Price's sermon was the subject of bitter attack in Edmund Burke's *Reflections on the Revolution in France* (1790).

Manchester Constitutional Society

Set up on 5 Oct 1790 to obtain shorter parliaments and more equal representation. Led by Manchester merchant Thomas Walker. Organised on basis of half-guinea subscriptions and monthly meetings. Corresponded with Jacobin Club of Paris in 1792. Followed by formation of Manchester Patriotic Reformation Societies. Ceased activity c.1794.

Sheffield Society for Constitutional Information

First address produced Dec 1791. A society of 'tradesmen and artificers', claiming over two thousand members by 1792. Originally pledged to non-violence in pursuit of reform and equal representation, produced cheap editions of Paine's *Rights of Man*. Its divisional organisation into 'tythings' provided the model for the London Corresponding Society. Evidence of arming alleged in 1794. Active in anti-war campaign 1794–5. Ceased open activity c.1797.

London Corresponding Society

Formally constituted on 25 Jan 1792 on the initiative of Thomas Hardy, a master shoemaker. Open to 'members unlimited' for a fee of one shilling and subscriptions of one penny per week. Adopted a programme of correspondence with other reform societies to promote universal suffrage and annual parliaments. Organised in divisions of 30 members with a secretary. Delegates and sub-delegates elected to a Central Committee. Delegates sent to British Convention in Edinburgh in October 1793. Organised a series of mass meetings in the capital, 1794–7. Papers seized and Hardy arrested in May 1794 on charge of high treason. By 1795 at least 70 divisions and 2,000 members in the capital. Committee members seized and imprisoned 19 Apr 1798. Formally suppressed in July 1799 under provisions of 39 Geo. III, c.79.

The Friends of the People

Aristocratic Whig Society, founded with advice of Major Cartwright in Apr 1792. Guinea and a half subscription. Objects 'To restore the freedom of election, and a more frequent exercise of their right of electing their representatives'. Members included Charles Grey, Richard Brinsley Sheridan, Thomas Erskine, George Lambton, George Tierney, and Charles Whitbread. Satellite societies formed in Southwark, Aldgate, and Royston in Hertfordshire. Criticised by both radicals and conservatives for its moderation, it became defunct in 1796.

The Union for Parliamentary Reform

Grew out of 'friends to parliamentary reform' formed in 1811 by Major Cartwright. Supporters included Christopher Wyvill, Henry Hunt, Sir Francis Burdett, William Cobbett, Lord Cochrane and Thomas Coke. Declared for annual parliaments and taxpayer suffrage.

The Hampden Club

First projected by London reformers in May 1811 and formally constituted at the Thatched House Tavern on 20 Apr 1812. A dining society limited to those possessing or heir to £300 a year in land, with £2 a year subscription. Declared itself in favour of 'a reform in the representation of the people' and eventually adopted the same programme as the Union for Parliamentary Reform. Although the London Hampden Club was soon virtually defunct, Hampden and Union Clubs sprang up in the provinces on a more open basis, usually adopting a penny per week subscription. A conference of delegates to coordinate a national reform campaign held in Jan 1817 with Cartwright in the chair led to the adoption of a programme of manhood suffrage and secret ballot.

Birmingham Political Union

Founded on 14 Dec 1829 by Thomas Attwood and fifteen others as the Birmingham 'Political Union for the Protection of Public Rights'. Termed a 'General Political Union between the Lower and the Middle Classes of the People' and pledged to 'an effectual Reform in the Commons House of Parliament'. Opening meeting held on 25 Jan 1830. Played a leading part in orchestrating the extra-parliamentary reform agitation in the years 1830–2. Revived in 1837 to support Chartist demands.

Biographical Details of Major Reformers

Attwood, Thomas (1783–1856)
MP Birmingham from 1832. Birmingham banker and currency reformer. Led campaign in Birmingham against the Orders in Council in 1812. In Dec 1829 set up the Birmingham Political Union, to press for parliamentary and currency reform. Campaigned against the New Poor Law and revived BPU in 1837 to campaign on behalf of currency reform and the People's Charter. Delegate to Chartist convention of 1839.

Bentham, Jeremy (1748–1832)
Utilitarian theorist and philanthropist. Author of *Introduction to the Principles of Morals and Legislation* (1788), *Fragment on Government* (1776) and *Parliamentary Reform in the Form of a Catechism* (1817). After concentrating early life on penal reform and schemes for a model prison, turned to advocacy of parliamentary reform on the basis of utilitarian principles. Associate of James Mill, Samuel Romilly, Francis Place and Sir Francis Burdett amongst others.

Burdett, Sir Francis (1770–1844), 5th Bt
MP Boroughbridge 1796–1802, Middlesex 1802–4, 1805–6, Westminster 1807–37, North Wiltshire 1837–44. Leader of 'Westminster radicals' from 1807 and proposer of reform measures in 1809, 1817 and 1818. Imprisoned in Tower in 1810 for a libel on the House of Commons and for protests over Peterloo in 1821. Disagreements with more radical reformers led Burdett to play a less prominent part in reform activities after 1832.

Cartwright, John (1740–1824)
'The Father of Reform'. Son of a Nottinghamshire country gentleman; author of *Take Your Choice* (1776), outlining radical reform programme later adopted by the London Corresponding Society and the Chartists. Helped to form and manage the Constitutional Society and Society of the Friends of the People. Tours of the manufacturing districts in 1813 and 1815 helped to revive the cause of parliamentary reform. Involved in formation of 'the Union for Parliamentary Reform' and the Hampden Club in 1812. Active reformer until his death.

Cobbett, William (1762–1835)
MP Oldham 1832–5. Radical journalist. Started political career as loyalist writer, but moved into opposition after the resumption of war with France in 1803 and espoused the cause of parliamentary reform. Impris-

oned for two years in 1810 for his protests over the flogging of a soldier, he took refuge in America from 1817 to 1819. As author of the *Political Register* and several influential pamphlets, he was especially noted for his attacks on 'Old Corruption'. His writings on rural life, especially *Rural Rides* (1830), contained a bitter attack on agricultural change and the pauperisation of the rural labourer.

Hardy, Thomas (1752–1832)
Master shoemaker. Founded London Corresponding Society in Jan 1792. Advocate of radical but constitutional reform. Arrested in May 1794 and charged with high treason. Acquitted in Nov after a trial of nine days at the Old Bailey. Ceased active politics shortly afterwards.

Horne Tooke, John (1736–1812)
MP Old Sarum 1801–2. Rev. John Horne assumed name Horne Tooke in 1782. Son of a London poulterer. Educated at Cambridge and started career in the church. Resigned living 1773. Defender of Wilkes and founder member of Society of Supporters of the Bill of Rights. Quarrelled with Wilkes and founded Constitutional Society in 1771. In 1790 stood as an independent candidate for Westminster and polled 1,679 votes. Member of London Revolution Society and Society for Constitutional Information. Arrested in May 1794 on charge of high treason. Acquitted after trial in Nov 1794. Continued to support reform during late 1790s.

Hunt, Henry (1773–1835)
MP Preston 1830–2. A wealthy gentleman-farmer who rose to prominence as a Radical candidate for Bristol in 1812. The leading radical orator of the post-1815 period and main speaker at St Peter's Fields in Aug 1819 for which sentenced to 30 months in Ilchester Gaol. Continued to support manhood suffrage until his death in 1835.

Paine, Thomas (1737–1809)
Republican political theorist. Born in Norfolk of Quaker father. Originally worked as stay-maker and revenue officer. Emigrated to America in 1774 where wrote *Common Sense* (1776) in support of American independence. Returned to Europe in 1787 and joined Society for Constitutional Information. Produced *The Rights of Man, Part I* (1791) and *Part II* (1792) in reply to Burke's *Reflections on the Revolution in France* (1790), advocating a republican constitution and extensive social welfare. Extensive circulation of Paine's work did much to stimulate popular radicalism and alarm the government. Elected member of French National Convention and granted French citizenship. Fled to France in Sep 1792 and tried *in absentia* for seditious libel. Imprisoned in France during the Terror, where completed *The Age of Reason* (1795) and *Agrarian Justice* (1796). Returned to the United States in 1802.

Place, Francis (1771–1854)
Radical London tailor. Joined Corresponding Society in 1794, left 1797. Leading member of Westminster Committee to elect Sir Francis Burdett in 1807. Active parliamentary reformer and utilitarian who managed the campaign to repeal the Combination Acts in 1824. In 1831 formed National Political Union and in reform crisis coined the slogan 'To stop the Duke, go for Gold'. Helped to draft the 'People's Charter' and acted as London business manager for the Anti-Corn Law League from 1840.

Price, Dr Richard (1723–91)
Leading Unitarian and reformer. Campaigned for repeal of the Test Acts and parliamentary reform. Member of Society for Constitutional Information and London Revolution Society. Printed sermon *A Discourse on the Love of Our Country* (1789) provoked Burke's reply in *Reflections on the Revolution in France* (1790).

Spence, Thomas (1750–1814)
Newcastle schoolmaster. Developed theories of division of all land amongst the population. Based on London from 1792 where sold tracts and produced periodical *Pig's Meat*. Imprisoned in 1794 and 1801. Followers, known as the 'Spencean Philanthropists', included Dr Watson, Arthur Thistlewood and Thomas Evans, who were involved in insurrectionary plotting in the years after his death.

Thistlewood, Arthur (1770–1820)
The illegitimate son of a Lincolnshire land-agent; visited France during the Terror. Served as a lieutenant in the militia; became a Spencean in 1814. Took part in Spa Fields riots of Dec 1816. Charged with high treason in 1817 but acquitted. Imprisoned 1818–19. Plotted a *coup d'état* with aid of government *agent provocateur* involving the assassination of the cabinet while at dinner. Seized Feb 1820 and executed in May.

Wilkes, John (1727–97)
MP Aylesbury 1757–64, Middlesex 1768–9, 1774–90. Joint editor of *North Britain*. Imprisonment on general warrant for seditious libel in issue No. 45 (23 Apr 1763) created popular following in London. Expulsion from Commons and replacement by Henry Luttrell as MP for Middlesex led to formation of The Society of the Supporters of the Bill of Rights (1769) and demands for parliamentary reform. Alderman of London 1769, Sheriff 1771, and Lord Mayor 1774. Unsuccessfully moved reform in the House of Commons in 1776 and thereafter devoted himself to London politics.

Wollstonecraft, Mary (1759–97)
Early feminist writer. Earned living first as a teacher and later as writer. Part of intellectual circle surrounding Dr Richard Price in London.

Author of first reply to Burke's *Reflections* with a *Vindication of the Rights of Men* (1790) and also *A Vindication of the Rights of Women* (1792). Visited Paris in 1794 and married William Godwin in 1797. Mother of Mary Shelley.

Wyvill, Christopher (1740–1822)

Rector of Black Notley, Essex, until 1806, but from 1774 lived on wife's estates at Burton Constable, Yorkshire. Leading promoter of 'economical reform' movement in Yorkshire from 1779. Organised Yorkshire petition of 1780 and Yorkshire Association. Adopted programme of limited reform of parliament and advised Pitt on reform scheme of 1785. Continued to urge moderate reform after 1789, but increasingly discouraged by the divisions between radicals and other reformers.

SOURCES: H. Pelling, *A History of British Trade Unionism* (Harmondsworth, 1963); A. E. Musson, *British Trade Unionism, 1800–1875* (London, 1972); A. Aspinall, *The Early English Trade Unions* (London, 1949); J. L. and B. Hammond, *The Skilled Labourer, 1760–1832* (London, 1919); G. D. H. Cole, *A Short History of the British Working Class Movement* (London, 1948); M. D. George, 'The Combination Laws', *Economic History Review*, VI (1936) and 'The Combination Laws Reconsidered', *Economic History* (supplement to *Economic Journal*), no. 2 (May, 1927). See also J. Stevenson, *Popular Disturbances in England, 1700–1970* (London, 1979). For the reform movement, the best general account with considerable detail of particular debates, bills and acts is J. Cannon, *Parliamentary Reform, 1640–1832* (Cambridge, 1972). For reform societies in the later eighteenth century see especially G. S. Veitch, *The Genesis of Parliamentary Reform* (London, 1913) and P. A. Brown, *The French Revolution in English History* (London, 1918). For the reform crisis of 1830–2, see M. Brock, *The Great Reform Act* (London, 1973) and J. R. M. Butler, *The Passing of the Great Reform Bill* (London, 1914). For the biographies of major reformers and radicals, see *Dictionary of National Biography*. J. Saville and J. M. Bellamy, *Dictionary of Labour Biography*, Volumes I, II, III, and IV (London, 1972–7) which is the essential source for trade union and radical activists in the period.

10 Law and Order

Principal Judges

Lord Chancellor

1737–61	Ld Hardwicke	1778–93	Ld Thurlow
1761–6	Ld Henley (E of Northington from 1764)	1793–1801	Ld Loughborough
		1801–6	Ld Eldon
1766–71	Ld Camden	1806–7	Ld Erskine
1771–8	Ld Apsley (Earl Bathurst from 1775)	1807–27	Ld Eldon
		1827–30	Ld Lyndhurst

Chief Justice of the Court of King's Bench

1760–88	Ld Mansfield	1818–32	C. Abbot (Ld Tenterden from 1827)
1788–1802	Ld Kenyon		
1802–18	Ld Ellenborougn		

Chief Justice of the Court of Common Pleas

1760–2	J. Willes	1801–4	Ld Alvanley
1762–6	C. Pratt (Ld Camden from 1765)	1804–14	J. Mansfield
		1814–18	V. Gibbs
1766–71	J. E. Wilmot	1818–24	R. Dallas
1771–80	W. De Grey	1824	Ld Gifford
1780–93	Ld Loughborough	1824–9	W. D. Best
1793–9	J. Eyre	1829–47	N. C. Tindal
1799–1801	Ld Eldon		

Chief Baron of the Court of Exchequer

1760–72	T. Parker	1813–14	V. Gibbs
1772–7	S. S. Smythe	1814–17	A. Thomson
1777–87	J. Skynner	1817–24	R. Richards
1787–93	J. Eyre	1824–30	W. Alexander
1793–1813	A. Macdonald		

Master of the Rolls

1754–64	Sir T. Clarke	1818–24	Sir T. Plumer
1764–84	Sir T. Sewell	1824–?	Ld Gifford
1784–8	Sir L. Kenyon	1826–7	Sir J. S. Copley
1788–1801	Sir R. P. Arden	1827–34	Sir J. Leach
1801–18	Sir W. Grant		

Vice-Chancellor of England

1813–18	Sir T. Plumer	1827	Sir A. Hart
1818–27	Sir J. Leach	1827–50	Sir L. Shadwell

Major Developments in Public Order

1769   Attacks upon mills brought within the compass of the Riot Act of 1715 by 9 Geo III, st. 2, c.5.

1780   Lord Mansfield authorised the use of troops against rioters without directions from the civil magistrate.

1785   Failure of Pitt's Police Bill for the Metropolitan district.

1792   Proclamations against seditious publications (21 May and 1 Dec). Formation of loyalist associations (first founded at London in Nov).

Middlesex Justices Act (32 Geo. III, c.53) provides 21 professional magistrates and a force of constables for the Metropolitan district (excluding the City of London).

Thomas Paine tried and found guilty *in absentia* for seditious libel (Dec).

1793   John Frost convicted of sedition (May).

Daniel Isaac Eaton tried for publishing seditious literature (June and July).

James Muir convicted of sedition (Aug).

Thomas Fyshe Palmer convicted of sedition (Sep).

1794   William Skirving convicted of sedition (Jan).

Maurice Margarot convicted of sedition (Jan).

Arrest of Thomas Hardy, Horne Tooke, John Thelwall and nine other reform leaders (May).

Suspension of Habeas Corpus (34 Geo. III, c.54) (May).

Appointment and first report of the Secret Committee of the House of Commons (May).

Second report of the Secret Committee of the House of Commons. First and second reports from the Committee of Secrecy appointed by the House of Lords (June).

Robert Watt and David Downie convicted of high treason (Aug–Sep).

Trial and acquittal of Hardy, Tooke and Thelwall on charges of high treason (Oct–Nov).

1795   The 'Two Acts': Treasonable and Seditious Practices Act (36 Geo. III, c.7), extending law of treason to spoken and written words; and Seditious Meetings Act (36 Geo. III, c.8) restricting public meetings and political lectures (Dec).

1797   Unlawful Oaths Act (37 Geo. III, c.123). Oaths of secrecy and secret ceremonies made unlawful. Directed against political clubs but also used against trade unions.

Trials and executions of naval mutineers, including Richard Parker (June–Aug).

Incitement to Mutiny Act makes seduction of the armed forces from their duty or incitement to mutiny a felony (37 Geo. III, c.70).

1798   Trials and conviction of United Scotsmen (Jan–Sep).

Seizure of United Englishmen and committee of the London Corresponding Society (Apr).

Trials of John Binns, Arthur O'Connor and Rev. James O'Coigley for high treason; execution of O'Coigley (May–June).

1799   Reports of the Committees of Secrecy of the House of Commons and House of Lords (Mar).

Act for the more effectual Suppression of Societies established for Seditious and Treasonable Purposes, and for better preventing Treasonable and Seditious Practices (39 Geo. III, c.79). Suppressed by name the United Irishmen, United Englishmen, United Scotsmen, United Britons, and London Corresponding Society (July).

Combination Act (39 Geo. III, c.81) See pp. 129–30.

1800   Combination Act (39 and 40 Geo. III, c.106). See p. 130.

Thames Police Office permanently established at Wapping to police riverside districts of London.

1801   First Report of the Secret Committee of the House of Commons on treasonable and seditious practices in Great Britain and Ireland (Apr).

Second Report of the Committee of the House of Lords (Apr).

Second report of the Secret Committee of the House of Commons (May).

1802   William Lee and William Ronkesley of Sheffield tried and convicted for swearing illegal oaths (Dec).

1803   Execution of Colonel Marcus Despard for high treason (Feb).

1810   Sir Francis Burdett imprisoned in the Tower of London for a libel of the House of Commons (Mar–Apr).

1812   Framebreaking Act (52 Geo. III, c.16) and Nottingham Peace Act (52 Geo. III, c.17) (Feb). Unlawful Oaths Act (May). Preservation of Public Peace Act and Act of Indemnity (July). Committees of Secrecy appointed (June).

1813   Renewal of Nottingham Peace Act (remained in force until 1815).

1817   Reports of the Committees of Secrecy of the Houses of Commons and Lords (Feb).

'Gag' Acts. Suspension of Habeas Corpus; seditious meetings act; act to prevent seduction of armed forces, and act to make perpetual parts of the statute 36 Geo. III, c.7, respecting treasonable attempts on the Prince Regent (57 Geo. III, c.3, 55, 7, 19 and 6) (Feb–Mar). Trial and imprisonment of radical journalists T. J. Wooler and W. Hone for seditious libel.

Flight of Cobbett to America (Mar).

Trial and acquittal of Spa Fields conspirators on charges of high treason (June).

Trial and execution of Jeremiah Brandreth at Derby for Pentrich 'rising' (Nov).

1819   Peterloo 'Massacre'. Arrest of Henry Hunt and organisers.
'Six Acts': (i) Act to prevent delays in trials for misdemeanour (60 Geo. III and 1 Geo. IV, c.4); (ii) Act to authorise seizures of arms in disturbed districts (60 Geo. III and 1 Geo IV, c.2); (iii) Act to prevent meetings for the training of persons in the use of arms (60 Geo. III and 1 Geo. IV, c.1); (iv) Act to prevent seditious assemblies of more than fifty persons except under specific circumstances (60 Geo. III and 1 Geo. IV, c.6); (v) Act to prevent blasphemous and seditious libels by permitting seizure of libellous material and banishment of authors on second offence (60 Geo. III and 1 Geo IV, c.8); (vi) Newspaper Stamp Duties Act. Some pamphlets subjected to stamp duty and sureties to be given for payment of fines incurred as blasphemous or seditious libels (60 Geo. III and 1 Geo. IV, c.9).

1820   Seizure of Cato Street conspirators (Feb).
Trial and execution of Arthur Thistlewood and four other conspirators (Apr–May).

1823   Peel's Gaol Act (4 Geo. IV, c.64). Laid down rules for the running of local gaols by Justices of the Peace; inmates to be classified and separated according to sex, age and type of offence.

1829   Metropolitan Police Act (10 Geo. IV, c.44). Established paid, uniformed police for the 'Metropolitan Police District', covering a radius of about 7 miles from the centre of London, excluding the City of London, controlled by two Justices (or 'Commissioners') under the authority of the Home Secretary.

SOURCES: Sir W. Holdsworth, *A History of English Law*, Vol. XIII (London, 1952); G. S. Veitch, *The Genesis of Parliamentary Reform* (London, 1913).

Popular Disturbances in Britain (excluding Ireland)

1761	Mar	Disturbances at Gateshead, Morpeth, Whittingham and Hexham against Militia Act.
		Anti-enclosure riot at North Leigh Heath (Oxon).
1762	July	Food riot in Manchester.
	Aug	Disturbances amongst Spitalfields weavers.
	Nov–Dec	Sailors' riots in Liverpool and Ormskirk.
1763	Oct	Machine-breaking by Spitalfields weavers.
1765	Jan	Houses attacked by mob in Devizes.
	May	Attack on Duke of Bedford's house in London by Spitalfields weavers.

July	Anti-enclosure riot at West Haddon in Northamptonshire.
Aug	Anti-workhouse riots at Wickham Market, Bulcamp, Sibston, Yoxford and Nacton Heath in Suffolk.
Sep	Anti-enclosure riot at Walkworth near Banbury.
	Pit machinery broken during colliers' strike on Tyneside.
1766 Jan–Nov	Widespread food rioting in England. Major centres of disturbance in the West Country, Thames valley, Midlands and East Anglia.
1768 Mar–May	Disturbances in London in support of John Wilkes.
Apr	Demonstrations by seamen of Newcastle, Sunderland and Shields in pursuit of a wage dispute.
Apr–May	Disturbances during wage disputes of sailors and coal-heavers in London.
May	'Massacre' of St George's Fields outside King's Bench Prison.
Aug	Disturbances amongst Spitalfields weavers during wage dispute.
1769 Feb–Mar	Attacks on spinning and carding machines at Blackburn.
Mar	'Battle of Temple Bar': pro-Wilkes demonstration in London.
Mar–Sep	Widespread disturbances amongst Spitalfields weavers.
1771 Mar–Apr	Pro-Wilkes riots in London.
Oct	Anti-enclosure disturbances at Swinehead, near Boston, Lincolnshire.
1772 Apr	Anti-enclosure disturbance at Redditch.
Apr–June	Food riots, mainly centred in East Anglia and the West Country.
Dec–Jan	Meal riots on Tayside.
1773 July–Aug	Renewed food rioting in England, especially in the Midlands and Cornwall.
Aug	Disturbances during strike of shipwrights' apprentices in Liverpool.
1775 June	Weavers' disturbances at Keighley during industrial dispute.
Aug	Rioting during sailors' wage dispute in Liverpool.
1776 Apr	Tinners' riots at Redruth and Falmouth over introduction of Staffordshire earthenware.
July	Riots in Shepton Mallet over the introduction of machinery in the woollen industry.
Oct	Riots at Wrexham over the employment of English colliers.

1778	Mar	Food riot at Flint.
	May–Aug	Anti-militia riots at Henfield (Sussex) and Merioneth-shire.
1779	Jan–Feb	Anti-Popery riots in Glasgow, Edinburgh and several other towns in Scotland.
	June	Machine-breaking in Nottingham.
	Oct	Cotton-spinning machinery broken at Chorley, Wigan, Bolton, Blackburn and Preston.
1780	June	Gordon riots in London.
		Anti-Catholic riots in Bath.
1781	June	Machine-breaking at Frome.
1782	Oct	Food riots at Wolverhampton and Stourbridge.
1783	Mar–July	Food riots, mainly in Staffordshire and Yorkshire.
	July	Disturbances amongst stocking weavers in Nottingham.
1784	May	Election riots at Westminster, Liverpool, Coventry, Leicester and Buckingham.
1785	June	Disturbances amongst seamen, keelmen and labourers in Sunderland.
1787	Feb-Mar	Riot at Bradford (Wilts) and Trowbridge over organisation of looms in single shops.
1788	July	Riots at Westminster election.
	Nov	Disturbances at Stamford because of attempts to end bull-running.
1789	June	Food riots near Truro.
1790	June	Election riots at Carlisle, Leicester, Nottingham, York and Beverley.
	Oct	Disturbances at Nottingham during framework knitters' dispute.
1791	July	Priestly riots in Birmingham by 'Church and King' mobs.
		Anti-enclosure riot in Sheffield.
1792	Mar	Destruction of power-loom factory in Manchester.
	Apr	Attacks on dissenters in Nottingham.
	May	Disturbance between soldiers and civilians in Sheffield.
		Machine-breaking at Woodchester, near Worcester.
		Disturbances over the price of meat at Nottingham.
		Riot over the price of provisions at Leicester.
	June	Disturbance amongst the colliers at Leeds.
		'Church and King' demonstrations in Manchester.
		Anti-government riots at Edinburgh.
		Riots in Gloucester against introduction of gig-mills.
	June–Oct	Political disturbances at Aberdeen, Perth, Dundee, Peebles, Lanark and Duns.
	July	Anti-clearance riot in Ross-shire.

	Oct	Food riot at Great Yarmouth.
		Disturbances at Wigan during colliers' strike.
	Oct–Nov	Disturbances as a result of labour dispute amongst the seamen at Ipswich and South Shields.
	Dec	Anti-Jacobin disturbances in Manchester.
1793	Feb	Food riots in Cornwall and South Wales.
	Apr	Anti-enclosure disturbances in Flintshire.
	June	Disturbances at Liverpool and Sheffield over the price of butter.
	Aug	Political riots in Nottingham.
	Sep	Riot against toll-gates in Bristol.
	Oct	Disturbance in Birmingham against taxes levied for the Priestley riots.
		Disturbances during labour dispute amongst river-bank workers at Grantham.
1794	July	Political disorders in Nottingham between loyalists and reformers.
		Disturbances amongst Tyneside keelmen during labour dispute.
	Aug	Anti-'crimp-house' disturbances in London. Several recruiting houses attacked.
1795	Feb–Nov	Widespread food riots in England, Wales and Scotland.
		Disturbances against the use of the Winchester corn measure in South Wales.
	Apr	Anti-recruiting riots in North Wales.
	July	Food and anti-recruiting riots in London.
	Oct	Mobbing of the King's coach in London.
	Nov	Anti-recruiting disturbances in North Wales.
1796	Jan–Apr	Renewed food riots in Wales, Cornwall, Midlands and Yorkshire.
	July	Disturbances between recruiting parties and populace in Nottingham.
	Nov–Dec	Riots in Lincolnshire against operation of the Militia Act. Other disturbances in Norwich, Northampton, Wellingborough, Kettering, Wing, Oswestry, Barmouth, Ulverstone, Penrith, Bala, Machynlleth and Llanbrynmair.
1797	Apr–May	Mutinies amongst sailors at Spithead and the Nore.
	Nov	Cloth-mill destroyed at Beeston, Notts.
	Dec	Machine-breaking at Frome in Somerset.
1798	Aug	Anti-enclosure riot at Gringly on the Hill, near Nottingham.
1799	June	Anti-enclosure riots at Wilbarston in Northampton.
	Nov	Food riot at Huddersfield.

1800	Jan	Disturbances at St Clears, Carmarthenshire, over taxes.
	Feb–Nov	Widespread food rioting in England, Wales and Scotland.
1801	Jan–Apr	Renewed food rioting in England and Wales.
1802	Apr–Aug	Shearmen's riots in Wiltshire against the introduction of gig-mills.
	July–Aug	Election riots at Coventry and Liverpool.
	Aug	Disturbances amongst London shipwrights during an industrial dispute.
1803	Mar	Riots against press-gangs in Bristol.
	Apr–May	Disturbances against press-gangs in London.
1804	Aug	Riots in London during the Middlesex Election.
1806	Feb	Attack upon Excise officers at Llannon in Cardiganshire.
1807	May	Election riots in Liverpool.
1808	May–June	Disturbances following rejection of Minimum Wage Bill for weavers at several towns in Lancashire.
1809	Sep	Anti-enclosure disturbances in Carnarvonshire.
	Oct–Nov	'Old Price' riots at Drury Lane Theatre, London.
1810	Apr	Disturbances in London at the arrest of Sir Francis Burdett.
	July	Food riot in Wolverhampton market.
	Sep	Riot at Dartmouth prison.
	Oct	Riot in Porchester Castle prison. Disturbance amongst soldiers in Wakefield.
	Nov	Theatre riot in Plymouth.
1811	Mar	Beginning of Luddite disturbances in Nottinghamshire. Extensive frame-breaking in the county until Nov 1816.
	Aug	Disturbances at Peterborough Theatre.
	Nov	Disturbance at East India College, Hertford.
	Dec	Theatre riots in Liverpool.
1812	Jan–Sep	Luddite disturbances in Yorkshire.
	Mar–Apr	Machine-breaking in Lancashire and Cheshire.
	Apr–Nov	Widespread food riots in the industrial areas.
	Apr	Riots in Manchester when crowd wrecks the Exchange newsroom.
	May	Demonstrations in Nottingham to celebrate the assassination of Spencer Perceval.
	Sep	Riot at Dartmoor prison.
	Sep–Oct	Anti-enclosure disturbances at Pistyll on the Lleyn peninsula.
1813	Feb	Anti-clearance riots at Kildonan in Sutherland.
	Apr	Anti-enclosure riots in Carnarvonshire.
	July	Riots against induction of a clergyman at Assynt, Sutherland.

1814 June	Labour disturbances amongst Leicester stocking weavers.
1815 Mar	Riots in London against passing of the Corn Laws. Disturbances amongst Tyneside keelmen during labour dispute. Farm machinery broken at Gosbeck, Suffolk.
July–Aug	Further machine-breaking disturbances in Suffolk.
Oct	Disturbances at Hull, Sunderland and South Shields during seamen's strike.
Nov	Disturbances amongst Bilston colliers following a wage cut.
1816 Feb	Machine-breaking at Huddersfield.
Apr–June	Food riots, machine-breaking and arson in Norfolk, Suffolk, Cambridgeshire and Essex. Most serious disturbances at Bridport, Norwich, Downham Market, Littleport, Brandon and Ely.
July–Aug	Food riots at Frome, Stockport, Bolton, Coventry, Hinckley and Birmingham.
Oct	Disturbances in South Wales during strikes amongst colliers and ironworkers.
Nov–Dec	Food riots at Carlisle, Huddersfield, Oldham, Sheffield and Dundee.
Dec	Spa Fields riots in London when the followers of Thomas Spence attempt to seize the Tower and the Bank of England.
1817 Jan	Attack upon the Prince Regent's coach on return from the state opening of Parliament. Disturbances amongst South Wales iron-workers.
Feb	Food riots at Amlwch and Tremadoc in Wales.
Mar	Food riot at Maryport. Strikes and food riots at Radstock. 'March of the Blanketeers' sets off from Manchester. Broken up near Stockport. Further disturbances in South Wales.
June	Pentrich 'Rising' in Derbyshire led by Jeremiah Brandreth. Huddersfield 'Rising'. Minor skirmishes.
1818 July–Aug	Disturbances during strike of Manchester cotton spinners.
Aug	Riots at Stockport during strike of power-loom weavers. Squatters riots at Rhydoldog in Carnarvonshire.
Nov	Food riots amongst colliers at Whitehaven.
1819 July	Orange riots in Liverpool.
Aug	Peterloo 'Massacre' (16th).

		Reform disturbance at Macclesfield and Stockport.
	Oct	Disturbances during keelmen's strike at North Shields.
1820	Feb	Cato Street conspiracy uncovered.
	Mar	Election riot at Banbury.

Reform disturbance at Macclesfield and Stockport.

Oct — Disturbances during keelmen's strike at North Shields.

1820 Feb — Cato Street conspiracy uncovered.

Mar — Election riot at Banbury.

Disturbances at South Shields amongst seamen.

Anti-clearance disturbances at Culrain, Gruids and Achness in Ross-shire and Sutherland.

Mar–Apr — Disturbances amongst wool-croppers near Huddersfield and Barnsley 'Rising'.

Apr — 'Battle of Bonnymuir' near Glasgow between weavers and troops.

June — Demonstrations in London in support of Queen Caroline.

Nov — Widespread demonstrations in support of Queen Caroline.

1821 Jan — Disturbances in Shropshire during colliers' strike.

Mar — Anti-clearance disturbance at Gruids, Scotland.

Aug — Riots in London during funeral of Queen Caroline.

1822 May — Disturbances during colliers' strike in South Wales.

Riots in Frome and Warminster over use of the guy-shuttle.

July — Disturbances amongst Norwich weavers over a wage reduction.

Oct–Nov — Disturbances during keelmen's strike in the Tyne.

1824 Aug — Houses demolished by squatters at Fishguard.

1825 Aug — Disturbances during seamen's strike at Sunderland.

1826 Apr–May — Power-looms broken at Accrington, Blackburn, Bury, Chaddeston, Rawtenstall, Long Holme, Edenfield, Summerseat and Manchester. Also attacks on power-looms by Bradford worsted weavers.

1829 May — Attacks on weaving factories and provision shops in Manchester.

June–July — Food disturbances in Bolton, Wigan and Preston.

1830 Apr — Beginning of 'Captain Swing' disturbances in southern counties of England.

Nov — Reform disturbances in London.

Dec — Disturbances in the Ruabon area as a result of a strike amongst the North Wales colliers.

Sources: R. F. Wearmouth, *Methodism and the Common People of the Eighteenth Century* (London, 1945) ch. 1; R. Quinault and J. Stevenson (eds), *Popular Protest and Public Order* (London, 1974); J. L. and B. Hammond, *The Skilled Labourer, 1760–1832* (London, 1919): G. Rudé, *The Crowd in History* (New York, 1964) and *Hanoverian London, 1714–1808* (London, 1971); D. J. V. Jones, *Before Rebecca* (London, 1973); T. C. Smout, *A History of the Scottish People, 1560–1830* (London, 1969); E. P. Thompson, *The Making of the English Working Class* (London, 1968); F. O. Darvall, *Popular Disturbances and Public Order in Regency England*, 2nd ed (Oxford, 1969); M. Thomis, *The Luddites* (Newton Abbot, 1970).

Note: The list given above is not exhaustive. In general, incidents have been included which achieved contemporary notoriety or resulted in serious damage to persons or property.

Criminal Statistics

Commitals and Convictions for Indictable Offences in England and Wales, 1805–30

	Total Commitals, England and Wales	Convicted	Sentenced to Death	Executed
1805	4,605	2,783	350	68
1806	4,346	2,515	325	57
1807	4,446	2,567	343	63
1808	4,735	2,723	338	39
1809	5,330	3,238	392	60
1810	5,146	3,158	476	67
1811	5,337	3,163	359	45
1812	6,576	3,913	450	82
1813	7,164	4,422	593	120
1814	6,390	4,025	488	70
1815	7,818	4,883	496	57
1816	9,091	5,797	795	95
1817	13,932	9,056	1,187	115
1818	13,567	8,958	1,157	97
1819	14,254	9,510	1,206	108
1820	13,710	9,318	1,129	107
1821	13,115	8,788	1,020	114
1822	12,241	8,209	921	95
1823	12,263	8,204	914	54
1824	13,698	9,425	1,017	49
1825	14,437	9,964	986	50
1826	16,164	11,007	1,146	57
1827	17,921	12,564	1,456	70
1828	16,564	11,723	1,086	79
1829	18,675	13,261	1,311	74
1830	18,107	12,805	1,351	46

SOURCE: G. R. Porter, *The Progress of the Nation* (London, 1847) p. 642.

Capital Convictions and Executions in London, 1601–1830

Period	Annual Rate of Capital Conviction	Annual Rate of Executions	Executions %
1601–60	89	71	80
1661–1700	78	53	68
1701–50	66	35	53
1751–1800	73	32	44
1801–30	130	17	13

Capital Convictions and Executions in London and Middlesex, 1701–1820

Period	Capital Convictions	Executions	Percentage of Executions to Capital Convictions
1701–10	449	189	42
1711–20	1084*	514*	47
1721–30	733*	450*	61
1731–40	526*	243*	46
1741–50	531*	338*	64
1751–60	411	281	68
1761–70	505	263	52
1771–80	779	357	46
1781–90	1,162	517	44
1791–1800	779	197	25
1801–10	836	104	12
1811–20	1,648	120	13

* Approximate figure.
Source: *British Parliamentary Papers, 1818*, XVI, pp. 184–5.

Capital Punishment in London, 1701–1830

Period	Capitally Convicted	Executed	Percentage of Executed to Convictions
1701–50	3,323*	1,735*	52
1751–1800	3,636	1,615	44
1801–30	3,898	509	13

* Approximate figure.

The Abolition of Capital Offences, 1808–30

In 1800 there were about 200 capital offences on the statute book.

The Larceny Act, 1808 (48 Geo. 3, c.129) abolished the death sentence for larceny from the person, and broadened the definition of the offence. This was the first of the eighteenth-century capital statutes to be repealed, as a result of Romilly's campaign.

Stealing from Bleaching Grounds Act, 1811 (51 Geo, 3, c.39), and Stealing of Linen Act, 1811 (51 Geo. 3, c.41): two obsolete capital statutes repealed by Romilly.

Stealing in Shops Act, 1820 (1 Geo. 4, c.117) raised the minimum amount stolen in shops which would constitute a capital offence from 5s to £15.

Judgement of Death Act, 1823 (4 Geo. 4, c.48) gave discretion to the judge to abstain from pronouncing the death sentence on a person convicted of any crime except murder, if the judge felt the offender was fit to be recommended for the King's mercy.

Benefit of Clergy Act, 1823 (4 Geo. 4, c.53) abolished the death penalty for: (a) larceny of property to the value of 40s on ships on navigable rivers; (b) larceny of property to the value of 40s in shops.

'*Peel's Acts*': essentially consolidating statutes, codifying the statute law on a number of offences:

(1) Criminal Statutes (Repeal) Act, 1827 (7 and 8 Geo. 4, c.27) consolidated about 90 statutes relating to larceny and allied offences, and repealed obsolete statutes on this subject.

(2) Indemnity Act, 1827 (7 and 8 Geo. 4, c.30) consolidated about 50 statutes relating to malicious injuries to property.

(3) Offences against the Person Act, 1828 (9 Geo. 4, c.31) consolidated 56 statutes relating to offences against the person.

Criminal Justice Act, 1827 (7 and 8 Geo. 4, c.28). reversed the previous position on the punishment of felonies. Previously all felonies were automatically capital offences unless 'benefit of clergy' was allowed; by this Act, 'benefit of clergy' was abolished, and the death penalty restricted to those felonies from which 'benefit of clergy' had previously been excluded, or which new statutes would *expressly specify* should be capital. The punishment for non-capital felonies was to be transportation or imprisonment.

Larceny Act, 1827 (7 and 8 Geo. 4, c.29) abolished the separate offence of grand larceny (theft of over 12d) which had carried the death sentence for a second offence. Simple larceny was now to constitute a single offence, punishable by imprisonment or transportation. The only larcenies which remained capital were: (a) larceny in a dwelling-house of property worth £5 or more; (b) stealing horses, sheep or cattle.

Forgery Act, 1830 (11 Geo. 4 & 1 Will. 4, c.66) consolidated the law relating to forgery. It abolished the death sentence for a number of offences, but retained it for 42 kinds of forgery. This Act was repealed by the Forgery Act, 1832 (2 and 3 Will. 4, c. 123), which abolished the death sentence for all forgery offences, except forgery of wills and of powers of attorney for the transfer of government stock.

Sources: L. Radzinowicz, *A History of English Criminal Law and its Administration from 1750;* 4 vols; (London, 1948–68) remains the best overall analysis of criminal law in this period. For popular disturbances see R. F. Wearmouth, *Methodism and the Common People of the Eighteenth Century* (London, 1945); E. P. Thompson, *The Making of the English Working Class,* 2nd ed. (Harmondsworth, 1968); and J. Stevenson, *Popular Disturbances in England, 1700–1870* (London, 1979). For criminal statistics see *Parliamentary Papers, 1834,* Vol. X, p. 299 and G. R. Porter, *The Progress of the Nation* (London, 1847), p. 642.

11 The Press

Newspaper Legislation, Taxes and Prices

Until the middle of the nineteenth century, newspaper proprietors were obliged to pay stamp, advertisement and paper duties. Together they comprised what Radicals criticised as 'taxes on knowledge', resulting in small circulations of expensive newspapers. Their complete abolition by 1861 made possible the cheap daily provincial newspaper.

Year	Stamp Duty per Sheet	Advertisement Duty	Pamphlet Duty per Sheet	Postal Rate for 55 miles	Cost of a Newspaper in London
1712	1d	1s	2s	3d	2d
1757	1d minimum	2s	,,	,,	,,
1776	1½d	,,	,,	,,	3d
1780	,,	2s 6d	,,	,,	,,
1784	,,	,,	,,	4d	,,
1789	2d	3s	,,	,,	4d
1796	,,	,,	,,	5d	,,
1797	3½d	,,	,,	,,	4½d–6d
1801	,,	,,	,,	6d	,,
1805	,,	,,	,,	7d	,,
1812	,,	,,	,,	8d	5d–7d
1815	4d	3s 6d	3s	,,	7d
1833	,,	1s 6d	,,	,,	,,

SOURCE: J. Greenwood, *Newspapers and the Post Office 1635–1834.*

National Newspaper Press

Chronology of Main Events

1702 *Daily Courant*, first daily newspaper, published.
1711 *The Spectator* launched.
1712 Stamp Act passed.
1731 *Gentleman's Magazine* founded.
1763 Wilkes wins *North Briton* case.
1769 *Morning Chronicle* founded with W. Woodfall as editor and proprietor.
1772 *Morning Post* founded, with 12 shareholders led by James Christie, Tattersall and John Bell.

157

1780 *Morning Herald* founded, originally a radical paper.
1785 *Daily Universal Register* begun (became *The Times* in 1788).
1791 *The Observer* first appeared – a Sunday newspaper.
1792 *The Courier* founded, with John Parry as proprietor and J. Thelwell as editor. *The Sun* first appeared with William Pitt and friends as proprietors and George Rose as editor. A Government organ to 1815.
1794 *Morning Advertiser* founded, the organ of the Incorporated Society of Licensed Victuallers.
1795 Peter and Daniel Stuart became proprietors of the *Morning Post*.
1798 Newspaper Publication Act put publishers under close supervision of magistrates.
1799 Coleridge appointed literary editor of the *Morning Post*.
1800 *Bell's Weekly Dispatch* (later the *Sunday Dispatch*) founded, with Robert Bell as proprietor/editor. Liberal/radical in politics.
1802 *The Political Register* (weekly) first published.
1803 Nicholas Byrne became editor/proprietor of the *Morning Post*.
1808 *The Examiner*, a Sunday newspaper, founded, with John and Leigh Hunt as manager and editor.
c.1812 Dr (Sir) John Stoddart became editor of *The Times*.
1814 New steam presses used for printing *The Times*.
1815 Newspaper stamp duty became 4*d* per copy.
1816 Cobbett's 2*d Political Register* ('Tuppenny Trash') published.
1817 John Black becomes editor of the *Morning Chronicle*.
       Reformist Register published.
1820 Imprisonment of Richard Carlile of *The Republican*.
       Thwaites Wright became editor of the *Morning Herald*.
1821 *Manchester Guardian* first published: John Edward Taylor proprietor, Jeremiah Garnett editor.
1822 W. Mudford became editor of *The Courier*.
       Sunday Times first appeared, with D. W. Harvey MP as editor/proprietor. Liberal in politics before 1845.
1827 *The Standard* founded, with Dr Giffard as editor.
       Applegarth-Cowper four-cylinder press prints 5,000 copies per hour of *The Times*.
       Thomas Barnes appointed editor of *The Times* (until 1841).
1837 Newspaper Tax reduced from 4*d* to 1*d*; Isaac Pitman's simplified shorthand introduced.

Provincial Newspaper Press

The following lists the major provincial papers in existence by 1830, with the date of their foundation. Their general political affiliation after 1830 is designated by C (Conservative), L (Liberal) and I (Independent).

England

Bath	*Bath Journal* (Keene's) (1742) (L) weekly; *Bath Chronicle* (1757) (C) weekly; *Bath Herald* (1792) (L) daily after 1858.
Belfast	*Belfast News Letter* (1737) (C) daily in 1857; *Belfast Northern Whig* (1824) (L) daily in 1857.
Birmingham	*Aris' Birmingham Gazette* (1741) (C) weekly; *Midland Counties Herald* (1836) (I) bi-weekly.
Bradford	*Bradford Observer* (1834) (L) daily in the late 1860s.
Brighton	*Brighton Herald* (1806) (L) weekly; *Brighton Gazette* (1821) (C) bi-weekly; *Brighton Guardian* (1827) (C) weekly.
Bristol	*Bristol Times and Mirror* (1714) (C) daily in 1858, as was *Bristol Mercury* (1790) (L).
Cambridge	*Cambridge Chronicle and University Journal* (1744) (C) weekly; *Cambridge Independent Press, University and Huntingdonshire Herald* (1807) (L) weekly.
Canterbury	*Kentish Post* (1717) (I) weekly, became *Kentish Gazette and Canterbury Press* in 1768; *Kentish and Canterbury Chronicle* (1768) (L) weekly; *Kent Herald* (1792) (L) weekly; *Kentish Observer and Surrey and Sussex Chronicle* (1832) (C) bi-weekly.
Carlisle	*Carlisle Journal* (1798) (L) bi-weekly; *Carlisle Patriot* 1815 (C).
Derby	*Derby Mercury* (1732) (C) weekly; *Derby Reporter* (1823) (L) weekly.
Doncaster	*Doncaster Gazette* (1786) (L) weekly.
Exeter	*Trewman's Exeter Flying Post* (1763) (C) weekly; *Western Times* (1828) (L), became *Daily Western Times* in the 1860s.
Halifax	*Halifax Guardian* (1832) (C) weekly.
Hull	*Hull Daily Mail* (1787) (C) daily in 1860s as was the *Eastern Morning News* (1794) (I).
Ipswich	*Ipswich Journal* (1720) (C) weekly; *Suffolk Chronicle* (1810) (L) weekly.
Leeds	*Leeds Mercury* (1718) (L) daily in 1861; *Yorkshire Weekly Post* (1854) (C) weekly; became *Yorkshire Post* (1866) (C) daily.
Leicester	*Leicester Journal* (1753) (C) weekly; *Leicester Chronicle* (1810) (L) bi-weekly.
Liverpool	*Liverpool Courier* (1808) (C) became *Daily Courier* 1863; *Liverpool Mercury* (1811) (L) daily in 1857.
Manchester	*Manchester Guardian* (1821) (L) daily in 1855; *Manchester Courier* (C) daily in 1861.
Newcastle-upon-Tyne	*Newcastle Courant* (1711) (I) weekly; *Newcastle Weekly Chronicle* (1764) (I) weekly; *Newcastle Journal* (1832) (C).

Northampton	*Northampton Mercury* (1720) (L) weekly; *Northampton Herald* (1831) (C) weekly.
Nottingham	*Nottinghamshire Weekly Express* (1710) (L).
Oxford	*Jackson's Oxford Journal* (1753) (C) weekly.
Plymouth	*Plymouth Herald* (I), *Plymouth Journal* (L) and *Plymouth Times* (C), 1820, 1820 and 1832 respectively, all weeklies.
Portsmouth	*Hampshire Telegraph* (1799) (L) weekly.
Sheffield	*Sheffield Register* (1787) (L) weekly, became *Sheffield Iris* 1794, expired 1848; *Sheffield Mercury* (1807–48) (C) weekly *Sheffield and Rotherham Independent* (1819) (L) daily in 1861.
Southampton	*Hampshire Advertiser* (1823) (C) bi-weekly; *Hampshire Independent* (1835) (I) weekly.
Stamford	*Rutland and Stamford Mercury* (1695).
Worcester	*Berrow's Worcester Journal* (1690) (C) weekly; *Worcester Herald* (1794) (I) weekly.
York	*Yorkshire Chronicle* (1772) (I) weekly; *Yorkshire Weekly Herald* (1790) (L) became *Daily Herald* 1874; *Yorkshire Gazette* (1819) (C) weekly.

Wales

Bangor	*North Wales Chronicle* (1807) (C) weekly.
Carmarthen	*Carmarthen Journal* (1810) (C) weekly.
Carnarvon	*Carnarvon Herald* (1831) (L) weekly.
Newport (Mon)	*South Wales Times* and *Star of Gwent* (1829) (C) weekly.
Swansea	*Cambrian* (1804) (L) weekly.

Scotland

Aberdeen	*Aberdeen Weekly Journal* (1748) (C); *Aberdeen Weekly Free Press* (1806) (L) became *Daily* in 1853.
Glasgow	*Glasgow Herald* (1782) (I) daily in 1859.
Dundee	*Dundee Advertiser* (1801) (L) daily in 1861.
Edinburgh	*Edinburgh Caledonian Mercury* (1660) (L) bi-weekly in 19th century; *Edinburgh Weekly Journal* (c.1744) (C) bi-weekly in 19th century; *Edinburgh Advertiser* (1764) (C) bi-weekly; *Scotsman* (1817) (L) daily in 1855.
Perth	*Perthshire Courier* (1809) (I) weekly; *Perthshire Constitutional and Journal* (1832) (C) bi-weekly; *Perthshire Advertiser* (1829) (L) tri-weekly.

Bibliography

No attempt has been made in this survey to cover the radical presses, particularly the famous 'unstamped'. Sources marked * below should be consulted for this information.

A. Andrews, *The History of British Journalism*, 2 vols (London, 1859)

*A. Aspinall, *Politics and the Press, 1780–1850* (London, 1949)

—— 'The Circulation of English Newspapers in the Early Nineteenth Century', *Review of English Studies*, XII (1946)

—— 'The Social Standing of Journalists at the Beginning of the Nineteenth Century', ibid. (July 1945)

G. A. Cranfield, *The Press and Society: From Caxton to Northcliffe* (London, 1978)

H. F. Fox-Bourne, *English Newspapers*, 2 vols (London, 1887)

J. Grant, *The Newspaper Press*, 3 vols (London, 1871–2)

W. Hindle, *The Morning Post, 1772—1937* (London, 1937)

*P. Hollis, *The Pauper Press* (Oxford, 1970)

H. W. Massingham, *The London Daily Press* (London, 1892)

S. Morison, *The English Newspaper, 1622–1932* (Cambridge, 1932)

C. Peabody, *English Journalism and the Men who Have Made It* (London, 1882)

D. Read, *Press and People, 1790–1850* (London, 1960)

*J. H. Rose, 'The Unstamped Press, 1815–1836', *English Historical Review*, XII (1897)

The Times, *History of the Times*, 5 vols

A. P. Wadsworth, 'Newspaper Circulations, 1800–1954', *Transactions of the Manchester Statistical Society* (1954–5)

*W. H. Wickwar, *The Struggle for the Freedom of the Press, 1819–1832* (London, 1928)

12 Religion

Religious Statistics

The Church of England

Churches, clergy, and Easter Day communicants, 1801–31

Year	Churches and chapels	Clergy	Easter Day communicants ('000s)	Easter Day communicant density
1801	11,379	–	535	9.9
1811	11,444	14,531	550	8.9
1821	11,558	–	570	7.9
1831	11,883	14,933	605	7.2

SOURCE: A. Gilbert, *Religion and Society in Industrial England* (London, 1976).

Regional variation in the average size of an Anglican parish in 1811

Region	Total number of parishes	Area in acres	Average size of parish in acres
East	1,634	3,240,000	1,980
South-east	1,048	2,594,000	2,475
South Midlands	1,379	3,558,000	2,580
North Midlands	1,236	3,517,000	2,840
South-west	940	2,703,000	2,880
South	873	2,541,000	2,910
West Midlands	1,253	4,021,000	3,200
Cornwall	205	868,000	4,230
Yorkshire	630	3,898,000	6,190
North	290	3,419,000	11,790
North-west	156	1,852,000	11,860

SOURCE: ibid.

The Catholic Church

Year	Estimated Catholic population	Churches and chapels	Actual Mass attendants
1720	115,000	–	61,600
1780	69,376	–	37,200
1800	–	–	–
1840	700,000	469	371,500

Figures are for England and Wales only.

SOURCE: ibid.

The New Dissent

Congregational, Particular Baptist, and New Connexion General Baptist membership 1750–1838

Year	Congregational		Particular Baptist		General Baptist New Connexion	
	Members	Density	Members	Density	Members	Density
1750	15,000		10,000		–	
1772	–		–		1,221	
1780	–		–		1,800	
1790	26,000		17,000		2,843	
1800	35,000	0.65	24,000	0.45	3,403	
1810	–		–		5,322	
1820	–		–		7,673	0.11
1830	–		–		10,869	0.13
1838	127,000	1.38	86,000	0.94	13,947	0.15

Total Methodist Membership as a Percentage of the adult English Population 1801–36

1801	1.6
1806	1.9
1811	2.3
1816	2.8
1821	2.9
1826	3.3
1831	3.4
1836	4.0

Year	Wesleyan Membership	New Connexion	Combined Total
1767	22,410		
1771	26,119		
1776	30,875		
1781	37,131		
1786	46,559		
1791	56,605		
1796	77,402		
1801	87,010	4,815	91,825
1806	103,549	5,586	109,135
1811	135,863	7,448	143,311
1816	181,631	8,146	189,777
1819	184,998	9,672	194,670

The Church of England

Archbishops and Bishops

Province of Canterbury

Canterbury
1758	Thomas Secker
1768	Hon. Frederick Cornwallis
1783	John Moore
1805	Chas. Manners Sutton
1828	William Howley
1848	John Bird Sumner

London
1748	Thomas Sherlock
1761	Thomas Hayter
1762	Richard Osbaldeston
1764	Richard Terrick
1777	Robert Lowth
1787	Beilby Porteus
1809	John Randolph
1813	William Howley
1828	Charles James Blomfield
1856	Archibald Campbell Tait

Winchester
1734	Benjamin Hoadly
1761	John Thomas
1781	Hon. Brownlow North
1820	Sir George Pretyman Tomline, Bt
1827	Charles Richard Sumner
1869	Samuel Wilberforce

Bath and Wells
1743	Edward Willes

1774	Charles Moss
1802	Richard Beadon
1824	George Henry Law
1845	Hon. Richard Bagot

Bristol
1758	Philip Yonge
1761	Thomas Newton
1782	Lewis Bagot
1783	Christopher Wilson
1792	Spencer Madan
1794	Henry Reginald Courtenay
1797	Folliot H. W. Cornwall
1803	Hon. George Pelham
1807	John Luxmore
1808	William Lort Mansel
1820	John Kaye
1828	Robert Gray
1834	Joseph Allen

Chichester
1754	Sir William Ashburton
1798	John Buckner
1824	Robert James Carr
1831	Edward Maltby

Ely
1754	Matthias Mawson
1770	Edmund Keene
1781	James York

1808 Thomas Dampier
1812 Bowyer E. Sparke
1836 Joseph Allen

Exeter
1747 George Lavington
1762 Frederick Keppel
1778 John Ross
1792 William Buller
1797 Henry Reginald Courtenay
1803 John Fisher
1807 Hon. George Pelham
1820 William Carey
1830 Christopher Bethell
1831 Henry Phillpotts

Gloucester
1752 James Johnson
1760 William Warburton
1779 James Yorke
1781 Samuel Halifax
1789 Richard Beadon
1802 Geo. Isaac Huntingford
1815 Hon. Henry Ryder
1824 Christopher Bethell
1830 James Henry Monk
        (1836 united with Bristol)

Hereford
1746 Lord James Beauclerk
1787 Hon. John Harley
1788 John Butler
1803 Folliott H. W. Cornwall
1808 John Luxmoore
1815 George Isaac Huntingford
1832 Hon. Edward Grey

Lichfield
1750 Hon. Frederick Cornwallis
1768 John Egerton
1771 Brownlow North
1774 Richard Hurd
1781 James Cornwallis
1824 Hon. Henry Ryder
1836 Samuel Butler

Lincoln
1744 John Thomas
1761 John Green
1779 Thomas Thurlow
1787 George Pretyman
1820 Hon. George Pelham
1827 John Kaye
1853 John Jackson

Norwich
1749 Thomas Haytor
1761 Philip Yonge
1783 Lewis Bagot
1790 George Horne
1792 Charles Manners Sutton
1805 Henry Bathurst
1837 Edward Stanley

Oxford
1758 John Hume
1766 Robert Lowth
1777 John Butler
1788 Edward Smallwell
1799 John Randolph
1807 Charles Moss
1812 William Jackson
1815 Hon. Edward Legge
1827 Charles Lloyd
1829 Hon. Richard Bagot
1846 Samuel Wilberforce

Peterborough
1757 Richard Terrick
1764 Robert Lambe
1769 John Hinchcliffe
1794 Spencer Madan
1813 John Parsons
1819 Herbert Marsh
1839 George Davys

Rochester
1756 Zachariah Pearce
1774 John Thomas
1793 Samuel Horsley
1802 Thomas Dampier
1809 Walter King
1827 Hugh Percy
1827 George Murray
1860 Joseph Cotton Wigram

Salisbury
1757 John Thomas
1761 Robert Hay Drummond
1761 John Thomas
1766 John Hume
1782 Hon. Shute Barrington
1791 John Douglas
1807 John Fisher
1825 Thomas Burgess
1837 Edward Denison

Worcester
1759 James Johnson

1774	Brownlow North	1808	F. H. W. Cornwall
1781	Richard Hurd	1831	Robert James Carr

Province of York

York

1757	John Gilbert
1761	Hon. R. Hay Drummond
1777	William Markham
1808	Hon. Edward V. Vernon Harcourt
1848	Thomas Musgrave

Durham

1752	Richard Trevor
1771	John Egerton
1787	Thomas Thurlow
1791	Hon. Shute Barrington
1826	William Van Mildert
1836	Edward Maltby

Carlisle

1747	Richard Osbaldeston
1762	Charles Lyttleton
1769	Edmund Law
1787	John Douglas
1791	Edward Venables Vernon
1808	Samuel Goodenough
1827	Hugh Percy

1856	Henry Montagu Villiers

Chester

1752	Edmund Keene
1771	William Markham
1776	Beilby Porteus
1788	William Cleaver
1800	Henry William Majendie
1810	Bowyer Edward Sparke
1812	George Henry Law
1824	Charles James Blomfield
1828	John Bird Sumner
1848	John Graham

Sodor and Man

1755	Mark Hildesley
1773	Richard Richmond
1780	George Mason
1784	Claudius Crigan
1813	George Murray
1828	William Ward
1838	James Bowstead

Plurality and Non-residence

1704 Of 9,180 benefices paying first fruits and tenths 5,082 were worth less than £80; 3,826 less than £50 and 1,200 less than £20 a year.

1802 2,500 benefices in patronage of bishops, deans and chapters
1,100 benefices in patronage of Crown
2,000 benefices in patronage of lay corporations, e.g. Oxford and Cambridge colleges
6,500 benefices in patronage of county families and individuals

1805 Clergy freed from ban under 21 Hen. VIII, c.13, now allowed to lease land for farming and to buy and sell for profit.

1807 4,412 resident incumbents for 11,164 parishes.

1810 About 1,500 resident incumbents had income under £150; 3,998 livings worth under £150, including 12 under £10 and 72 under £20. About 2,500 livings left to curates paid at £30–£40 a year.

1835 *The Extraordinary Black Book or Corruption Unmasked* gives the following distribution of Church revenues of £9,459,565 – 2 archbishops at £26,465 each; 24 bishops at £10,174; 28 deans at £1,580; 61 archdeacons at £739; 26 chancellors at £494; 844 prebendaries, canons, etc., at £338; 2,886 pluralist parsons holding 7,037 livings at £1,863; and 4,305 incumbents, half resident, at £764.

Revenues from Bishoprics, 1760
(in order of revenue)

See	Revenue p.a. £	See	Revenue p.a. £
Canterbury	7,000	Rochester	600 (+ 900)
Durham	6,000	Lincoln	1,500
Winchester	5,000	Lichfield and	1,400
York	4,500	Coventry	
London	4,000	St Asaph	1,400
Ely	3,400	Bangor	1,400
Worcester	3,000	Chichester	1,400
Salisbury	3,000	Carlisle	1,300
Oxford	500 (+ 1,800)	Hereford	1,200
Norwich	2,000	Peterborough	1,000 +
Bath and Wells	2,000	Llandaff	500 (+ 450)
Bristol	450 (+ 1,150)	Gloucester	900 (+ rich Durham
Exeter	1,500		prebend)
Chester	900 (+ 600)	St Davids	900 (+ two livings)

SOURCE: *A List of the Archbishops, Bishops, Deans, and Prebendaries in England and Wales, in His Majesty's Gift, with the reputed Yearly Value, of Their Respective Dignities* (London, 1762).

Missionary and Benevolent Societies

1698   Society for the Promotion of Christian Knowledge.
1701   Society for the Propagation of the Gospel in Foreign Parts.
1740   Foundling Hospital, London (Capt. Thomas Coram, 1668–1751).
1758   Magdalen Hospital, London, for penitent prostitutes.
1780   Sunday Schools started by Robert Raikes of Gloucester.
1787   Quakers start Society for Abolition of Slave Trade.
       Proclamation Society against vice and immorality.
1793   Baptist Missionary Society (William Carey, 1761–1834).
1795   London Missionary Society, undenominational.
1796   Quakers' Retreat at York, first humane asylum with efforts to cure insane.
1799   Church Missionary Society for Africa and the East.
       Sunday School Union.
       Religious Tract Society.
1802   Society for Suppression of Vice.
1804   British and Foreign Bible Society.
1807   Abolition of Slave Trade.
       British and Foreign School Society.
1809   London Society for Promoting Christianity among the Jews.
1811   National Society to open Christian schools.
1813   Wesleyan Missionary Society.
1833   Emancipation of slaves.

The Clapham Sect

Many High Churchmen (Tory), precluded from advancement, gave devoted service in their parishes. Evangelicals (Low Church, Whig), who remained in the Church of England but worked with dissenters, had considerable political influence and organised great philanthropic campaigns, e.g. the Clapham Sect fought for the abolition of slavery. Some members of the Clapham Sect were:

Henry Martyn (1781–1812), missionary in India
Hannah More (1743–1833), writer, organiser of Sunday schools
Charles Simeon (1759–1836), Cambridge vicar and preacher
Lord Teignmouth (1751–1834), Governor-General of India
Henry Thornton (1760–1815), banker, MP for Southwark
Henry Venn the Elder (1725–97), Vicar of Yelling, Hunts
William Wilberforce (1759–1833), MP, leader against slavery.

Chronology of the New Dissent

Protestant Dissenters

1689   Protestant dissenters allowed to build conventicles.
1711   Occasional Conformity Act.
1714   Schism Act to prevent dissenters controlling their children's education.
1718   Act of quieting and establishing corporations: dissenters could retain seat without taking Sacrament if not challenged within six months.
1719   Repeal of Schism Act and Occasional Conformity Act.
1723   Regium donum of royal bounty for ministers' widows.
1727   Annual Indemnity Act enabling dissenters to take Sacrament after, not before, election.
1727   Ministers of Presbyterian, Independent and Baptist congregations around London formed General Body of Protestant Dissenting Ministers.
1732   Parallel organisation of Protestant Dissenters' Deputies.
1767   Judgement by Lord Mansfield stopped City of London mulcting dissenters to raise funds to build the Mansion House.
1760 onwards   Distinguished dissenting academies: Morton's at Stoke Newington (Defoe a pupil); Doddridge's at Northampton; Dr John Taylor's at Warrington; Samuel Jones's at Tewkesbury.
1787–90   Bills for repeal of Test and Corporation Acts in 1787, 1789 and 1790 defeated in House of Commons.
1812   Formal repeal of Conventicle Act and Five Mile Act.
1813   Unitarian Relief Act.
1828   Repeal of Test and Corporation Acts.

Methodists

1729 John Wesley (1703–91), junior fellow of Lincoln College, Oxford, became leader of strict religious society formed by brother Charles Wesley (1707–88) and dubbed Methodists.

1738 John Wesley's 'new birth' in Aldersgate 24 May.

1739 George Whitefield (1714–79) started open-air preaching at Hanham-mount, Rose Green, Kingswood, Bristol.

1739 Methodist Society, meeting in Old Foundry, Moorfields, London.

1740 Wesley (Arminian) and Whitefield (Calvinist) agree to differ.

1743 Rules for Classes.

1744 First Methodist Conference.

1747 Societies grouped into circuits.
First of John Wesley's 42 visits to Ireland.

1760 Lay preachers at Norwich administer Holy Communion.

1771 Francis Asbury (1745–1816) sailed for America as Wesleyan missionary. First Methodist bishop in America.

1781 Lady Huntingdon's Connexion (Calvinist) separates from the Church of England.

1784 Deed of Declaration, beginning of modern Methodism (Arminian). Conference control over ministers and churches throughout Connexion.
Thomas Coke (1747–1814) ordained by John Wesley as 'superintendent' of Methodist Society in America. Bishops of Methodist Episcopal Church of America derived their orders from Coke.

1791 Death of Wesley.

1795 Separation of Methodists from Church of England.

1797 Methodist New Connexion.

1808 Expulsion by Wesleyan Methodist Conference of Hugh Bourne (1772–1852) for open-air preaching.

1812 Primitive Methodist Connexion formed by Hugh Bourne and William Clowes (1780–1851).

1818 Bryanites or Bible Christians separated from Methodists.

Baptists

1727 Joined Presbyterians and Independents around London in General Body of Protestant Dissenting Ministers.

1732 Parallel lay organisation of Protestant Dissenters' Deputies.

1770 Orthodox General Baptists formed the separate General Baptist New Connexion. The old connexion gradually merged with Unitarians.
Bristol Education Society formed to enlarge Baptist college in Bristol; colleges in Nottingham (1797), Bradford (1804), Stepney (1810).

1792 Baptist Missionary Society.

Roman Catholicism

Popes with Family Name

1758   Clement XIII (Rezzonico)   1775   Pius VI (Braschi)
1769   Clement XIV (Ganganelli)   1800   Pius VII (Chiaramonti)

Chronology of Principal Events

In 1685 England was divided into four districts by the Papacy – London, Midland, Western, Northern – in each of which a papal vicar exercised the authority normally possessed by the ordinary (bishop). Eight districts instituted in 1840 and hierarchy restored in 1850.

Roman Catholic priests faced the penalties of high treason for saying Mass. Unlicensed teachers could be fined 40s a day. Laymen refusing to take an oath denying the spiritual authority of the Pope were guilty of recusancy. This meant they could not hold any office, keep arms, go to law, travel more than five miles without licence, or be executor, guardian, doctor or lawyer. They could not sit in Parliament nor on corporations. The nearest protestant kin could claim lands from a Roman Catholic heir. Roman Catholics were subject to double land tax.

In practice the treatment of Roman Catholics was not so savage as the laws allowed. Few were punished for saying or hearing Mass. Magistrates seldom tendered the recusancy oath.

1700   Act 'for preventing growth of popery'. A Roman Catholic could not inherit or buy land unless he swore to abjure his religion; could not send children abroad for education.
1714   Ultramontane Roman Catholics (but not Howards, Blounts, Stonors, etc.) refused to abandon claim of Pope Sixtus V (1585–90) to release subjects of a heretic monarch from oath of fealty.
1716   In North Riding of Yorkshire 350 people convicted of recusancy.
1723   Levy of £100,000 on Roman Catholics.
1729   A priest, Matthew Atkinson, died in Hurst Castle after 30 years' imprisonment.
1739   Fear of Papists and Inquisition was revived during the war with Spain.
1747   Duke of York, the brother of Bonnie Prince Charlie (and King Henry IX to Jacobites) made a cardinal. Cardinal for 60 years 10 days, a record. Died 13 July 1805.
1778   Roman Catholic worship permitted. Purchase of land allowed and forfeiture of estates repealed. New oath of allegiance.
1780   No-Popery riots in London led by Lord George Gordon (1751–93). Similar riots in Scotland.
1791   Further relief for Roman Catholics.

1808   Roman Catholics given commissions in army and navy under
        stress of Napoleonic Wars.
1813   Catholic Emancipation defeated by Speaker's vote.
1817   Grattan's Catholic Relief Bill defeated.
1819   Catholic Emancipation Bill defeated by two votes.
1823   Burdett's Catholic Relief Bill rejected by Lords.
1829   Catholic Emancipation.

Main Centres of Roman Catholic Refugees, 1794

Some 8,000 Roman Catholic priests and nuns, driven from the Continent
by the French Revolution, were given sanctuary in Britain, e.g. 1,000
welcomed at Winchester by Anglicans. Main centres were:

Benedictines	Acton Burnell, Salop; Downside, Som., 1814; Ample-forth, Yorks.
Cistercians	1794–1817 Lulworth, Dorset.
Dominicans	1794–1810 Carshalton, Surrey; novitiate Hinckley, Leics.
Franciscans	1794 Novitiate at Osmotherley, Yorks.
Jesuits	1794 Stonyhurst, Lancs.

Nuns

Benedictine	1794–1857 at Winchester; Preston, Lancs.; after 1811 Caverswall Castle, Staffs.
Canonesses	1794 Regular (Winderheim) English convent from Bruges at Hengrave Hall, Suffolk, till 1802, then back to Bruges. From Louvain to Hammersmith, then Amesbury, Wilts, 1799, and Spettisbury, Dorset.
Carmelites	1794 from Antwerp to Lanherne, Cornwall; St Helen's Auckland, Co. Durham. From Hoogstraet to Acton, Middlesex, then Canford House, Dorset, till 1825.
Cistercians	1794 Hammersmith till 1801, then Stapehill, Wimborne, Dorset.
Dominicans	1794–1839 from Spellekens Convent to Hartpury Court, nr. Gloucester.
Franciscans (enclosed)	1794–1804 Abbey House, Winchester; then Taunton.
Mary, Institute of the Blessed Virgin	School at Hammersmith till 1796. Nuns moved to Bar Convent, York, oldest existing convent in England (1686).

SOURCE: Anson, Peter F., *The Religious Orders and Congregations of Great Britain and Ireland* (Stanbrook Abbey, Worcester, 1949).

Wales

Wales was neglected by the Church of England. Only one bishop between 1702 and 1870 could speak Welsh. Most bishops were absentees, e.g. Hoadly visited Bangor once in six years; Watson, Bishop of Llandaff, lived in Westmorland for 34 years.

1715   Thirty-five Nonconformist chapels in Wales.

1730   Circulating schools started by Griffith Jones (1683–1761).

1735   'Conversion' of Howell Harris of Trevecca (1714–1773) who led movement to revitalise established church.

1746   SPCK Welsh Bible and Prayer Book.

1761   13,000 circulating schools opened.

1767   Lady Huntingdon (1707–91) rented Trevecca House, North Wales, as training centre for her Connexion.

1770   1st edition (Carmarthen) of Welsh family Bible published by Peter Williams (1722–96).

1784   Thomas Charles (1755–1814), Anglican curate, joined Methodists and organised his Sunday schools in Wales which had no age limit. 'Charles taught Wales to read.'

1800   Welsh Wesleyan Methodist Church (Arminian doctrines). One thousand chapels in Wales.

1811   First ordination of Welsh Methodists (Calvinist doctrines).

1818   Revival at Beddgelert, Carnarvonshire, led by Richard Williams.

1823   Confession of Faith of Welsh Methodists formulated.

1826   Constitutional deed gave Welsh Methodist Church legal existence but forbade any alteration in faith or doctrine.

Scotland

Chronology

1690   Episcopal Church in Scotland disestablished and disendowed. Presbyterian Church took its place. Episcopalians still strongly supported in east and north-east.

1700   Out of 900 parishes, ministers in 165 adhered to Episcopal Church.

1707   Act of Union gave full rights to Church of Scotland (Presbyterian). No religious test. Rise of Moderates, as reaction from fanaticism of Covenanters.

1712   Toleration Act for Scotland. Right of nominating ministers restored to ancient patrons, unless Roman Catholic. This deprived kirk sessions of right of electing ministers, an important part of presbyterian system.

1725   Holy Bounty to protestantise the Highlands.

1732 Secession from Church of Scotland, led by Ebenezer Erskine (1680–1756) in protest at patronage, growth of toleration and threatened abolition of penal statutes against witches. (Law punishing witchcraft with death repealed for Great Britain, 1736.)

1746 Penal statutes against episcopalians: illegal to have churches or chapels, public services banned, clergy not allowed to minister to above 5 people at a time. Penalties imprisonment or banishment.

1747 Secession Church split into Burghers, led by Erskine, and anti-Burghers.

1752 Compromise on patronage: presbytery could satisfy itself on life, learning and doctrine of patron's nominee. But unrest continued into 19th century.

1763 Historian William Robertson (1721–93) Moderator of General Assembly.

1779 No-Popery riots in Edinburgh.

1784 Scottish Episcopal Church gave episcopate to American Church by consecration in Aberdeen of Samuel Seabury (1729–96), first Bishop of Connecticut.

1811 Congregational Union of Scotland.

Dioceses of the Episcopal Church

Fife (1726–1844); Dunkeld (1808 with Fife); Dunblane (1808 with Fife); Edinburgh; Aberdeen; Orkney (with Caithness 1733–69, with Ross 1769); Brechin; Moray; Ross (1762 with Caithness, 1769–1819 with Moray); Caithness (1733–1864 with Orkney); Glasgow (after 1721); Galloway or Candida Casa; The Isles or Sodor (1773 with Caithness).

Between 1705 and 1727 fourteen bishops were consecrated without sees to preserve the succession.

Primus of Episcopal Church

1704 Alexander Rose (Edinburgh)
1720 John Fullarton (Edinburgh)
1727 Arthur Millar (Edinburgh)
1731 Daniel Freebairn (Edinburgh)
1739 Thomas Rattray (Dunkeld)
1743 Robert Keith (Caithness, Orkney)
1757 Robert White (Dunblane)
1761 William Falconar (Moray, Edinburgh)
1782 Robert Kilgour (Aberdeen)
1788 John Skinner (Aberdeen)

Roman Catholics

1694 Roman Catholic vicariate established; two districts – Lowland and Highland; 1827 three districts – Eastern, Western, Northern.

1773   12 Jesuit fathers in Scotland when the Pope suppressed order.
1780   Bill to allow Roman Catholic priests to exercise office in Scotland withdrawn after riots in Edinburgh.

Ireland

Church of Ireland claimed it was successor of ancient Celtic Church. Identical in doctrine, worship and government with Church of England. The Commons of the Irish Parliament represented wealthy members of the established Church. Twenty-eight spiritual peers in House of Lords. By Act of Union Church of Ireland became part of the Church of England, with four spiritual peers in the House of Lords. Disestablished 1871.

After the Surrender of Limerick (1691) penal laws excluded Roman Catholics, three-quarters of the population, from professions, education, civil office, juries, vote, right to arms and horse. Priests were proscribed. Many Roman Catholics left Ireland but a body of rich Roman Catholic provision merchants grew up.

Chronology

1727   Roman Catholics deprived of vote.
1747   Wesley's first visit to Ireland; made 42 visits altogether.
        First Methodist church Whitefriars Street, Dublin.
1750   Roman Catholics admitted to lower grades of army.
1771   Bogland Act enabled Roman Catholics to take lease for 61 years of not more than 50 acres of unprofitable land, free of taxes for 7 years.
1774   Act denying the Pope had any civil or temporal authority in Ireland, following declaration by Munster bishops, accepted by most Roman Catholics.
1778   Act to allow Roman Catholics on simple oath to inherit land and take leases.
1779   Roman Catholics supported the Volunteers with equipment and upkeep.
        Irish Protestant Dissenters relieved from Test Act.
1782   Protestant Volunteers' congress at Dungannon, Ulster, supported freedom of conscience and declared sympathy with Roman Catholics.
        Catholics allowed to purchase land freely and have own schools.
1791   Society of United Irishmen, started by protestant Theobald Wolfe Tone (1763–98) welcomed Roman Catholics.
1793   Act by Irish Parliament conferred franchise on Roman Catholics on same terms as Protestants. But Catholics could not be MPs nor hold most important offices. They could receive degrees and fellowships at Dublin University.

1795 Religious disorders, e.g. at Armagh. Coalition between Roman
      Catholics and Presbyterians. Catholics harried.
1798 Insurrection Wicklow, Wexford. Catholics led by priests.
1800 Catholic Emancipation, with commutation of tithe and provision
      for Roman Catholic clergy, expected as price of Union with Eng-
      land, but not granted owing to the opposition of George III.
1808 Endowment of Maynooth College.
1829 Catholic Emancipation.

Division of Population among Creeds
1800 Roman Catholic Irish 3,150,000
      Protestant Anglo-Irish   450,000
      Presbyterians   900,000
      Roman Catholics paid about £500,000 a year in tithes to Protes-
      tant clergy.

Dioceses of Church of Ireland 1714–1830
Province of Armagh: Meath, Clogher, Kilmore or Tir Briuin, Ardagh
                      (1692–1751 held by bishops of Kilmore,
                      1751–1839 held by archbishops of Tuam, then
                      united to Kilmore), Down, Dromore, Derry,
                      Raphoe, Tuam (archbishop till 1839), Killala,
                      Elphin, Clonfert (united to Killaloe 1804) Kil-
                      macduagh (1627–1836 held *in commendam* by
                      bishops of Clonfert, united to Killaloe 1752).
Province of Dublin: Kildare, Ossory, Ferns, Cashel (archbishop until
                      1839) Waterford, (united to Cashel 1832), Cork,
                      Cloyne (united to Cork 1835), Limerick, Killaloe,
                      Kilfenora (1661–1741 held by Archbishop of
                      Tuam, 1742–52 held by Bishop of Clonfert, 1752
                      united to Killaloe).

13 Selected Holders of Local Government Office

Lord Lieutenants, England

Bedfordshire
Apr 1745 D of Bedford
Jan 1771 E of Upper Ossory
Feb 1818 Ld Grantham
Nov 1859 D of Bedford

Berkshire
Dec 1751 D of St Albans
1761 Ld Vere
July 1771 D of St Albans
Mar 1786 Ld Craven
Dec 1791 E of Radnor
Nov 1819 E of Craven
May 1826 E of Abingdon (5th)
Feb 1855 E of Abingdon (6th)

Buckinghamshire
Dec 1758 Earl Temple
1763 Ld Le Despenser
Nov 1781 E of Chesterfield
Mar 1782 Earl Temple (M of Buckingham
Feb 1839 Ld Carrington

Cambridgeshire
Aug 1757 Vt Royston (2nd E of Hardwicke)
June 1790 3rd E of Hardwicke
1834 Thomas Clifton

Cheshire
Nov 1727 Vt Malpas (3rd E of Cholmondeley)
1771 4th E (1st M) of Cholmondeley
May 1783 5th E of Stamford and Warrington
June 1819 6th E of Stamford and Warrington
June 1845 M of Westminster

Cornwall
1740 Hon. Richard Edgcumbe (1st Ld)
1761 Ld Edgcumbe (Vt, later E of Mount-Edgcumbe)
1795 E of Mount-Edgcumbe
1840 Sir William Trelawny

Cumberland
Dec 1759 Sir James Lowther (later E of Lonsdale)
June 1802 Vt Lowther (1st E of Lonsdale, 2nd creation)
Apr 1844 2nd E of Lonsdale

Derbyshire
Jan 1756 4th D of Devonshire
Feb 1764 M of Granby
June 1766 Ld George Cavendish
June 1782 5th D of Devonshire
Aug 1811 6th D of Devonshire
May 1858 7th D of Devonshire

Devonshire
June 1751 D of Bedford
Jan 1771 Earl Poulett
May 1788 Ld (1st Earl) Fortescue
Nov 1839 Vt Ebrington (2nd Earl Fortescue)

Dorset
Mar 1733 4th E of Shaftesbury
June 1771 Ld (Earl) Digby
Oct 1793 Ld Rivers
June 1803 E of Dorchester
Mar 1808 Earl Digby
June 1856 7th E of Shaftesbury

Durham
1758 2nd E of Darlington

176

1792		3rd E of Darlington (D of Cleveland)
Apr	1842	M of Londonderry

Essex

Apr	1756	E of Rochford
Oct	1781	Earl Waldegrave
Nov	1784	Ld Howard de Walden
Jan	1798	Ld Braybrooke
Apr	1825	Vt Maynard
Nov	1865	Ld Dacre

Gloucestershire

Feb	1754	2nd Ld Ducie
	1761	Ld Chudworth
	1762	Norbonne Berkeley (Ld Bottetourt)
July	1766	E of Berkeley
Aug	1810	D of Beaufort
Feb	1836	Ld Seagrave (Earl Fitzhardinge)

Hampshire

Oct	1759	D of Bolton
June	1763	M of Carnarvon (D of Chandos)
Aug	1764	E of Northington
Jan	1771	M of Carnarvon (D of Chandos)
May	1780	Ld Rivers
Apr	1782	D of Bolton
	1793	Geoffrey Powlett, Sir William Heathcote and William Chute
	1798	E of Wiltshire
Feb	1800	Ld Bolton
Aug	1807	E of Malmesbury
Dec	1820	D of Wellington
Nov	1852	M of Winchester

Herefordshire

	1747	Vt Bateman
Mar	1802	E of Essex
Aug	1817	Ld Somers
	1841	Ld Bateman

Hertfordshire

	1714	Earl Cowper
Oct	1764	E of Essex
Mar	1771	Vt Cranborne (M of Salisbury)
July	1823	1st E of Verulam
Jan	1846	2nd E of Verulam

Huntingdonshire

Nov	1739	D of Manchester
	1762	D of Manchester
May	1789	D of Montagu
June	1790	M of Graham (D of Montrose)
Mar	1793	D of Manchester
Sep	1841	E of Sandwich

Kent

July	1746	D of Dorset
Feb	1766	D of Dorset
	1769	D of Dorset
	1797	Ld (E of) Romney
May	1808	Earl (M) Camden
	1841	E of Thanet

Lancashire

July	1771	12th E of Derby
Nov	1834	13th E of Derby

Leicestershire

Apr	1721	3rd D of Rutland
July	1779	4th D of Rutland
Dec	1787	D of Beaufort
July	1799	5th D of Rutland
Mar	1857	6th D of Rutland

Lincolnshire

Jan	1742	3rd D of Ancaster and Kesteven
Dec	1778	4th D of Ancaster and Kesteven
Aug	1779	5th D of Ancaster and Kesteven
Mar	1809	Ld (Earl) Brownlow
Aug	1852	M of Granby (D of Rutland)

Middlesex

Oct	1714	D of Newcastle
	1762	3rd D of Northumberland
1762–86		office in commission
Aug	1794	M of Titchfield (D of Portland)
Feb	1842	M of Salisbury

Monmouthshire

June	1732	Thomas Morgan
Dec	1771	5th D of Beaufort
Oct	1803	6th D of Beaufort
Feb	1836	Capel Hanbury Leigh

Norfolk

June	1757	E of Orford
Feb	1792	Marquess Townshend

Mar 1808	Ld Suffield	
Mar 1822	Ld Wodehouse	
Aug 1846	E of Leicester	

Northamptonshire
Nov 1749	E of Halifax
July 1771	E of Northampton
1796	E of Northampton
June 1828	E of Westmorland
Feb 1842	M of Exeter

Northumberland
Mar 1753	E (3rd D) of Northumber-land
Sep 1786	4th D of Northumberland
1798–June 1798	office in commission
1798 –1817	4th D of Northumberland (again)
July 1817	5th D of Northumberland
Feb 1847	Earl Grey

Nottinghamshire
Jan 1763	D of Kingston
Sep 1765	1st D of Newcastle
Dec 1768	2nd D of Newcastle
Apr 1794	3rd D of Newcastle
June 1795	3rd D of Portland
Dec 1809	4th D of Newcastle
1840	E of Scarborough

Oxfordshire
Mar 1760	4th D of Marlborough
1817	7th E of Macclesfield
Apr 1842	6th D of Marlborough

Rutland
June 1751	9th E of Exeter
Mar 1779	E of Winchilsea and Nottingham
Mar 1826	4th M of Exeter
Mar 1867	E of Gainsborough

Shropshire
1761	E of Bath
Aug 1764	E of Powis
Oct 1772	Ld Clive
Apr 1775	Ld Clive (E of Powis)
Aug 1839	D of Sutherland

Somerset
Jan 1744	2nd Earl Poulett
Nov 1764	E of Thomond
Feb 1773	E of Egmont
Mar 1774	Ld North (E of Guildford)

Oct 1792	4th Earl Poulett
Feb 1819	2nd M of Bath
Apr 1837	E of Ilchester

Staffordshire
Jan 1755	Earl Gower (M of Stafford)
Oct 1800	Earl Gower (M of Stafford and D of Sutherland)
June 1801	E of Uxbridge
Apr 1812	Earl Talbot

Suffolk
Feb 1763	Ld (Vt) Maynard
June 1769	D of Grafton
June 1790	D of Grafton
Jan 1844	E of Stradbroke

Surrey
Jan 1741	3rd Ld Onslow
Oct 1776	4th Ld Onslow (Earl Onslow)
May 1814	Vt Middleton
Nov 1830	Ld Arden
Aug 1840	E of Lovelace

Sussex
1759	in commission
1762	E of Egremont
Oct 1763	3rd D of Richmond
Jan 1807	D of Norfolk
Jan 1816	4th D of Richmond
Nov 1819	3rd E of Egremont
1835	5th D of Richmond

Warwickshire
June 1750	E (1st M) of Hertford
Jan 1795	E of Warwick and Brooke
June 1816	2nd M of Hertford
July 1822	E of Warwick and Brooke
Mar 1854	3rd E of Craven

Westmorland
Aug 1758	Sir James Lowther (E of Lonsdale)
June 1802	Vt Lowther (1st E of Lonsdale, 2nd creation)
Apr 1844	2nd E of Lonsdale

Wiltshire
Mar 1761	10th E of Pembroke
Feb 1780	E of Ailesbury
Mar 1782	10th E of Pembroke (again)
Jan 1794	E of Pembroke
Nov 1827	M of Lansdowne
Mar 1863	M of Ailesbury

Worcestershire

June	1751	6th E of Coventry
Nov	1808	Vt Deerhurst (7th E of Coventry)
Apr	1831	Ld Foley
May	1833	Ld Lyttleton

Yorkshire: East Riding

July	1778	M of Carmarthen (D of Leeds)
Feb	1780	E of Carlisle
Mar	1782	M of Carmarthen (D of Leeds) (again)
Feb	1799	E of Carlisle
Aug	1807	Ld Mulgrave
Nov	1824	Vt Morpeth (E of Carlisle)
Jan	1840	Ld Wenlock

Yorkshire: North Riding

Apr	1740	E of Holdernesse
Dec	1777	Earl Fauconberg
Apr	1802	D of Leeds
Feb	1839	Ld Dundas (E of Zetland)
Mar	1873	M of Ripon

Yorkshire: West Riding

	1762	E of Huntingdon
Aug	1765	M of Rockingham
Sep	1782	E of Surrey (D of Norfolk)
Feb	1798	Earl Fitzwilliam
Nov	1819	Vt Lascelles (2nd E of Harewood)
	1842	Ld Wharncliffe

Lord Lieutenants, Wales

Anglesey

	1771	Sir Nicholas Bayley
July	1782	E of Uxbridge
	1813	E of Uxbridge (1st M of Anglesey)

Breconshire

Dec	1771	Charles Morgan
June	1787	D of Beaufort
Oct	1803	D of Beaufort (also for Monmouthshire)
Feb	1836	Penry Williams

Cardiganshire

	1763	Vt (E) of Lisburne
July	1800	Thomas Johnes
Oct	1816	William Edward Powell
Oct	1854	Thomas Lloyd

Carmarthenshire

	1779	Thomas Johnes
Mar	1780	Jonathan Vaughan
June	1804	Ld Dynevor
May	1852	1st Earl Cawdor

Carnarvonshire

	1761	Thomas Wynne (Ld Newborough)
Nov	1781	Vt Bulkeley
Sep	1822	Thomas Assheton Smith
Feb	1829	Ld Willoughby de Eresby
Feb	1851	Sir Richard Bulkeley

Denbighshire

	1792	Watkin Williams
	1793	Richard Myddelton
	1795	Sir Watkin Williams Wynn
	1840	Middleton Biddulph

Flintshire

	1761	Sir Roger Mostyn
	1797	Ld Kenyon
	1798	Vt Belgrave (Earl Grosvenor and M of Westminster)
	1845	Sir Stephen Glynne

Glamorgan

Nov	1752	E of Plymouth
Mar	1772	Ld Mountstewart (E and 1st M of Bute)
Mar–Dec	1794	3 Dep Lts during vacancy
Dec	1794	1st M of Bute (again)
June	1812	2nd M of Bute
Apr	1848	Christopher Talbot

Haverfordwest

Jan	1770	Sir Richard Philipps (Ld Milford)
Apr	1824	Richard Philipps (Ld Milford)
July	1857	Sir J. H. Philipps-Scourfield

Merionethshire

	1775	Sir Watkin Williams Wynn, 4th Bt
Aug	1789	Watkin Williams

June 1793	Sir Watkin Williams Wynn, 5th Bt	
Dec 1830	Sir Watkin Williams Wynn, 6th Bt	
June 1840	Hon. Edward Mostyn Lloyd (Ld Mostyn)	

Montgomeryshire

Oct 1772	Ld Clive
Apr 1775	E (1st M) of Hertford
Nov 1776	E of Powis
June 1804	E of Powis
1839	E of Powis

Pembrokeshire

Feb 1778	Hugh Owen
1780	Ld Milford
1824	Sir Jonathan Owen
Apr 1861	3rd Ld Kensington

Radnorshire

1766	E of Oxford
1792	Hon. Thomas Harley
Mar 1805	Ld Rodney
Aug 1842	Sir Jonathan Benn Walsh (Ld Ormathwaite)

14 The Economy

Population, 1761–1831

	England and Wales	Scotland	Ireland	United Kingdom
			(millions)	
1761	6.569	–	–	–
1771	7.052	–	3.530	–
1781	7.531	–	4.048	–
1791	8.247	1.500	4.753	14.500
1801	9.156	1.599	5.216	15.972
1811	10.322	1.824	5.956	18.102
1821	12.106	2.100	6.802	21.008
1831	13.994	2.374	7.767	24.135

SOURCE: P. Deane and W. A. Cole, *British Economic Growth, 1688–1959*, 2nd ed. (Cambridge, 1969) p. 6; and B. R. Mitchell and P. Deane, *Abstract of British Historical Statistics* (Cambridge, 1962) p. 8.

Principal Urban Populations, 1801 and 1831

	1801	1831		1801	1831
	(thousands)			(thousands)	
London	959*	1,656	Paisley	25	46
Manchester (and Salford)	89	223	Sunderland	24	39
Edinburgh (and Leith)	83	162	Bolton	18	42
Liverpool	82	202	Exeter	17	28
Glasgow	77	202	Yarmouth	17	25
Birmingham	71	144	Leicester	17	41
Bristol	61	104	Stoke-on-Trent	17†	35
Leeds	53	123	York	17	26
Sheffield	46	92	Stockport	17	36
Plymouth (and Devonport)	40	66	Greenock	17	27
Norwich	36	61	Coventry	16	27
Bath	33	51	Chester	15	21
Portsmouth (and Portsea)	33	50	Shrewsbury	15	21
Newcastle-upon-Tyne	33	54	Wolverhampton	13	25
Hull	30	52	Oldham	12	32
Nottingham	29	50	Preston	12	34
Aberdeen	27	57	Oxford	12	21
Dundee	26	45	Colchester	12	16

* London County Council Area
† Estimate. Figure for 1831 includes the townships of Hanley, Longton, Stoke and Burslem.

Prices

The Schumpeter-Gilboy Price Index (1701 = 100)*

1760	98	1776	114	1792	122	1808	204
1761	94	1777	108	1793	129	1809	212
1762	94	1778	117	1794	136	1810	207
1763	100	1779	111	1795	147	1811	206
1764	102	1780	110	1796	154	1812	237
1765	106	1781	115	1797	148	1813	243
1766	107	1782	116	1798	148	1814	209
1767	109	1783	129	1799	160	1815	191
1768	108	1784	126	1800	212	1816	172
1769	99	1785	120	1801	228	1817	189
1770	100	1786	119	1802	174	1818	194
1771	107	1787	117	1803	156	1819	192
1772	117	1788	121	1804	161	1820	162
1773	119	1789	117	1805	187	1821	139
1774	116	1790	124	1806	184	1822	125
1775	113	1791	121	1807	186	1823	128

The Rousseaux Price Index (average of 1865 and 1885 = 100)†

1800	175	1808	189	1816	144	1824	122
1801	188	1809	206	1817	161	1825	133
1802	152	1810	193	1818	160	1826	117
1803	161	1811	178	1819	147	1827	117
1804	159	1812	196	1820	132	1828	112
1805	170	1813	203	1821	121	1829	110
1806	166	1814	202	1822	116	1830	109
1807	161	1815	164	1823	120		

* Index for consumers' goods based on prices for food and household items.
† Unweighted average of indices for agricultural products and principal industrial products.

SOURCES: E. B. Schumpeter, 'English Prices and Public Finance, 1660–1822', *Review of Economic Statistics* (1938); P. Rousseaux, *Les Mouvements de Fond de L'Economie Anglaise, 1800–1913* (Brussels, 1938).

Average Price of Wheat in England and Wales, 1771–1830 (per imperial quarter)

	s	d		s	d		s	d
1771	48	7	1784	50	4	1797	53	9
1772	52	3	1785	43	1	1798	51	10
1773	52	7	1786	40	0	1799	69	0
1774	54	3	1787	42	5	1800	113	10
1775	49	10	1788	46	4	1801	119	6
1776	39	4	1789	52	9	1802	69	10
1777	46	11	1790	54	9	1803	58	10
1778	43	3	1791	48	7	1804	62	3
1779	34	8	1792	43	0	1805	89	9
1780	36	9	1793	49	3	1806	79	1
1781	46	0	1794	52	3	1807	75	4
1782	49	3	1795	75	2	1808	81	4
1783	54	3	1796	78	7	1809	97	4

	s	d		s	d		s	d
1810	106	5	1817	96	11	1824	63	11
1811	95	3	1818	86	3	1825	68	6
1812	126	6	1819	74	6	1826	58	8
1813	109	9	1820	67	10	1827	58	6
1814	74	4	1821	56	1	1828	60	5
1815	65	7	1822	44	7	1829	66	3
1816	78	6	1823	53	4	1830	64	3

SOURCE: Mitchell and Deane, p. 488.

Industrial Production, 1801–30 (1913 = 100)

The Hoffman Index
(including building)

1801	6.64	1809	8.08	1817	9.51	1825	12.50
1802	6.85	1810	8.22	1818	9.81	1826	12.89
1803	7.06	1811	8.36	1819	10.13	1827	13.30
1804	7.27	1812	8.49	1820	10.46	1828	13.71
1805	7.42	1813	8.63	1821	10.83	1829	14.14
1806	7.64	1814	8.80	1822	11.25	1830	14.60
1807	7.80	1815	8.99	1823	11.66		
1808	7.94	1816	9.24	1824	12.08		

SOURCE: W. G. Hoffman, *British Industry, 1700–1950* (Oxford, 1955).

Raw Cotton Imports and Consumption

	Imports (in thousand lb)	Consumption (in million lb)		Imports (in thousand lb)	Consumption (in million lb)
1760	2,359	–	1782	11,828	–
1761	2,996	–	1783	9,736	–
1762	3,519	–	1784	11,482	–
1763	2,707	–	1785	18,400	–
1764	3,870	–	1786	19,475	–
1765	3,777	–	1787	23,250	–
1766	6,918	–	1788	20,467	–
1767	3,623	–	1789	32,576	–
1768	4,131	–	1790	31,448	–
1769	4,406	–	1791	28,707	–
1770	3,612	–	1792	34,907	–
1771	2,547	–	1793	19,041	–
1772	5,307	–	1794	24,359	–
1773	2,906	–	1795	26,401	–
1774	5,707	–	1796	32,126	–
1775	6,694	–	1797	23,354	–
1776	6,216	–	1798	31,881	–
1777	7,037	–	1799	43,379	–
1778	6,569	–	1800	56,011	52
1779	5,861	–	1801	56,004	54
1780	6,877	–	1802	60,346	56
1781	5,199	–	1803	53,812	52

	Imports (in thousand lb)	Consumption (in million lb)		Imports in thousand lb	Consumption (in million lb)
1804	61,867	61	1818	177,282	110
1805	59,682	59	1819	149,740	109
1806	58,176	57	1820	–	120
1807	74,925	73	1821	–	129
1808	43,606	42	1822	–	145
1809	92,812	88	1823	–	154
1810	132,489	124	1824	–	165
1811	91,577	89	1825	–	167
1812	63,026	73	1826	–	150
1813	50,996	78	1827	–	197
1814	60,060	74	1828	–	218
1815	99,306	81	1829	–	219
1816	93,920	89	1830	–	248
1817	124,913	107			

SOURCES: A. P. Wadsworth and J. de L. Mann, *The Cotton Trade and Industrial Lancashire, 1600–1780* (Manchester, 1931); E. Baines, *History of the Cotton Manufacture* (London, 1835); T. Ellison, *The Cotton Trade of Great Britain* (London, 1886).

Enclosure Acts, 1760–1830

1760–9	385	1770–9	660	1780–9	246	1790–9	469
1800–9	847	1810–19	853	1820–9	205		

SOURCE: G. R. Porter, *The Progress of the Nation* (London, 1836) pp. 155–6.

The Corn Laws

13 Geo III, c.43 (1773)

Export prohibited at or above average of 44s per quarter; 5s bounty when price under 44s. Imports at or above 48s subject to 6d duty; over 44s and under 48s, duty of 17s; duty of 22s on imports when average price under 44s.

31 Geo III, c.30 (1791)

Export prohibited at or above 46s; average 44s to 46s, export allowed without bounty; export with 5s bounty when average prices under 44s. Imports, when average price at or above 54s, subject to 6d duty; between 50s and 54s, import duty of 2s 6d; at average of under 50s, duty of 24s 3d.

44 Geo III, c.109 (1804)

Export, when average price above 54s, prohibited; export permitted but without bounty when average price of wheat over 48s and under 54s; 5s bounty on exports when prices at or under 48s 7½d; duty on imports when prices at or above 66s; duty of 3s 1½d when prices between 63s and under 66s; duty of 30s 3¾d when prices under 63s.

55 Geo III, c.26 (1815)
Full freedom of import without duty when price of wheat at or above 80*s*
per quarter. All imports prohibited when price below 80*s*.

9 Geo IV, c.60 (1828)
Introduction of sliding scale of duties with steep fall in the duty on
imported corn after the price of corn rose above 66*s*; at 66*s* the duty
payable was 20*s* 8*d*, at 73*s* only 1*s*.

Sources: C. R. Fay, *The Corn Laws and Social England* (Cambridge, 1932); D. G. Barnes, *The History of the English Corn Laws from 1660–1846* (London, 1930).

Trade (£'000: official values)*

	Imports	Exports	Re-exports
1760–9	10,719	10,043	4,790
1770–9	12,104	9,287	5,136
1780–9	13,820	10,200	4,262
1790–9	21,797	17,520	9,350
1800–9	28,740	25,380	12,150
1810–19	31,640	35,050	11,680
1820–9	38,310	46,530	9,980

* Annual averages per decade. Figures for 1760–91 relate to England and Wales; for 1791–1829 to Great Britain.

Shipping and Shipbuilding
Shipping registered in the United Kingdom, 1788–1830

	Number	Thousand tons		Number	Thousand tons
1788	12,464	1,278	1810	20,253	2,211
1789	12,801	1,308	1811	20,478	2,247
1790	13,557	1,383	1812	20,637	2,263
1791	13,960	1,415	1813	20,951	2,349
1792	14,334	1,437	1814	21,550	2,414
1793	14,440	1,453	1815	21,869	2,478
1794	14,590	1,456	1816	22,026	2,504
1795	14,317	1,426	1817	21,775	2,421
1796	14,458	1,361	1818	22,024	2,453
1797	14,405	1,454	1819	21,997	2,452
1798	14,631	1,494	1820	21,969	2,439
1799	14,883	1,551	1821	21,652	2,356
1800	15,734	1,699	1822	21,238	2,315
1801	16,552	1,797	1823	21,042	2,303
1802	17,207	1,901	1824	21,280	2,349
1803	18,068	1,986	1825	20,595	2,327
1804	18,870	2,077	1826	20,968	2,411
1805	19,027	2,093	1827	19,524*	2,181*
1806	19,315	2,080	1828	19,646	2,193
1807	19,373	2,097	1829	19,110	2,200
1808	19,580	2,130	1830	19,174	2,202
1809	19,882	2,167			

* New register introduced which removed many ships that had been lost and retained on old register.

THE ECONOMY

Ships built and first registered in Britain ('000 tons)*

	Sailing ships	Steam ships		Sailing ships	Steam ships
1790–9	79.8	–	1810–19	90.8	0.4
1800–9	97.1	–	1820–9	81.0	3.0

* Yearly average per decade   SOURCE: Mitchell and Deane, pp. 220–1.

Public Income and Expenditure
Great Britain, 1760–1801 (£'000)

	Income	Expenditure		Income	Expenditure
1760	9,207	17,993	1781	13,280	25,810
1761	9,594	21,112	1782	13,765	29,234
1762	9,459	20,040	1783	12,677	23,510
1763	9,793	17,723	1784	13,214	24,245
1764	10,221	10,686	1785	15,527	25,832
1765	10,928	12,017	1786	15,246	16,678
1766	10,276	10,314	1787	16,453	15,484
1767	9,868	9,638	1788	16,779	16,338
1768	10,131	9,146	1789	16,669	16,018
1769	11,130	9,569	1790	17,014	16,798
1770	11,373	10,524	1791	18,506	17,996
1771	10,987	10,106	1792	18,607	16,953
1772	11,033	10,726	1793	18,131	19,623
1773	10,487	9,977	1794	18,732	28,706
1774	10,613	9,566	1795	19,053	38,996
1775	11,112	10,365	1796	19,391	42,372
1776	10,576	14,045	1797	21,380	57,649
1777	11,105	15,259	1798	26,946	47,422
1778	11,436	17,940	1799	31,783	47,419
1779	11,853	19,714	1800	9,674	12,383
1780	12,524	22,605	1801	31,585	50,991

United Kingdom, 1802–30 (in £ million)

	Income	Expenditure		Income	Expenditure
1802	39.1	65.6	1817	69.2	71.5
1803	41.2	54.8	1818	57.6	58.7
1804	42.4	53.0	1819	59.5	57.6
1805	50.2	62.8	1820	58.1	57.5
1806	55.0	71.4	1821	59.9	58.4
1807	60.1	72.9	1822	61.6	58.4
1808	64.8	73.3	1823	59.9	56.5
1809	68.2	78.0	1824	58.5	54.3
1810	69.2	81.5	1825	59.7	55.5
1811	73.0	81.6	1826	57.7	54.1
1812	71.0	87.3	1827	55.2	56.1
1813	70.3	94.8	1828	54.7	55.9
1814	74.7	111.1	1829	56.5	53.5
1815	77.9	112.9	1830	55.3	53.7
1816	69.2	99.5			

SOURCE: Mitchell and Deane, pp. 387–96.

The National Debt (£ million)

1760	101.7	1778	143.1	1796	310.4	1814	725.5
1761	114.2	1779	153.4	1797	359.2	1815	744.9
1762	126.6	1780	167.2	1798	391.2	1816	778.3
1763	132.6	1781	190.4	1799	426.6	1817	766.1
1764	134.2	1782	214.3	1800	N.A.	1818	843.3
1765	133.6	1783	231.8	1801	456.1	1819	844.3
1766	133.3	1784	242.9	1802	498.6	1820	840.1
1767	133.9	1785	245.5	1803	516.4	1821	838.3
1768	132.6	1786	246.2	1804	523.8	1822	831.1
1769	130.3	1787	245.8	1805	539.6	1823	836.1
1770	130.6	1788	245.1	1806	564.4	1824	828.6
1771	128.9	1789	244.3	1807	583.1	1825	820.2
1772	128.7	1790	244.0	1808	591.3	1826	811.0
1773	128.9	1791	243.2	1809	599.0	1827	810.0
1774	127.7	1792	241.6	1810	607.4	1828	806.4
1775	127.3	1793	242.9	1811	609.6	1829	801.3
1776	131.2	1794	249.6	1812	626.9	1830	798.2
1777	136.6	1795	267.4	1813	652.3		

SOURCE: *State Papers*, 1898, LII, 1786–1890; *State Papers*, 1890–1, XLVIII.

Yield on Consols (per cent)

1760	3.8	1778	4.5	1796	4.8	1814	4.9
1761	3.9	1779	4.9	1797	5.9	1815	4.5
1762	4.3	1780	4.9	1798	5.9	1816	5.0
1763	3.4	1781	5.2	1799	5.1	1817	4.1
1764	3.6	1782	5.3	1800	4.7	1818	3.9
1765	3.4	1783	4.8	1801	4.9	1819	4.2
1766	3.4	1784	5.4	1802	4.2	1820	4.4
1767	3.4	1785	4.8	1803	5.0	1821	4.1
1768	3.3	1786	4.1	1804	5.3	1822	3.8
1769	3.5	1787	4.1	1805	5.0	1823	3.8
1770	3.6	1788	4.0	1806	4.9	1824	3.3
1771	3.5	1789	3.9	1807	4.9	1825	3.5
1772	3.3	1790	3.9	1808	4.6	1826	3.8
1773	3.5	1791	3.6	1809	4.6	1827	3.6
1774	3.4	1792	3.3	1810	4.5	1828	3.5
1775	3.4	1793	4.0	1811	4.7	1829	3.3
1776	3.5	1794	4.4	1812	5.1	1830	3.5
1777	3.8	1795	4.5	1813	4.9		

SOURCE: T. S. Ashton, 'Some Statistics of the Industrial Revolution', *Transactions of the Manchester Statistical Society* (1947–8).

Income Tax: Rates and Yields, 1799–1816

	Net Produce (£ million)	Standard Rate in the £		Net Produce (£ million)	Standard Rate in the £
1799	1.9	2s	1803	–	–
1800	5.7	2s	1804	4.9	1s
1801	5.9	2s	1805	3.9	1s
1802	5.3	2s	1806	5.0	1s 3d

	Net Produce (£ million)	Standard Rate in the £		Net Produce (£ million)	Standard Rate in the £
1807	12.0	2s	1812	13.6	2s
1808	11.2	2s	1813	14.6	2s
1809	12.7	2s	1814	14.9	2s
1810	12.8	2s	1815	14.3	2s
1811	13.6	2s	1816	14.7	2s

SOURCE: Mitchell and Deane, p. 427.

Country Banks in England and Wales, 1784–1830

Number of banks, excluding branches

1784	119	1804	414	1814	657	1824	660
1793	280	1805	438	1815	626	1825	684
1794	272	1806	478	1816	575	1826	597
1796	301	1807	515	1817	577	1827	600
1797	230	1808	573	1818	596	1828	615
1798	312	1809	631	1819	595	1829	640
1800	370	1810	654	1820	606	1830	628
1801	383	1811	656	1821	609		
1802	397	1812	646	1822	623		
1803	410	1813	660	1823	641		

SOURCE: *English Historical Documents, 1783–1832* Vol. XI (London, 1959) p. 596.

Canal Acts, 1759–1827

1759 Acts: First Bridgewater Act passed.

1760 Acts: Amended Bridgewater (including provision for the aqueduct at Barton).

1761 Construction: Bridgewater completed.

1762 Acts: Bridgewater extension to Runcorn.

1766 Acts: Trent and Mersey: Staffordshire and Worcestershire.

1768 Acts: Coventry; Droitwich, Birmingham (Birmingham to Auther-ley); Forth and Clyde; Borrowstowness.

1769 Acts: Oxford.
Construction: Birmingham canal completed from Wednesbury to Birmingham.

1770 Acts: Leeds and Liverpool; Monkland.

1771 Acts: Chesterfield; Bradford.

1772 Acts: Chester; Market Weighton.
Construction: Staffordshire and Worcestershire completed; Bridgewater joined to Mersey.

1774 Acts: Huddersfield Broad (Sir John Ramsden's); Bude.
Construction: Bradford completed.

1775 Acts: Gresley.

1776 Acts: Stourbridge; Dudley.
Construction: Chesterfield completed.

1777   Acts: Erewash.
       Construction: Trent and Mersey completed; work stopped on
       Leeds and Liverpool (Leeds and Liverpool ends were both open).
1778   Acts: Basingstoke.
       Construction: work stopped on Oxford (open to Banbury).
1779   Construction: Stroudwater open.
1780   Acts: Thames and Severn.
1783   Acts: Birmingham and Fazeley.
1786   Construction: work restarted on Oxford.
1788   Acts: Shropshire (Tub Boat) Canal.
       Construction: First canal inclined plane built by William
       Reynolds on Ketley Canal.
1789   Acts: Andover; Cromford.
       Construction: Thames and Severn completed.
1790   Acts: Glamorganshire.
       Construction: Oxford; Birmingham and Fazeley; Forth and Clyde
       completed; work restarted on Leeds and Liverpool.
1791   Acts: Royal Military; Worcester and Birmingham; Hereford and
       Gloucester; Manchester, Bolton and Bury; Kington and Leomin-
       ster; Neath.
1792   Acts: Nottingham; Ashton; Lancaster; Wryley and Essington;
       Coombe Hill; Monmouthshire.
       Construction: Shropshire completed.
1793   Acts: Oakham; Grantham; Ulverston; Nutbrook; Derby; Grand
       Junction; Caistor; Shrewsbury; Stainforth and Keadby; Dearne
       and Dove; Stratford-upon-Avon; Brecknock and Abergavenny;
       Ellesmere; Warwick and Birmingham; Old Union; Gloucester
       and Berkeley; Aberdare; Barnsley; Crinan.
1794   Acts: Montgomeryshire; Somersetshire Coal Canal; Wisbech;
       Peak Forest; Huddersfield Narrow; Swansea; Grand Junction
       (branches to Buckingham, Aylesbury and Wendover); Warwick
       and Braunston; Rochdale; Kennet and Avon; Ashby.
       Construction: Glamorganshire Canal opened from Merthyr Tyd-
       fil to Cardiff.
1795   Acts: Bridgewater (extension to Leigh); Grand Junction (Pad-
       dington branch; Wiltshire and Berkshire; Newcastle-under-Lyme;
       Ivelchester and Langport.
1796   Acts: Salisbury and Southampton: Grand Western; Warwick and
       Napton; Aberdeenshire.
       Construction: Lune aqueduct completed.
1797   Acts: Polbrock.
       Construction: Ashton; Shrewsbury completed.
1798   Construction: Swansea completed; Huddersfield Narrow (Hud-
       dersfield to Marsden and Ashton to Stalybridge opened;
       Hereford and Gloucester (Gloucester to Ledbury) opened.

1799   Construction: Warwick and Birmingham; Warwick and Napton; Barnsley completed.
1800   Acts: Thames and Medway.
        Construction: Peak Forest completed.
1801   Acts: Croydon; Grand Surrey; Leven.
        Construction: Grand Junction (Buckingham and Paddington branches) completed.
1802   Construction: Nottingham completed.
1803   Acts: Tavistock; Caledonian.
        Construction: Pontcysyllte aqueduct completed.
1804   Construction: Dearne and Dove: Rochdale completed.
1805   Construction: Grand Junction (main line from Brentford to Braunston) completed.
1806   Acts: Glasgow, Paisley and Johnstone.
1807   Acts: Isle of Dogs.
1808   –
1809   Construction: Perpendicular lift invented by John Woodhouse, erected at Tardebigge on Worcester and Birmingham.
1810   Acts: Grand Union.
        Construction: Kennet and Avon completed.
1811   Acts: Bridgewater and Taunton.
1812   Acts: Regent's; North Walsham and Dilham; London and Cambridge Junction.
1813   Acts: Wey and Arun Junction; North Wilts.
        Construction: Grand Junction (Aylesbury branch) completed.
1814   Acts: Newport Pagnell.
        Construction: Grand Western (Loudwell to Tiverton) completed.
1815   Acts: Pocklington; Sheffield.
        Construction: Grand Junction (Northampton branch) completed.
1816   Construction: Leeds and Liverpool completed.
1817   Acts: Portsmouth and Arundel; Edinburgh and Glasgow Union.
1819   Acts: Bude; Carlisle.
        Construction: North Wiltshire completed.
1820   Construction: Regent's completed.
1821   Act passed for Stockton and Darlington Railway.
1822   Construction: Caledonian; Edinburgh and Glasgow Union completed.
1823   Acts: Harecastle New Tunnel.
1824   Acts: Kensington; Hertford Union.
1825   Acts: Baybridge; Liskeard; English and Bristol Channels Ship Canal.
1826   Acts: Birmingham and Liverpool Junction; Macclesfield; Alford.
        Construction: Lancaster completed.

1827   Construction: Harecastle New Tunnel; Gloucester and Berkeley
        completed.

SOURCES: H. R. De Salis, *A Chronology of Inland Navigation in Great Britain* (London, 1897); J. Priestley, *Historical Account of the Navigable Rivers, Canals and Railways of Great Britain* (London, 1831); and C. Hadfield, *The Canal Builders* (Newton Abbot, 1962).

Distribution of the Labour Force, 1801–31
(estimated percentage of the total occupied population)

	Agriculture, Forestry, Fishing	*Manufacture, Mining, Industry*	*Trade and Transport*	*Domestic and Personal*	*Public, Professional and other*
1801	35.9	29.7	11.2	11.5	11.8
1811	33.0	30.2	11.6	11.8	13.3
1821	28.4	38.4	12.1	12.7	8.5
1831	24.6	40.8	12.4	12.6	9.5

SOURCE: P. Deane and W. A. Cole, *British Economic Growth, 1688–1959* (Cambridge, 1969) p. 142.

SOURCES: The essential and most readily available source for statistics on the economy in this period is B. R. Mitchell and P. Deane, *Abstract of British Historical Statistics* (Cambridge, 1962). See also P. Deane and W. A. Cole, *British Economic Growth, 1688–1959* (Cambridge, 2nd ed. 1969).

15　Social Developments

Major Social Legislation and Developments

1773　Spitalfields Weavers Act (13 Geo. III, c.68).
Act empowering magistrates to regulate wages of persons employed in silk manufacture.

1782　Gilbert's Act (22 Geo. III, c.83).
Parishes permitted to combine for more effective administration; able-bodied and infirm to be separated and only latter to be sent to the workhouse; work to be provided for able-bodied poor with wages supplemented from poor rate if necessary; 'Guardians' of the poor to be appointed to administer relief.

1795　The 'Speenhamland system'. Adopted by the Berkshire justices at Speenhamland (6 May 1795) to supplement wages on a sliding scale dictated by the price of bread. Elements of this system had been operated by individual parishes as early as the 1780s under the provisions of Gilbert's Act.

1802　The Health and Morals of Apprentices Act (42 Geo. III, c.87).
Applied to cotton mills only. Male and female apprentices to have separate accommodation; all to have two suits of clothes a year and daily instruction. All night working of children to stop and day-work limited to twelve hours, exclusive of meals. A local magistrate and clergyman (not mill-owners) appointed by magistrates at Quarter Sessions to act as visitors and enforce the Act.

1819　Cotton Factory Act (59 Geo. III, c.66).
No children to be employed in spinning cotton or its preparation under age of nine. Hours for children and youths between nine and eighteen limited to twelve hours per day exclusive of meals.

Hospital Foundations, 1714–1830

1720	Westminster	
1726	Guy's	
1734	St George's London	
1738	Bath General	
1739	Foundling	
1739	Queen Charlotte's	
1740	London Hospital	
1740	York County	

1745	Durham, Newcastle-upon-Tyne and Northumberland Infirmary	
1745	Gloucester Infirmary	
1745	Liverpool Royal Infirmary	
1745	Middlesex	
1745	Shrewsbury Infirmary	
1746	Middlesex County	
1746	Worcester Royal Infirmary	

1746	London Lock	1796	Royal Sea Bathing Hospital (Margate)
1750	City of London Maternity		
1751	St Luke's London	1802	House of Recovery (Grays Inn Road)
1752	Manchester Royal Infirmary		
1753	Devon and Exeter	1802	London Fever
1758	Magdalen	1805	Moorfields
1765	Westminster Lying-in	1806	Exeter Eye
1766	Manchester Royal Lunatic Asylum	1810	Taunton and Somerset
1767	Leeds Infirmary	1814	Royal Hospital for Diseases of the Chest
1769	Lincoln County		
1770	Radcliffe Infirmary, Oxford	1816	Royal Ear
1771	Leicester Infirmary	1816	Royal Westminster Ophthalmic
1776	Hereford General Infirmary	1816	Royal Waterloo Hospital for Children and Women
1777	York Lunatic Asylum		
1782	Nottingham General	1818	West London Infirmary (Charing Cross Hospital)
1784	Hull Royal Infirmary		
1787	Wakefield	1828	Royal Free
1792	Liverpool Royal Lunatic Asylum	1829	Manchester Hospital for Children
1796	Manchester Fever		

Charities and Philanthropic Societies

1699	Society for Promoting Christian Knowledge
1701	Society for the Propagation of the Gospel in Foreign Parts
1756	Marine Society
1769	Relief of the Infant Poor (London)
1773	Thatched House Society (for aid to those in debtors' prisons)
1785	Sunday School Society
1788	Philanthropic Society (for Children)
1790	Liverpool School for the Indigent Blind
1793	Baptist Missionary Society
1795	London Missionary Society
1800	St Giles in the Fields School for the Indigent Blind; Society for Bettering the Condition of the Poor
c.1800	Church Missionary Society
1804	British and Foreign Bible Society
1809	National Society for Promoting Education
1811	Association for the Relief of the Manufacturing and Labouring Poor
1814	British and Foreign School Society
1818	Church Building Society
1823	Anti-Slavery Society
1824	Royal National Life-boat Institution
1824	Royal Society for the Prevention of Cruelty to Animals
1830	Liverpool Night Asylum for the Houseless

Education

Number of schools and children attending, 1819

	England	Wales	Scotland
Parochial schools			
Number	–	–	942
Children	–	–	54,161
Endowed schools			
Number	4,167	209	212
Children	165,433	7,625	10,177
Unendowed schools			
Number	14,282	572	2,479
Children	478,849	22,976	112,187
Sunday schools			
Number	5,162	301	807
Children	452,817	24,408	53,449

Source: *Parliamentary Papers*, 1820, XII, pp. 342–55.

Poor Relief, 1783–1831

	£		£
Average of 1783–85	1,912,241	Average of 1821–22	6,358,703
1803	4,077,891	1822–23	5,773,096
1812–13	6,656,105	1823–24	5,736,898
1813–14	6,294,584	1824–25	5,786,989
1814–15	5,418,845	1825–26	5,928,501
1815–16	5,724,506	1826–27	6,441,088
1816–17	6,918,217	1827–28	6,298,000
1817–18	7,890,148	1828–29	6,332,410
1818–19	7,531,650	1829–30	6,829,042
1819–20	7,329,594	1830–31	6,798,889
1820–21	6,958,445		

Source: G. R. Porter, *The Progress of the Nation* (London, 1851) p. 517.

Friendly Societies

Counties	Total Population in 1801	Members of Friendly Societies 1803	1815
Middlesex	818,129	72,741	60,579
Lancaster	682,731	104,776	137,655
Yorks, West Riding	563,953	59,558	74,005
Devon	343,001	31,792	48,607
Kent	307,624	12,633	15,640
Somerset	273,750	19,848	23,883
Norfolk	273,371	14,821	13,587
Surrey	269,049	19,199	21,805
Gloucester	250,803	19,606	24,567
Stafford	239,152	32,852	41,213
Essex	226,437	14,890	34,425
Southampton	219,656	4,733	11,013
Suffolk	210,431	11,448	13,335

Counties	Total Population in 1801	Members of Friendly 1803	Societies 1815
Lincoln	208,557	7,530	8,658
Warwick	208,190	17,000	26,330
Chester	191,751	14,828	19,626
Cornwall	188,269	16,736	21,390
Wiltshire	185,107	11,330	15,302
Salop	197,639	19,144	23,638
Derby	161,142	22,681	22,412
Durham	160,861	11,556	13,115
Sussex	159,311	4,419	4,790
Northumberland	157,101	11,606	12,193
Yorks, North Riding	155,506	9,718	8,885
Nottingham	140,350	15,202	19,149
Yorks, East Riding	139,433	11,248	11,371
Worcester	139,333	12,845	13,458
Northampton	131,757	8,062	10,150
Leicester	130,081	10,889	15,425
Cumberland	117,230	7,788	9,807
Dorset	115,319	3,795	5,952
Oxford	109,620	5,010	5,922
Berkshire	109,215	2,843	3,558
Buckingham	107,444	4,079	5,917
Hertford	97,577	8,622	10,477
Cambridge	89,346	3,173	4,524
Hereford	89,191	2,811	2,854
Bedford	63,393	2,730	3,647
Monmouth	45,582	3,799	7,923
Westmorland	41,617	2,435	1,278
Huntingdon	37,568	1,740	2,470
Rutland	16,356	1,704	1,398
Wales	541,546	30,130	45,097
Total	8,872,980	704,350	861,657

SOURCES: No single source exists for social statistics in the period 1760–1830. A guide to administrative developments can be found in a number of works including U. R. Q. Henriques, *Before the Welfare State: Social Administration in early Industrial Britain, 1780–1850* (London, 1979) and J. Roach, *Social Reform, 1750–1850* (London, 1978). G. Porter, *The Progress of the Nation* (London, 1847) contains much useful statistical material.

Bibliographical Note

The period 1760 to 1830 witnessed significant changes in the operation of cabinet government and only a gradual evolution of a body of ministers who regularly transacted business together. As J. Steven Watson suggested in Volume XII of the *Oxford History of England, The Reign of George III, 1760–1815* (Oxford, 1960), to print lists of cabinets it is necessary that there should be some certainty about those entitled to attend and a sense of collective cabinet opinion. For much of this period the question of whether a minister was of the cabinet depended as much upon his own strength as upon the office he held. As a result it has been necessary to adopt a slightly different approach to lists of Ministries from that employed in *British Historical Facts: 1830–1900*. Between 1760 and 1782 we have included only the most important holders of office under successive administrations, but have followed J. Steven Watson in choosing the second Rockingham administration as the point at which to begin to indicate which office-holders were outside the cabinet. For further discussion of this issue, see J. B. Owen, *The Eighteenth Century, 1714–1815* (London, 1974) and A. Aspinall, *The Cabinet Council, 1783–1835* (London, 1954). There is an extremely useful discussion of the situation in the early years of George III's reign in I. R. Christie, *Myth and Reality in Late Eighteenth-century British Politics, and Other Papers* (London, 1970).

There are considerable difficulties involved in discovering precisely when an individual was appointed to an office and for how long he held it. In some cases it has not been possible to determine the date of appointment to office and a gap appears in the list. In general we have followed the practice of the authoritative work on office-holders by J. C. Sainty, *Office-Holders in Modern Britain* (London, 1972–   ) in dating appointments:

I   *Treasury Officials 1660–1870*
II   *Officials of the Secretaries of State 1660–1782*
III *Officials of the Board of Trade 1660–1870*
IV   *Admiralty Officials 1660–1870*
V   *Home Office Officials 1782–1870*

All officials are taken to have remained in office until the appointment of their successors unless otherwise stated.

For certain appointments additional information can be found in F. M. Powicke and E. B. Fryde, *Handbook of British Chronology* (London, 2nd ed. 1961) which lists English Officers of State, some Irish and Scottish appointments, and many ecclesiastical dignitaries. Joseph Haydn, *The Book of Dignities* (London, 1890) is the only comprehensive work on appointments for the period and, in spite of some errors and omissions, remains the best single work on offices and office-holders. G. P. Judd IV, *Members of Parliament, 1734–1832* (New Haven, 1955) provides an indispensable guide to the careers of individual members of parliament.

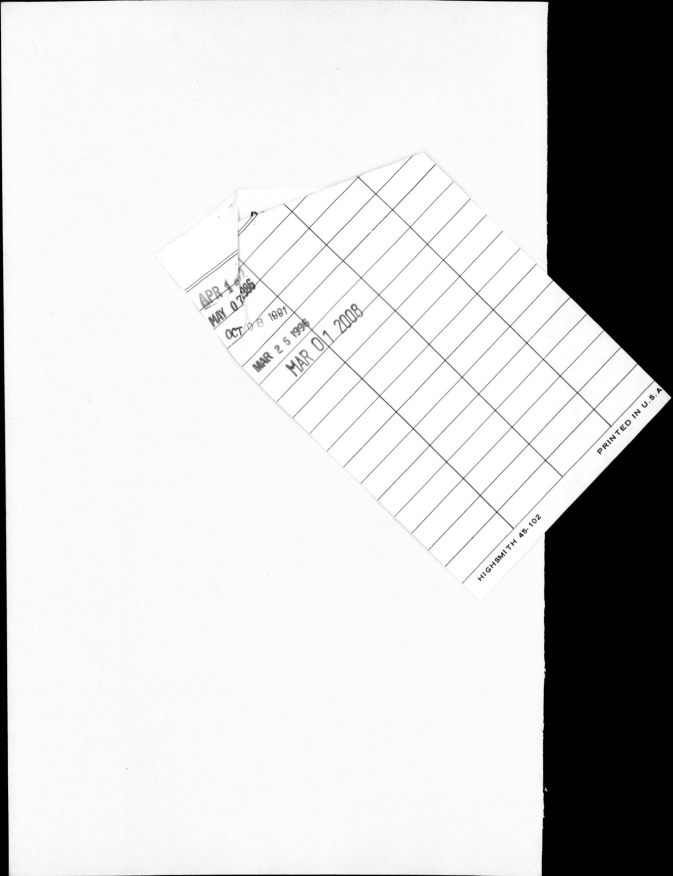